CHICAGO STUDIES IN THE HISTORY OF AMERICAN RELIGION

Editors
JERALD C. BRAUER
AND MARTIN E. MARTY

A CARLSON PUBLISHING SERIES

For a complete listing of the titles in this series,
please see the back of this book.

The Catholic Parish as a Way-Station of Ethnicity and Americanization

CHICAGO'S GERMANS
AND ITALIANS, 1903-1939

Stephen J. Shaw

PREFACE BY MARTIN E. MARTY

CARLSON
Publishing Inc

BROOKLYN, NEW YORK, 1991

Please see the end of this volume for a listing of all the titles in the Carlson Publishing Series *Chicago Studies in the History of American Religion*, edited by Jerald C. Brauer and Martin E. Marty, of which this is Volume 19.

Copyright © 1991 by Stephen Joseph Shaw

Library of Congress Cataloging-in-Publication Data

Shaw, Stephen Joseph, 1944-
    The Catholic parish as a way-station of ethnicity and Americanization : Chicago's Germans and Italians, 1903-1939 / Stephen J. Shaw ; preface by Martin E. Marty.
        p. cm. — (Chicago studies in the history of American religion ; 19)
    Originally presented as the author's thesis (Ph.D. —University of Chicago, 1981) with title: Chicago's Germans and Italians, 1903-1939.
    Includes bibliographical references and index.
    ISBN 0-926019-55-4 (alk. paper)
    1. Catholics—Illinois—Chicago—Cultural assimilation. 2. German Americans—Illinois—Chicago—Cultural assimilation. 3 Italian Americans—Illinois—Chicago—Cultural assimilation. 4. Chicago (Ill.)—Ethnic relations. 5. Ethnicity—Illinois—Chicago--History—20th century. I. Title. II. Series.
F548.9.C3S53   1991
305.6'2077311'09041—dc20   91-26847

Typographic design: Julian Waters

Typeface: Bitstream ITC Galliard

Case design: Alison Lew

Index prepared by Scholars Editorial Services, Inc., Madison, Wisconsin, using NL Cindex, a scholarly indexing program from the Newberry Library.

Printed on acid-free, 250-year-life paper.

Manufactured in the United States of America.

Contents

An Introduction to the Series xi
Preface *by Martin E. Marty* xv
Acknowledgments xvii

I.   Chicago: The City and Its People 1

II. The German and Italian City 29

III. The German Parish 71

IV. The Italian Parish 101

V.   The Decline and Perseverance of Ethnicity: 1930 and Beyond ... 131

Notes 143
Bibliography 177
Index 197

Tables

1. German and Italian National Parishes, 1880-1903 14
2. Principal Italian Wards, 1910-1920 50
3. German Immigration to Chicago by Provinces, 1870-1880 59
4. Decline of St. Boniface Parish, 1901-1914 79
5. St. Boniface *Vereine*, 1904 89
6. Growth of German Parochial School System, 1903-1940 93
7. Italian Societies, St. Philip Benizi, 1937 113
8. Growth of Italian Parochial School System, 1920-1940 121

An Introduction to the Series

The *Chicago Studies in the History of American Religion* is a series of books that deal with topics ranging from the time of Jonathan Edwards to the 1970s. Three or four deal with colonial topics and three or four treat the very recent past. About half of them focus on the decades just before and after 1900. One deals with blacks; two concentrate on women. Revivalists, fundamentalists, theologians, life in the suburbs and life in heaven and hell, the Beecher family of old and a monk of new times, Catholics adapting to America and Protestants fighting one another—all these subjects assure that the series has scope. People of every kind of taste and curiosity about American religion will find some books to suit them. Does anything serve to characterize the series as a whole? What does the stamp of "Chicago studies" mean?

Yale historian Sydney Ahlstrom in *A Religious History of the American People*, as influential as any twentieth-century work in its field, pays respect to the "Chicago School" of American religious historians. William Warren Sweet, the pioneer in such studies (beginning in 1927) at Chicago and, in many ways, in America at large represented the culmination of "the Protestant synthesis" in this field. Ahlstrom went on to name two later generations of Chicagoans, including the seminal Sidney E. Mead and major figures like Robert T. Handy and Winthrop Hudson and ending with the two editors of this series. He saw them as often "openly rebellious" in respect to Sweet and his synthesis.

If, as Ahlstrom says, "a disproportionate number" of historians have some connection with the Chicago School, it must be said that the new generation represented in these twenty-one books carries on both the lineage of Sweet and something of the "openly rebellious" character that scholars at Chicago are encouraged to pursue. This means, for one thing, that the "Protestant synthesis" does not characterize their work. These historians question the canon of historical writing produced in the Protestant era even as many of them continue to pursue themes shaped in a Protestant culture. Few of them concentrate on the old "frontier thesis" that marked the early years of the school. The shift for most has been toward the urban and pluralist scene. They call into question, not in devastating rage but in steady patterns of inquiry, the received wisdom about who matters, and why, in American religion.

So it is that this series of books focuses on blacks, women, dispensationalists, suburbanites, members of "marginal" denominations, "ethnics" and immigrants as readily as it does on white men of progressive urban bent in mainstream denominations and of long standing in America. The authors relish religious diversity and enjoy discovering the power of people once considered weak, the centrality to the American plot of those once regarded as peripheral, and the potency of losers who were once disdained by winners. Thus this series enhances an understanding of an America overlooked by the people of Sweet's era two-thirds of a century ago when it all, or most of it, began.

Rebellion for its own sake would not long hold interest; it might tell more about the psychology of rebels and revisers than about their subject matter. Revision, better than rebellion, characterizes the scholars. Re+vision: that's it. There was an original vision that characterized the Chicago School. This was the contention that in secular America and its universities religion mattered, as a theme in the national past and as a presence in the present. Second, it argued that the study of religious history belonged not only in the seminaries and archives of denominations, but also in the rough-and-tumble of the secular university, where no religious meanings were privileged and where each historian had to make a case for the value of his or her story.

Other assumptions from the earliest days pervade the books in this series. They are uncommonly alert to the environment in which expressions of faith occur. That is, they do not take for granted that religion comes protected in self-evidently important and hermetically sealed packages. Churches and denominations are porous, even when they would be sealed off; they cannot be understood apart from the ways the social environs effect them, but their power to effect change in the environment demands equal and truly unapologetic treatment. These writers do not shuffle and mumble and make excuses for their existence or for the choice of apparently arcane subject matter. They try to present their narrative in such ways that they compel attention.

A fourth characteristic that colors these works is a refusal in most cases to be typed in a fashionable slot labeled, variously, "intellectual" or "institutional" history, "cultural" or "social" history, or whatever. While those which concentrate on magisterial thinkers such as Jonathan Edwards are necessarily busy with and devoted to his intellectual achievement, most of the books deal with figures who cannot be understood only as exemplars in a sequence of studies of "the life of the mind." Instead, their biographies and circumstances come very much into play. On the other hand, none of these writers is a reductionist who sees religion as "nothing but" this or that—"nothing but" the working out of believers' Oedipal urges or expressing the economic and class interests of the subjects. Social history becomes in its way intellectual history, even if the intellects are focused on something other than the theologians in the traditions might like to see.

Some years ago *Look* magazine interviewed leaders in various denominations. One was asked if his fellow believers considered that theirs was the only true faith. Yes, he said, but they did not believe that they were the only ones who held it. The editors of this series of studies and the contributors to it do not believe that the "Chicago School," whenever and whatever it was, is the only true approach to American religious history. And, if they did, they would not hold that Chicagoans alone held it. To do so would imply a strange solipsistic or narcissistic impulse that would be the death of collegiality in the historical field. They have welcomed the chance to be in a climate where their inquiries are given such encouragement, where they find a company of fellow scholars in the Divinity School, the History Department, and the Committee on the History of Culture, whence these studies first emerged, and elsewhere in a university that provides a congenial home for massed and massive concentration of a special sort on American religious history.

While the undersigned have been consistently involved, most often together, in all twenty-one books, we want to single out a third person mentioned in so many acknowledgment sections, historian Arthur Mann. He has been a partner in two or three dozen religious history dissertation projects through the years and has been an influential and decisive contributor to the results. We stand in his debt.

Jerald C. Brauer
Martin E. Marty

Editor's Preface

Late in this century the descendants of earlier immigrants often express aloud, especially during battles over "bilingualism" in public schools, some bewilderment over why the newcomers, especially the millions of Latinos or Hispanics, are not content to have English alone taught in public schools. The Poles and Ukrainians, the Galician Jews and Russians all had to learn English, and so did the Germans and Italians who receive notice in this book. What is different about then and now? Why cannot the newcomers do like the oldcomers and adapt straightaway to American ways?

There is, of course, no single and simple answer to such questions, but this book, by focusing on two immigrant groups in one city and by devoting attention to one church, the Roman Catholic, throws significant light on the issues involved. Early in this century, urban Catholicism was strong as an institution and a framer of ways of life for millions of recent arrivals to America. Key to this church movement were the local parishes with their range of festivals and services performed for members and especially their parochial schools. Today many descendants of those urban Catholics have turned prosperous and entered a suburban dispersion. There by the tens of millions they remain faithful to the church, but their ways of life are diffused into the general population mix. They left behind for blacks, Latinos, and Asians, great shells of buildings for congregations now Pentecostal, now Baptist. They found few women becoming nuns and lost the work force and the means to keep the parochial schools strong, or even to help them all survive. So the newer Spanish-speaking immigrants have no choice but public schools. No wonder they use these to keep their customs and language intact.

Were the old parochial schools, then, instruments of German and Italian language expression and cultural intention? Not so, or not quite, as Shaw shows. An interesting dialectic occurred between the parishes and the diocese. The archdiocesan office had a synoptic and pragmatic view. The young Catholics, in order to remain Catholic, had to find ways to move with ease in the larger culture. They had to be Americanized, and that meant they needed instruction in English language and in American ways. Parents sent their children to these schools and allowed or perhaps even encouraged some of the changes thus to occur.

However, they were not simply Americanized, stirred into a melting pot, dispersed and diffused into a Protestant-Jewish-secular culture of nondescript character. They used the parishes as agencies where they could practice the old, imported, European ways. The dramas, clubs, festivals, folk practices all served to help them reinforce their ethnicity, to honor where it was whence they came, to remember ancestral ways, to preserve dignity among populations that so often scorned their ways.

In short, the parishes were, as Shaw effectively demonstrates, way-stations between ethnic and immigrant phases to Americanized status. This did not mean that there was one-way traffic at whose exit they became ex-Catholic. The archdiocese would not have stood for Americanization on such terms. Instead, they were given tools for bringing together their past and present, their old ways and new, Old World and New, old faith and new circumstance. The system was imperfect, often randomly established and maintained, and probably not as defined as Shaw's story reveals it to be. But by focusing on one city, Chicago, he has projected onto the screen of national consciousness one important if not normative way by which immigrants of old "made it"—a way that (many will share my conviction) has lessons for today even as it aids in appreciation of the people and ways of yesterday.

Martin E. Marty

Acknowledgments

Completion of this work would have been impossible without the assistance and cooperation of many individuals. Martin E. Marty patiently saw it through three drafts to its final form. His expert critique, as well as his constant enthusiasm for this project, are deeply appreciated. Fr. Wencelaus J. Madaj, archivist for the Archdiocese of Chicago, allowed free use of the archdiocesan archives. The staff of the *New World*, the official archdiocesan newspaper, generously supplied a complete set of microfilms for this research. Fr. Conrad Borntrager, O.S.M., archivist for the Servite Order, generously provided access to the Servite Archives as well as supplementary material at Our Lady of Sorrows Basilica. The Fathers of St. Boniface Parish were most helpful in allowing access to their personal parish archives. Fr. Marion A. Habig, O.F.M., provided valuable information on Chicago's German parishes as well as a complete set of parish *Pfarrbote* from St. Augustine's Parish. Mr. and Mrs. Anthony Serritella, as well as their son James, were most hospitable and generous with their time and provided invaluable information on Chicago's Italian community. Theresa Krutz, a member of the Chicago Historical Society, shared her considerable knowledge of Chicago's German community. In the final stages of preparation, the typing of Patricia Hickey was most appreciated. Lastly, I wish to acknowledge the patient endurance of my wife, Dorothy, who not only provided valuable editorial comment, but the loyalty and encouragement needed to complete such a project.

The Catholic Parish as a Way-Station

ONE

Chicago: The City and Its People

Chicago traces its history to colonial days, when French explorers met the "Iliniwek," or Illinois tribes on the banks of the Illinois and Des Plaines rivers. The word "Chicago" (variously spelled che-cau-gou, Chikagu, Chicaqu) reputedly meant place of the wild garlic, skunkweed, or "something great."[1] Whatever its real meaning, Chicago remained an isolated outpost until the first half of the nineteenth century. Father Jacques Marquette, who visited the region in the summer of 1673, returned in 1674 to minister to the needs of the Indians.[2] He was the first recorded European to stay in the area.[3] Recognizing the strategic importance of the area, George Rogers Clark captured Vincennes for the Americans in 1779.[4] The Northwest Ordinance (1787) opened the area to further exploration. Chicago's first settler was Jean Baptiste Point Du Sable, a black man, born in Santo Domingo around 1750. Starting a settlement on the north side of the Chicago River, Du Sable transported food and materials from one side of the river to the other. Although the settlement grew into a thriving trading center, Du Sable and his family suddenly moved, without any explanation, to East Peoria, Illinois.[5]

But the city was destined to grow—and the army was the first to arrive. A detachment of United States soldiers erected a fort at Michigan and Wacker in July 1803. Named after Henry Dearborn, fifth secretary of war, the compound spawned a thriving settlement, which attracted many emigrants from the East Coast. John Kinzie, who purchased the Du Sable trading post in early 1803, acted as a liaison between the soldiers and Indians. A few miles southwest, the community of Bridgeport welcomed its first resident, Charles Lee, who cultivated a farm in that area shortly after 1803. But the Battle of Tippecanoe (1811) was a harbinger of bad times. The War of 1812 left Fort Dearborn far beyond the American line of settlement, a week's march from the closest fort. On August 15, a band of Indians, attacking a group of retreating soldiers and civilians, killed fifty-two and captured forty-two as prisoners. They burned Fort Dearborn the same day.[6]

But Chicago again rose like a phoenix from the ashes of war. Soldiers rebuilt the fort in 1816; Illinois became a state on December 3, 1818; legislatures created Cook County on January 15, 1831; and Chicago, which received a town charter in 1833, became a city on March 4, 1837.[7] The town first attracted real estate speculators as well as Irish and German immigrants. The Irish, who were the largest foreign-born group through the first half of the century, numbered 6,096 by 1850. The majority, who were Catholic, soon supplanted the French as the most important ethnic group within Catholicism. Germans numbered 5,035 by midcentury, with the majority coming from the upper Rhine Valley.[8] A Yankee who came to Chicago in 1847 noted the "Dutch, who talk very bad English . . . you could understand them about as well as you could a flock of cackling geese."[9] While the Irish worked as laborers, the better-educated Germans opened shops and businesses. The English, Welsh, and Scotch, who numbered 2,493 in 1850, completed the ethnic side of the city.

Illinois changed from a frontier state to an emerging economic power between 1848 and 1871.[10] The railroads began to cross the state like a giant web in the late forties and fifties. Illinois's population grew from 851,470 in 1850, to 2,539,891 in 1870. Towns like Springfield, Alton, Peoria, Cairo, Quincy, Belleville, Beardstown, and Ottawa became thriving cities during these two decades.[11] But it was Chicago that grew the most during this period. The city numbered 29,963 in 1850; by 1860, it was a metropolis of 109,260. The Old Northwest contributed one-fourth of the total population of Chicago during the 1850s, and one-third during the 1860s. Foreign-born immigrants were 50 percent (54,586) of the total population by 1860. Germans were now the largest foreign-born element, with 22,230 inhabitants. The Irish followed, with 19,889.[12]

But Chicago was still a frontier town during the fifties and sixties. An 1849 cholera epidemic claimed thirty-six lives. Dysentery and tuberculosis were common, as mud and dirt plagued the city. But the native and foreign-born alike continued to flow into this rough city. They literally raised the streets out of the mud in 1857; they built sewers and public works to make life more amenable; they manned the factories and warehouses that made Chicago the packing center of the country by 1860.[13] The city suffered the traumas of the Civil War like the rest of the country, as 5,857 men lost their lives for the Union cause.[14] Chicago quickly recovered, and became the railroad hub of the nation by 1865. But this recovery was short-lived, as a terrible fire consumed the city on October 8, 1871, destroying three and a half square miles and left 104,500 homeless.

The decades between 1870 and 1900 were critical for Chicago and Illinois.[15] The state as a whole changed from a largely rural area to an urban and manufacturing center. Twenty-eight farm counties lost population between 1870 and 1890, as more and more emigrants were drawn to Chicago. By 1890, 28.7 percent of the total state population lived in Illinois's largest city. Chicago grew from a city of 298,977 in 1870, to a major American city of 1,698,575 by 1900. The immigrant population continued to flow into the city, as Germans, Poles, and Italians came to this promising metropolis. Chicago was America for these immigrants, a place where they could nourish their traditions and live with their compatriots, but at the same time, find the dream that was America. Germans increased from 52,316 in 1870, to 170,238 in 1900. The Polish element increased dramatically from 1,205 in 1870, to 59,713 at the turn of the century. Italians also grew from a mere 552 in 1870, to 16,008 in 1900. Czechs, Slovaks, and Hungarians were also present by the beginning of the twentieth century. By 1910, first- and second-generation immigrants accounted for 77 percent of the total population.[16] Max Weber noted the "maddening mixture" of Chicago's peoples in 1904: "The Greek shining the Yank's shoes for five cents, the German acting as his waiter, the Irishman managing his politics, and the Italian digging his dirty ditches."[17]

Chicago grew enormously during the last three decades of the nineteenth century; the city became the second largest urban area in the country and the sixth largest in the world. Industrial areas rose on the Chicago and Calumet rivers on the far southeast side. Chicago's elite lived on Prairie Avenue, between Eighteenth and Twenty-first streets. Chicago's immigrants worked at McCormick's reaper plant and the Union Stockyards, as well as in the steel mills that arose to the north and south. Germans, who were prominent in the labor struggles of the 1880s and 1890s, fiercely opposed the low wages and working conditions of Chicago's factories. While many espoused anarchism and communism, the vast majority simply struggled to survive.[18] But most immigrants, who continued to improve their lot, moved to better homes or apartments on the fringes of the city. The fantastic growth of three- and four-story apartment buildings during this period testifies to the gradual improvement of living conditions; indeed, contractors built over 1,142 units in 1883 alone.[19]

Illinois and Chicago grew from 1900 to 1940. In 1900, Illinois had a population of 4,821,550; by 1940, it had 7,897,241. Chicago grew from 1,698,575 in 1900, to 3,396,808 in 1940. Its area increased from 190 square miles in 1910, to 213 square miles in 1940. The most notable ethnic change was the emergence of the black as a significant and powerful force in Chicago life. In 1900, there were only 30,150 blacks in the city (1.07 percent of the whole); by 1940, this number had risen to 277,731 (8.1 percent). The percentage of immigrants to total population decreased, as native-born population and immigration restriction laws outpaced new arrivals. In 1900, Chicago had a foreign-born population of 587,112 (or 34.5 percent of the whole); by 1940, the actual number of foreign born had increased to 677,218, but the percentage had dropped to 20.5 percent of the whole. German foreign-born decreased from 170,738 in 1900, to 83,424 in 1940. The Irish decreased from 73,912 to 35,156 during the same period of time. Polish increased dramatically from 59,713 in 1900, to 119,264 in 1940. Italians also increased from 16,008 to 66,472 during the same forty years. Lithuanians, who were scarcely noticeable at the turn of the century, numbered 26,254 by 1940. Other groups, who were no more than traces in 1900, also made their appearance. Yugoslavians and Greeks numbered 12,659 and 13,972, respectively, in 1940. Mexicans, who first began to appear at the beginning of the century, grew from 102 in 1900, to 4,211 in 1930. Thus, Chicago continued to be an immigrant city, as new nationalities came to take the place of the old. It remained a city of promise, a place where the hopes, dreams, and aspirations could come true.[20]

New means of transportation enabled Chicago's citizenry to move north and south. Electric streetcars and the elevated replaced older cable cars by 1906. The el looped around the downtown area in a giant arch, as it spread its tentacles north, south, and west. Extending as far south as Sixty-ninth Street by 1915, the elevated encouraged the development of Sixty-third and Halsted as the largest outlying shopping center in Chicago. But the North Side quickly surpassed the South in the development of new residential neighborhoods. Both the Northwestern Railroad and the el furthered the northern movement of German and Irish immigrants. As early as 1907, the *Pfarrbote* (parish bulletin) of St. Boniface Parish (921 North Noble Street) observed that the city was becoming a place for business, while people were moving to the suburbs (January 1907). Between 1910 and 1916, the population within four miles of the Loop remained stationary (about one million), while the population from four to seven miles jumped from 460,000 to 1,076,000; the population from seven to ten miles increased from 189,000 to 332,000.[21] Chicago's elite now lived on the Near North Side, while older areas such as Ashland Boulevard on the West Side and Prairie Avenue on the South declined. Blacks moved into these areas as early as 1910, with significant pockets at Thirty-first and State and Ashland and Lake Streets. While segregation was complete, the problems of blacks were quite different from other immigrant groups.[22]

As older immigrants moved north (especially the Irish and Germans), newer ones took their place just beyond the central business district. Living conditions were deplorable, since much of the housing dated from the early 1880s. Three- and four-story apartment buildings appeared by 1900, "in rooms where the sun never enters. The air he breathes must reach him through dark passages and foul courts. He must be content with two yards square of earth's space for himself, for each one of his children, for each of his thousand close neighbors, and for each one of their children."[23] Rear tenements were even worse than the double-deckers; the front apartments cut off all light, the rooms were dark, and the conditions filthy. The worst area at the beginning of the century was the West Side, where thousands of Italians, Greeks, and other eastern Europeans settled. Crime, which was notorious in this part of the city, affected the Italians and Greeks in particular. The Twenty-second Precinct of the Nineteenth Ward, popularly known as the Bloody Maxwell District, was a den of murderers, thieves, burglars, and the worst gangs in the city. Irish hoodlums ruled the area until the 1880s; Bohemian, Jewish, and German gangs took over during the last two decades of the century. As Italians entered the district at the beginning of the century, men like Jim Colosimo monopolized the gambling and prostitution rackets.[24] But it was the poor immigrant who bore the brunt of criminal activity.

Chicago remained a city of immigrants through World War I. Immigration reached a four-year peak from 1911 to 1914, when 129,813 foreign-born entered Chicago. In 1910, first- and second-generation immigrants accounted for 77 percent of Chicago's population; the foreign-born alone were 35 percent of the total number. Graham Taylor, founder of Chicago Commons Settlement, watched his own community change from English, Irish, and German in the 1880s and 1890s, to Italian and Eastern European in the 1900s. Taylor, who never doubted the value of these new Americans, stated that he "was thus prepared to appreciate the hyphens of other people, whose love of their old fatherlands made them no less loyal, but all the more valuable to their adopted country, into whose fabric they weave themselves and their racial heritages."[25]

Chicago was poised for prosperity after World War I.[26] A new skyline rose in the Loop, suburbs mushroomed around the city like emerging flowers, and the automobile changed the face of Chicago forever. The city spent over three billion dollars on internal improvements alone during the 1920s. Electrical consumption increased 133 percent, and the number of cars quadrupled. Immigrants joined in the prosperity of the times, as a number of major business areas emerged away from the Loop. Lawrence and Broadway (Uptown), Lincoln-Ashland-Belmont, Madison and Pulaski, Sixty-third and Halsted (Englewood), Sixty-third and Cottage Grove (Woodlawn), and 111th and Michigan Avenue (Roseland) became commercial centers for Chicago's daily needs. Sears, Roebuck and Montgomery Ward, which opened several outlets at these regional centers, soon became Chicago's leading retailers. Local communities, which became focal points of day-to-day living, offered all the practical goods needed for daily life.[27]

Manufacturing continued to spread outward from Chicago's center, as factories followed the path of population and commerce. The Pershing Road tract had already been established before the war, on the South Side of the city. The Clearing Industrial district grew out of vacant lots on the southwest side. Giant industries such as Zenith, Motorola, and Admiral grew tremendously during this period. Lake Calumet on the far South Side also emerged as a major manufacturing center. As new factories rose in Evanston, Skokie, Cicero, Berwyn, Harvey, Chicago Heights, Waukegan, Aurora, and Joliet, immigrants either moved to these cities or took public transportation to them.[28]

From 1917 to 1927, Chicago welcomed 910,000 new inhabitants. Crop disasters in the South forced thousands of blacks to move north after World War I. By 1920, there were 109,458 blacks in Chicago (4.05 percent of the total population); by 1930, they had increased to 233,903 (or 6.09 percent of the whole). The black community, which was relatively prosperous during the 1920s, spread along South Parkway (Martin Luther King, Jr. Drive) and Michigan Avenue, as it took over apartments and storefronts along the way.[29] The Immigration Restriction Laws of 1921 and 1924 limited new immigration, while older groups began to decline considerably. German foreign-born decreased from a high of 182,281 in 1910, to a low of 83,424 in 1940. Polish immigration also diminished, from 137,611 in 1920, to 119,264 in 1940. Italian foreign-born increased during the same period, from

59,215 in 1920, to 73,960 in 1930. Second- and third-generation immigrants continued to make Chicago an immigrant city. German stock numbered 377,975 in 1930, while Polish descendants were even larger, with 401,316 the same year. The city itself grew 25 percent during the 1920s, while the six collar counties increased 33 percent.[30]

The older residential areas within four miles of State and Madison lost 150,000 persons between 1920 and 1930. Housing in this area, which was over forty years old, provided shelter for only the poorest immigrants. Meanwhile, the Irish, Germans, and native-born moved upward into the better apartment buildings which were mushrooming around the city. Three-story apartments expanded rapidly both before and after World War I, on land where frame cottages used to stand. Vacant prairie lands were enriched by eighteen- to forty-two-family units. Single-family bungalows sprouted up on cheaper land beyond the apartment belt; it was a sign of the new prosperity that affected the entire country. Over 100,000 such homes were built in the 1920s. Subdivisions began to rise at the edge of the city, as farmlands gave way to sidewalks and three- and four-story apartment buildings.[31] New suburbs emerged as older ones prospered. Germans gradually moved north to Evanston, Wilmette, Skokie, and Kenilworth, while Italians moved west to Elmwood Park, River Forest, and Riverside. Chicago soon became a suburban metropolis.[32]

The general division of Chicago into north, west, and south was always unrealistic, for the city was basically a mosaic of ethnic and racial neighborhoods. Neighborhood consciousness remained strong through the 1930s, as eastern and southern Europeans clung to their native enclaves.[33] City census figures corroborate this. Germans remained the second leading ethnic group between 1930 and 1940.[34] The North Side remained heavily German, as thirty-one community areas within Chicago numbered over one thousand foreign-born. The leading Teutonic community in 1930 was Lakeview, with 7,768 foreign-born Germans (27.1 percent of the total population), followed closely by Lincoln Park, with 7,283 foreign-born (29.1 percent of the total) the same year. Other German communities included North Center (5,927 foreign-born), Uptown (3,677), and Logan Square (3,639). Of Chicago's seventy-five community areas, eighteen boasted Germans as the leading foreign-born group. Italians were the fifth largest foreign-born group in the city in 1930, with 73,960 foreign-born (8.8 percent of the total population). The Near West Side remained the leading Italian community—as it had been for decades—with 17,161 foreign-born (44 percent of the whole). West Town, which lay directly south of it, numbered 8,290 (11.5 percent of the whole) foreign-born, making it the second leading Italian community in 1930.

As the decade passed, these figures remained remarkably the same. While the total German foreign-born population declined from 111,366 in 1930 to 83,424 in 1940, twenty-six community areas still numbered more than one thousand foreign-born. Italians, whose total numbers declined from 73,960 in 1930 to 66,472 in 1940, became the fourth largest ethnic group by World War II. The Near West Side, with 11,849 foreign-born, and West Town, with 6,776, remained Chicago's strongest Italian communities. These statistics show a Chicago that was still divided into distinct ethnic and racial groups. Charles Merriam, an astute observer of Chicago's ethnic scene, observed in 1929 that two-thirds of Chicago's total population was either foreign-born or the children of foreign-born parents. He noted that "Pole, Irish, German, Czech, Italian, Slav, Jew; these are not the symbols of concord in Chicago any more than they are in Europe from which they came. On the contrary, the battles between them are often very bitter."[35] Hence, on the eve of World War II, Chicago was still a colorful mixture of diverse nationalistic groups. Although some turned to politics and nationalistic societies for support,[36] it was still the Catholic Church that best fulfilled their needs.

Catholicism grew with Illinois during the first half of the nineteenth century. Despite nativistic attacks, the Catholic Church was a leading force in the history of Illinois.[37] Bishop Stephen Flaget of Bardstown, Kentucky, learned of the existence of four French settlements around Chicago in 1815.

> I hear during my excursion that in the very midst of the Indians were four French congregations belonging to my diocese; one on the upper Mississippi, another in a place usually designated as Chicagou, still another on the shores of Lake Michigan and a fourth towards the source of the Illinois River; but lack of time and the prevalence of war have prevented me from visiting them.[38]

Father Gabriel Richard visited the area in September 1821.

> Thirty days in all from Macinac, I arrived at a post called Chicago, near a little river of the same name, ten leagues to the northwest of the southernmost point of Lake Michigan. I said Mass in the house of a Canadian and preached in the afternoon to an American garrison.[39]

Richard, who came to Chicago to witness a peace treaty between the governor and the Potawatomy Indians, was probably the first priest to preach in Chicago. Most of the city's Catholics were French or Indian—a reflection of Chicago's early ethnic beginnings.

But the church needed permanent priests if Catholicism was to succeed in Illinois. A group of Chicagoans petitioned Bishop Joseph Rosatti of St. Louis, Missouri, for permanent clergymen.

> We, the Catholics of Chicago, Cook Co., Ill., lay before you the necessity there exists to have a pastor in this new and flourishing city. There are several families of French descent, born and brought up in the Roman Catholic faith and others quite willing to aid us in supporting a pastor, who ought to be sent before other sects obtain the upper hand.[40]

Bishop Rosatti responded by appointing Father John Mary St. Cyr as Chicago's first permanent pastor. Conditions were primitive—there was no permanent church, money was scarce, and few had but a rudimentary knowledge of the faith. But St. Cyr managed to build Chicago's first Catholic church in 1837. Americans, Irish, French, and Germans met at a common altar for the first time, under the patronage of the Virgin Mary. As more and more immigrants inundated the city, ecclesiastical authorities wisely made it a diocese in its own right in 1844.[41]

The Right Reverend William Quarter, Chicago's first bishop, was consecrated by Archbishop John Hughes of New York and arrived in Chicago on May 5, 1844. The diocese included the entire state of Illinois, with only twenty-three native and foreign priests in residence. Quarter wrote Archbishop Joseph Purcell of Cincinnati that "a great spirit of liberality exists towards Catholics in all parts of this state and in the city. . . . I have already visited a large portion of the diocese and the prospects everywhere else are . . . bright for Catholicity. In almost every part of the state there are Catholics settled and although they are poor, yet they are willing to contribute of their scanty means."[42]

The new bishop was particularly concerned for the immigrants within his community. He appealed to the Leopold Association in Germany for financial assistance. German Catholics, who numbered about one thousand, were in dire need of German-speaking priests. The Reverend C. H. Ostlangenberg was sent to Chicago and another priest to Quincy, Illinois, for the German communities in those cities. Quarter established two German-speaking parishes in Chicago at this time: St. Joseph's Parish, at Chicago Avenue and Cass Street, was established on August 15, 1846, St. Peter's, at Wells and Franklin, was established five days later.[43] Bishop Quarter also founded other immigrant churches during his brief but busy episcopate. He established St. Patrick's Church at Adams and Desplaines, for the Irish in his community (1847); and St. Anne's, at Bourbonnais Grove near Kankakee, for the French of his diocese the very same year. But his premature death in 1848 robbed the city of a young and dynamic leader. The bishop left a diocese of 80,000 Catholics, 40 priests, and 56 churches.[44]

The Right Reverend James Oliver Van de Velde became Chicago's second bishop on February 11, 1849. His personal diary reflects the immigrant nature of the church at midcentury.

> In general, the emigrants who come to these parts and who make up almost the entire Catholic population, are not in a position to supply even their own wants. Poverty is so great that there is not a single parish . . . which is provided with the necessary equipment for the celebration of the sacred rites. A single priest has sometimes eight parishes to attend and as he has for those various stations only one chalice, one missal, one chasuble, one alb, one altar-stone, he must perforce carry all these articles with him, however long and distressing be the way.[45]

Bishop Van de Velde supervised the construction of Holy Name Church, first at Cass and Superior, then at State and Superior; it was destroyed by the Great Fire in 1871. Other churches moved as immigrant populations left their original neighborhoods. St. Peter's German Church picked up and moved to the southwest corner of Polk and Clark streets in 1853, while St. Patrick's Irish Church left for Desplaines and Adams the same year. Van de Velde established two new German parishes for his ever-increasing immigrant flock: St. Michael's, on the Near North Side, in 1852, and St. Francis of Assisi, on the West Side, in 1851. He also founded new parishes in Edwardsville, Rockville, Woodstock, Chester, and Buffalo Grove. Bothered by rheumatism, Van de Velde resigned his see in 1854; he became bishop of Natchez, Tennessee, the same year.

Bishop Anthony O'Regan succeeded Van de Velde as Chicago's third bishop. The diocese was now divided in half, with Quincy the second episcopal see. O'Regan, who admired the Jesuits, invited Father Arnold Damen and three other Jesuits to conduct a series of missions in 1856; the society soon established Holy Family Church, at 1019 South May, in 1857, and St. Ignatius College, at 1076 West Roosevelt Road (Twelfth Street), the same year. The Flemish bishop, who could not always control his nationalistic clergy, wrote to a friend in 1857:

> For the last nine years this diocese has been grievously afflicted by bad priests, Irish, French, and German. My predecessor was frustrated and tried to resign, he could not live here. I am suffering far, far more and know not what I shall do.[46]

When a dissident Frenchman even threatened his life, O'Regan exclaimed, "This has been more than once threatened and they are wicked enough to do it."[47] Tired out by strife and illness, O'Regan retired to Ireland in 1858 and died at Brompton, England, on November 13, 1866.[48]

Bishop James Duggan governed the Chicago diocese during the Civil War decade. Consecrated on May 3, 1857, he received news of his appointment on January 21, 1859. Catholicism spread rapidly in Chicago during his episcopate. New parishes sprang from older ones, as Chicago's Catholic immigrants filled up the vacant prairies and farmlands that made up this expanding city. By 1870, Chicago numbered twenty-seven parishes, averaging 11,074 parishioners per parish. Irish communities spread north and south, as the men of Eire and their families bettered their lives. St. Patrick's begot St. Jarlath's on the West Side, while St. Columbkille's bore Annunciation Parish on the North Side. St. James Parish, at 2942 South Wabash, established two missions during the 1860s: St. Thomas the Apostle in Hyde Park and St. Anne's on Garfield Boulevard.[49] There were 39,988 foreign-born Irish in Chicago at the end of the decade. Germans were now the leading foreign-born nationality, with 52,316 in 1870.[50] Bishop Duggan also established St. Boniface Parish, at 921 North Noble, in 1865, as Chicago's fifth German parish. Polish immigrants, who were also numerous, established St. Stanislaus Kostka Parish (1867), at 1351 West Evergreen Street, in 1867. Other ethnic parishes included Notre Dame de Chicago (French, 1865) and St. Wenceslaus (Bohemian, 1866).[51] By the end of the decade, Chicago Catholicism was largely foreign-born, with Irish and German immigrants dominating the scene.

The Reverend Thomas Foley succeeded Duggan as bishop of Chicago in 1870, after a lengthy battle against mental illness forced the former bishop to retire. Foley had scarcely arrived in Chicago when the Great Fire destroyed much of his predecessors' work. Hundreds of institutions perished—the Christian Brothers' Academy on Van Buren Street, the House of Providence, St. Joseph's Orphan Asylum, St. Benedict's Convent, St. Michael's and St.

Joseph's German Parish, and Holy Name Cathedral. Foley extended his help for rebuilding to all races and creeds. He allowed Protestant and Jewish congregations to use Catholic churches for worship until new congregations could be built.[52] He founded three German parishes to care for the thousands of immigrants forced south of their homes—St. Anthony of Padua Parish, at 518 West Twenty-eighth Place, in 1873; St. Paul's, at 2127 West Twenty-second Place, in 1876; and St. Augustine's, at 5045 South Laflin, in 1879. Bishop Foley also established two Polish and six English-speaking parishes during his eight-year episcopate. Worn out from his labors, Chicago's fifth bishop died from pneumonia and typhoid fever on February 19, 1879.

As Chicago entered the last two decades of the nineteenth century, Catholicism struggled to keep the immigrants' loyalty. There were numerous national schisms during this period. Laymen of Sacred Heart Parish in Scranton, Pennsylvania, took control of the parish when the bishop refused to give them a voice in church affairs. Poles from St. Adalbert's Parish in Buffalo, New York, took over their congregation when they failed to reconcile their differences with the local bishop over control of church property. Fifty of these independent parishes formed the Polish National Catholic Church of America, under the leadership of Bishop Francis Hodur, of Scranton, Pennsylvania.[53]

But the most important national issue involved German Americans.[54] The largest immigrant group within Catholicism, German Americans were the most vocal in demanding their rights. They consistently fought to maintain their language and culture. They equated language with faith, as Arthur Preuss so eloquently stated in the *Fortnightly Review*:

> English is for all practical purposes a Protestant language . . . in trying to preserve the faith of these people [the German Americans] it is necessary that we scrupulously abstain, and cause others to abstain from any attempt to rob them of their language . . . all too often faith is lost together with language.[55]

To maintain their *Deutschtum* (Germanity), native Germans petitioned Rome for German bishops and national parishes. Peter Paul Cahensly, a Catholic merchant from Limburg, Germany, requested Rome to create national bishops and reorganize the hierarchy along ethnic lines. James Cardinal Gibbons, archbishop of Baltimore and the leading American prelate of the day, rejected this petition and stated that "we cannot view without astonishment and indignation a number of self-constituted and officious gentlemen in Europe complaining of the alleged inattention which is paid to the spiritual wants of the foreign population and to the means of redress which they have thought proper to submit to the Holy See."[56] These issues troubled the American church through the 1890s as Germanophiles (and other nationalities) struggled to maintain their ethnic ways. While Rome consistently refused to divide the American church into separate nationalities, individual American bishops set up their own ethnic parishes to reconcile the differences within American Catholicism. Such a man was Chicago's first archbishop.

The Right Reverend Patrick A. Feehan guided Chicago Catholicism through the 1880s and 1890s.[57] His greatest accomplishment was to reconcile the various ethnic and national forces in his archdiocese. Feehan was an American pragmatist who sought practical solutions to Chicago's problems. While Pope Leo XIII essentially decreed against such ethnic parishes in 1886, Feehan, recognizing their necessity, supervised the establishment of a vast network of ethnic communities.[58] He managed to placate the three most powerful immigrant groups within the city—the Irish, the Germans, and the Poles. For the Irish, he supported nationalistic societies devoted to the liberation of Ireland. And for the Germans and Poles, he established fifty-three ethnic parishes on the North and South sides of the city (see Table 1).

Archbishop Feehan celebrated the silver jubilee of his episcopal ordination on November 19, 1890. The occasion was a celebration of Chicago's multiethnic but American church. A solemn Pontifical Mass, which was held at Holy Name Cathedral, began the festivities. Several hundred dignitaries gathered to honor Chicago's first archbishop. The next evening at the Auditorium Theater, the Reverend D. J. McCaffrey extolled the growth of the archdiocese:

> From the dying embers of Chicago's seven churches in 1871 was caught the spark of true devotion which inflamed the Catholic heart of Chicago with emulation and enthusiasm not only to rebuild but to beautify and multiply to sevenfold and seven the church buildings in our metropolis . . . the Catholic Church of Chicago, standing before the world so strong, so promising, surrounded by all the noble safeguards of religion, fortified by those 83 cross-crowned citadels, commanding 500,000 soldiers, marshalled by more than 200 fearless chieftains true to the cross—all commanded by . . . Archbishop Feehan.[59]

TABLE 1

German and Italian National Parishes, 1880-1903

German Parishes

SS. Peter and Paul	9041 South Exchange	1881
St. Alphonsus	1429 West Wellington	1882
Immaculate Conception	3111 South Aberdeen	1883
St. Aloysius	2300 West Lemonyne	1884
St. George	3924 South Wentworth	1884
St. Martin	5842 South Princeton	1885
Holy Trinity	916 South Wolcott	1885
St. Matthias	2310 West Ainslie	1887
St. Francis Xavier	2840 West Nelson	1888
St. Theresa	1037 West Armitage	1889
St. Maurice	3615 South Hoyne	1890
St. Nicholas	10809 South State	1890
St. Clara	6415 South Woodlawn	1894
Sacred Heart	7020 South Aberdeen	1894
St. Philomena	1921 North Kedvale	1895
Holy Ghost	2150 West Adams	1896
Our Lady of Perpetual Help	1300 South St. Louis	1898
St. Raphael	6012 South Laflin	1901
St. Benedict	2212 West Irving Road	1902

Italian Parishes

Assumption	323 West Illinois	1886
St. Mary of Mt. Carmel	6722 South Hermitage	1892
Holy Guardian Angel	860 West Cabrini	1899
Santa Maria Incoronata	218 Alexander Street	1899

SOURCE: *The Official Catholic Directory* (Milwaukee: M. H. Wiltzius Co., 1903-10; New York: P. J. Kennedy and Sons, 1920-40).

Archbishop Ryan of Philadelphia noted that though "there are some . . . who might think that he might have been more progressive, might have led more movements, might have gone on more in the spirit of this city. . . . [Yet] Chicago . . . needs something to restrain and direct her."[60] The French representative pointed out that French Canadians living in the United States preserved their maternal tongue while remaining fervent Catholics and loyal citizens.[61] The German delegate emphasized the close connection between language and faith:

> Each people . . . find the devout expression . . . only in their own language. In the union instituted by God there can be no confusion. . . . Our German language is to us the treasure that is inseparable with our being. We are better citizens, better men and better Christians if we give expression to our noblest feelings in our own tongue unhindered. It is the tie that holds us together, and it presents our duties to our country and even to our God and Church. . . . This treasure cannot and shall not be torn from us. For it and for the preservation of our German parish schools we stake our best powers. Upon these two rests our steadfastness in the faith and our loyalty to the Church.[62]

Feehan, who addressed the crowd last, stressed the gradual Americanization of his immigrant flock:

> But though speaking many tongues and representing many races, there is one common language which you all speak . . . for each one repeats the same credo—I believe in the 'Holy Catholic Church'. . . . That future will be when the children of many races shall form one great people united by a bond stronger than death—that of their Catholic faith. As the mountain streams uniting form at length the broad, deep river, so those streams of population coming from many sources will make great people. Strong, free, intelligent, Catholic. . . . They will be always found among the best and most devoted of our citizens . . . because their religion will continue to teach them that loyalty to the commonwealth is an imperative and conscientious duty.[63]

Like a mosaic of many colors, these speeches show a church that was in the very first stages of Americanization. Immigrant groups were still strong and vital, as they fostered their own languages and traditions. Germans, French, and Italians all vied for a place in the Catholic Church. Archbishop Feehan, who recognized these differences, allowed each nationality to develop its own brand of Catholicism. But he also realized that these groups could not remain separate forever; they would one day merge into a united American people.

Feehan's genius, which lay in his ability to recognize these differences, effectively reconciled disparate and often feuding elements.

The Chicago archdiocese grew considerably under Archbishop Feehan. The *New World* became Chicago's first diocesan newspaper in 1892.[64] The Visitation and Aid Society, the Illinois Charitable Relief Corps, the St. Vincent de Paul Society, and the National Catholic Women's League were also founded at this time. Feehan also established numerous benevolent societies to provide insurance for poor immigrants—e.g., the Catholic Order of Foresters, the Catholic Benevolent Legion, the Catholic Knights and Ladies of America, and the Catholic Mutual Benefit Association. Ethnic societies, which were already strong and numerous, included the Ancient Order of Hibernians (Irish), the German Roman Catholic Verein, and the Polish Roman Catholic Union. When Feehan died on July 12, 1902, he left Chicago a legacy of 137 parishes, 566 priests, and over one million Catholics. These parishes included 61 national communities—27 German, 15 Polish, 8 Bohemian, 4 French, 4 Italian, and 3 Lithuanian. The archdiocese also numbered 23 academies for girls, 8 colleges for boys, 7 orphan asylums, and 4 industrial and reform schools.[65] Feehan was clearly a man fit for the times. Judiciously guiding the Chicago church through a turbulent era, the archbishop led his foreign flock on the narrow path between ethnicity and Americanization.[66] His successors were able to build on his rich legacy.

Catholicism, which became a major force within the city by the end of the century, was already one-third of the total population in 1892.[67] German foreign-stock, 33 percent of whom were Catholic, accounted for approximately 25 percent of the total population in 1890. In the same year, Irish stock (76 percent Catholic) counted for 13 percent, and Polish ancestry (97 percent Catholic), 6.5 percent.[68] There were 107 Catholic parishes in the city by 1895, with an average 13,317 parishioners per parish. By 1900, German parishes averaged 7,302 registered members, while Italian parishes were somewhat behind with 4,002 parishioners each.[69] By 1929, there were 253 parishes in Chicago—36 of these were Polish, 31 German, 11 Italian, 9 Lithuanian, 7 Slovak, 7 Bohemian and 17 other national communities (altogether these parishes totaled 118). By 1930, German foreign-stock were 11 percent of the total population, while Italian descendants numbered 5.3 percent.[70] German parishes averaged 3,976 parishioners that year, while Italian communities averaged 6,724. By 1940, German parishes, which were still large, averaged 3,090 parishioners per parish; while Italian communities averaged 6,043 the same year. Chicago grew 113.4 percent from 1900 to

1940 (based on 1850 as a starting point), while Chicago's parishes grew 54.2 percent.[71] It is clear that Catholicism welcomed the new century in a strong position. Its ethnic affiliants were one-third of the total population, while its national parishes remained strong and vital. Germans and Italians, who were significant parts of the total Catholic population, maintained ethnically important parishes as way stations of tradition and Americanization.

The Reverend James Quigley led the Chicago archdiocese through the first four decades of the new century. Born in Osawa, Ontario, of Irish immigrant stock, Quigley came to the United States in 1864, when his parents moved to Buffalo, New York. Educated in Austria and Rome, he first assisted at St. Vincent Parish, in Attica, New York. After serving at various parishes, Quigley became bishop of Buffalo on February 24, 1897. Six years later, on March 10, 1903, he formally became Chicago's second archbishop.[72] Ethnics were prominent at his arrival. A committee of three Germans, one Italian, one Pole, one Hungarian, and seven Irishmen greeted the archbishop on his arrival in Chicago. The *New World* reported: "The thousand who were jubilantly singing contained hosts accustomed from childhood to chorales, a large proportion of the singers being from the most musical of nations, the Italians, the Germans, Poles, French, Bohemians, and the children of Ireland."[73]

Since Quigley had spent so much time in Europe, he understood better than most bishops the plight of the newcomers. Always taking a deep interest in ethnic minorities, Quigley preached to Germans, Italians, Poles, and Frenchmen in their own native tongues. He had helped to settle a longshoremen's strike in Buffalo along ethnic lines; he also reconciled the various ethnic groups of that city, "despite the various racial bloods" that flowed through his diocese. Quigley courageously spoke out in behalf of immigrants, at a time when many wanted to restrict their arrival. As he said, "A young people, a people of a composite stock, we have kinship with many different nations, but we are not identical with any of them, and are developing a separate national life."[74] While recognizing the need for temporary separation, Quigley also encouraged Americanization.

> Undoubtedly temporary segregation has its advantages; it protects, to some extent, religion and race. It is impossible, however, that such a status should continue. The friction resulting from association with other races will gradually disintegrate these colonies . . . the importance of having all these nationalities touch at certain points with the great Catholic body is apparent.[75]

Quigley consistently supported and established various immigrant organizations throughout the archdiocese. He headed the Catholic Colonization Society, which attempted to direct immigrants to agricultural communities. He was a member of the National Liberal Immigration League, which sought to counteract prejudice directed against foreigners. The archdiocesean *New World* consistently opposed immigration restriction. As it stated in 1908: "The great need of this country at present is not of men to read its laws but of men to keep them. Not of men who have been educated in the letter of the law, but of men who are imbued with its spirit because they have been brought up from their childhood in the atmosphere of genuinely Christian homes."[76] The foreign-language press followed Quigley in denouncing immigration restriction—the Poles and Czechs were most vehement, but the Irish and Germans also joined in opposition to any restrictive laws.

Contemporaries of Quigley agreed that America should be open to all immigrants. Frederick Siedenberg, S.J., founder of the Loyola University School of Sociology, published his views in a series of articles entitled "Immigration a Foe to America?" Writing in 1910, Siedenberg asked: "Why cannot the new immigrant and especially his children be assimilated? Has our melting pot lost its power? Today, all told, there are only fifteen million foreign-born persons in the country. Are the 85,000,000 native-born afraid of these?"[77] Bishop Peter J. Muldoon insisted that the new immigrant was "a mighty asset for the nation and for the Church if guided right."[78] The Reverend Edmund M. Dunne, Quigley's chancellor from 1905 to 1910, was attentive to Chicago's Italians. His basic principles were "(1) the immigrant must be kept faithful to his religion; (2) through his own language as long as necessary; and (3) he must at the same time be made a good American citizen." Dunne realized that an infinite continuation of racial differences was impossible, that "their progress is conditioned by their absorption into the American nation." At the same time, "it was never the Church's policy to obliterate the racial characteristics of her children coming here to enjoy liberty and advantages."[79]

Archbishop Quigley was a builder of immigrant churches. The city, which numbered 211 ecclesiastical communities by 1915, included numerous ethnic communities. There were 36 German, 33 Polish, 10 Italian, 9 Lithuanian, and 8 Slovenian parishes.[80] Quigley established two new German parishes during his episcopate: St. Gregory's, at 1634 West Gregory Street, in 1904; and St. Clement's, at 642 West Deming Street, in 1905. But it was the Italians whom Quigley understood the best. Having lived in their country for four years, he sympathized with their varying problems and understood their need to continue ethnic traditions.

The *New World* said of Quigley: "Many of the new churches were erected to accommodate the ever-increasing foreign population of the city. Archbishop Quigley was most zealous in seeing that these adopted children of America were well-cared for . . . if these thousands were to become useful and respected citizens of their new home. Archbishop Quigley's administration saw erected in the neighborhood of 20 new Italian churches alone."[81] Six of these were in Chicago:[82]

Santa Maria Addolorato	528 North Ada Street	1903
St. Michael Archangel	2325 West 24th Place	1903
St. Anthony of Padua	11533 South Prairie Street	1904
Holy Rosary	612 North Western Avenue	1904
Our Lady of Pompeii	1224 West Lexington Avenue	1911
St. Francis de Paula	7822 South Dobson Street	1911

Chicago remained an immigrant city throughout Quigley's twelve-year episcopate. The Reverend M. J. Madaj noted that "Chicago Catholics boasted that the Archdiocese had more Irish Catholics than Dublin, more German Catholics than Berlin, more Polish Catholics than Warsaw, more Bohemian Catholics than Prague, and more Italian Catholics than Pisa."[83] Bishop Paul Rhode of Green Bay, Wisconsin, extolled the archbishop's appreciation of immigrant groups in a eulogy:

> His main concern was at all times to understand his varied flock. I can consciously say that during the six years of my close association with him in the work of the pastorate, I never once heard a disparaging word regarding any of the nationalities that enter into the composition of our Catholic population, and I can equally conscientiously say that there is not one nationality but was possessed of some trait that the Archbishop in special praised and held up to admiration as offsetting and redeeming any shortcomings that otherwise might be noticed.[84]

Archbishop Quigley was a progressive and dynamic archbishop. He exhorted his parishioners to support Indian and black missions as early as 1904. He hosted the first Catholic Missionary Congress in 1908, under the auspices of the Catholic Church Extension Society. He contributed enormously to the institutional growth of the church by establishing various organizations, societies, and educational institutes. St. Mary's Training School for orphan boys and girls was one of his principal interests—an institute that was completely rebuilt after a fire destroyed it in 1899. Quigley also supported the first Catholic social settlements, which included the first day nurseries in Chicago. He established parish boards, which included lay trustees to supervise parish finances; he also divided larger parishes into smaller ones, as he founded seventy-four new parishes between 1903 and 1915. Grammar schools increased from 166 to 256 during the same period, while the total number of elementary students grew from 67,321 to 109,162. There were twelve boys' high schools by 1915, and twenty-five girls' academies the same year.[85] It was an episcopate marked by growth and consolidation, a time when Chicago Catholicism welcomed its immigrant flock and made them a part of the city and the church.[86]

The Roman Catholic Union participated at his funeral. Eight Germans and one Italian assisted Daniel McGann, the grand marshall of the funeral procession, as it wound its way through Chicago's Loop. The *New World* wrote in its obituary:

> This unanimous response of the societies proved that, regardless of individual society or nationality, all are one in Catholicity and good feeling. The great service rendered by our late Archbishop in welding together the various races and nationalities was wonderfully demonstrated on this occasion.[87]

Indeed, Chicago's second archbishop cautiously encouraged Americanization while courageously defending ethnic rights. While recognizing the value of all nationalities, Quigley particularly defended the right of Italians to maintain their own national parishes. He instinctively recognized the need for these way stations of ethnicity and Americanization. But his successor would not be so willing to accommodate his immigrant flock.

George William Mundelein became Chicago's third archbishop on November 29, 1915. A descendent of five generations of German Americans, he grew up on the East Side of New York City, where he attended De LaSalle Institute and Manhattan College.[88] Offered a midshipmanship at the Naval Academy by President Grover Cleveland, Mundelein turned it down for a career in the church. His studies at St. Vincent Abbey in Latrobe, Pennsylvania, and the Propaganda Fidei in Rome led to his ordination for the Brooklyn diocese in 1895. After nine years of service in various parishes and as chancellor of the diocese, Mundelein was consecrated auxiliary bishop of

Brooklyn on September 21, 1908. Seven years later, he was formally installed as archbishop of metropolitan Chicago on February 9, 1916.[89]

Mundelein was a much different man from Quigley. While Quigley essentially encouraged ethnicity, Mundelein merely tolerated it. While Quigley actively supported ethnic schools and institutions, Mundelein tried to hasten their Americanization. This can be seen in his attitude toward Catholic education.[90] One of his first acts as archbishop was to reform and reorganize the parochial school system. On April 28, 1916, he appointed three parish school supervisors—an Irishman, a German, and a Pole—to coordinate school activities and evaluate textbooks. Representatives from 250 parochial schools met with the new supervisors to select appropriate texts for the first four years. They recommended unified methods of teaching, common exams, and standardized report cards. Ethnic schools were required to teach the ordinary subjects in English, although they could conduct reading and catechism in their own language. Mundelein saw the parish school as "an anchor that steadies and holds the boat. A school will insure the continuation of a parish more than anything else. . . . More than that, it is the junior church." The parochial school was one of the principal instruments for Americanization. As Mundelein himself stated: "We know that education must not be one-sided, not of the intellect alone, but also of the heart, of the soul. It is for this reason that at so great a sacrifice, with so much labor at so great expense, we are erecting, maintaining and perfecting our schools."[91]

American parishes needed American priests. It was for this reason that Mundelein established one of the largest diocesan seminary systems in the world.[92] Announcing plans for Quigley Preparatory Seminary on May 14, 1916, he enthusiastically welcomed thirty young men that very same year. The seminary opened in 1919, the seventy-fifth anniversary of the diocese of Chicago. Shortly thereafter, Mundelein announced plans for St. Mary of the Lake Seminary. Mr. and Mrs. Edward Hines, prominent Catholic laity and owners of the Hines Lumber Company, donated $500,000 for the new seminary in memory of their son, Lieutenant Edward Hines, who had fallen in battle during World War I. Construction of the new seminary began in 1920 in Area, Illinois (the city was later renamed for Mundelein himself), with the first seminarians arriving in 1924. The seminary chapel opened on September 19, 1925, and by 1926, the first students were ordained to the priesthood. The institute, which continued to grow under Mundelein's supervision, ordained fifty seminarians in 1934. It continues to exist as the ultimate example of Mundelein's concern for Americanization.

Archbishop Mundelein encouraged assimilation through numerous archdiocesan organizations and societies. He elevated the Holy Name Society to one of the principal sodalities for men. Originally founded in 1274,[93] the society was largely a loose federation of parochial units until Mundelein made it a laymen's militia, for "the personal sanctification of the individual members."[94] He entrusted it with the care of juvenile delinquents through the Big Brother movement. He built Holy Name Technical School in Lockport, Illinois, to care for young men sent from Boys' and Juvenile Court. By 1921, there were over two hundred Big Brother groups, which cared for more than 4,000 boys.[95] The Holy Name Society also operated an employment bureau for young men, a lecture circuit, and a subscription service for the *New World*. By joining the Holy Name Society, ethnic parishes became more American and more Catholic. The records of the *New World* indicate that membership in the society increased dramatically during the 1920s and 1930s; by 1943, there were over 15,000 members. Indeed, Mundelein's efforts to coordinate parish activities through the Holy Name Society were largely successful.[96]

A small group of French Catholic laymen founded the St. Vincent de Paul Society in 1833.[97] Frederick Ozanam, a spokesman for the society, described its goals: "The visitation of the poor in their homes, if carried our prudently, would have a more salutary influence on themselves. If you are to serve the poor, turn your charity to the moral and spiritual improvement of the families visited."[98] The society came to the United States in 1845, where it organized its first conference in St. Louis, Missouri. By 1883, there were 4,000 conferences, with 45,000 members; by 1911, there were 7,500 conferences, with 100,000 members. Mundelein saw the society as one of the two great spiritual organizations in the church—the Holy Name offered personal sanctification and St. Vincent de Paul followed the example of the Good Samaritan. As the archbishop stated, "In the church today we have societies, sodalities, confraternities . . . but I have ever maintained that there is no body of laymen in the Church more Christian, more Catholic, more charitable, than the St. Vincent de Paul Conference."[99] Acting through the parish, these conferences brought immigrants into archdiocesan activities. Parish records clearly indicate that ethnic communities were just as involved in the St. Vincent de Paul Society as in diocesan parishes. German and Italian archives show that the men of these communities were active in the society—and their activity gradually Americanized them. But it was Mundelein who made the society a moving force in Catholic life. When the threat of Nazism was spreading throughout Europe, he called on all Catholics to support the St. Vincent de Paul Society:

> I have repeatedly said that one of our great assets, not only in the parish, but also in the diocese, is a flourishing St. Vincent de Paul Society . . . it would be disastrous indeed if through fault of ours, negligence or indifference, the field of the volunteer worker were restricted. . . . Vincentians continue to be apostles of Christian charity in a selfish, unbelieving world; you belong to an army which has its corps, its companies, its regiments in the Church Triumphant as well as our Church Militant.[100]

Indeed, the St. Vincent de Paul Society played a prominent role in Catholic life through the 1920s and beyond.

The Knights of Columbus was a national organization that also fostered Americanization on the parish level.[101] Founded in 1882 by Father Michael J. McGivney, the Knights of Columbus was a supraethnic society that accepted all men between eighteen and forty-five.[102] Its rituals and ceremonies stressed, charity, fraternity, and patriotism. With $8 million at the end of World War I, the society set up free employment bureaus, evening schools, and correspondence courses to help servicemen adjust to peacetime life; some 500,000 veterans received free academic, commercial, and technical training through the Knights of Columbus. The society, which increased steadily during the 1920s and 1930s, gave thousands of dollars for charitable relief during the Great Depression. Mundelein said that, "It needs no particular elaboration on my part to bring home to them [i.e., the Knights of Columbus] the great need of charitable assistance at this time in the general depression that exists in our midst."[103] Like the Holy Name and St. Vincent de Paul Society before them, the Knights of Columbus acted admirably to alleviate the general suffering of the 1930s.

The Catholic Youth Organization (CYO) was the most significant archdiocesean organization in Chicago after 1930. Organized by Bishop Bernard Sheil (an auxiliary to Mundelein) in 1930, the CYO Americanized thousands of immigrant children in scores of Chicago parishes.[104] The *Chicago Herald-American* praised its efforts on its tenth anniversary in 1940:

> The Catholic Youth Organization, ten years old tomorrow, is and has always been a completely, unwaveringly, proudly American youth organization.
> It has helped to shape the lives of hundreds of thousands of boys and young men in the past 10 years, and it has shaped them into thoroughly American ways of life.

> It has provided education and opportunities for those who lack them . . . it has combined, in perfect balance, practical help with training in the finest ideals of Christianity and Americanism . . . instead of helplessly fearing for the future of America, it has gone practically to work to insure a good future for America by training thousands of boys and young men into Good Americans. . . . Following that policy, CYO has become, in ten short years, *one of the most powerful influences for good citizenship in Chicago and one of the great forces for Americanism in America.*[105]

The organization operated a Working Boys' Home, at 1140 West Jackson Boulevard, where young men provided a motor delivery service, a garage, a candle factory, and a mimeo and stencil-cutting business. Summer schools were set up in the city parks to provide recreation for Chicago's children. The St. Rose of Lima CYO enrolled 1,600 boys and girls in its varied program of gymnastics, arts and crafts, and education at Sherman Park on the South Side. But it was boxing that became the most popular event sponsored by the organization. Parishes from north, south, and west participated in the annual Christmas Fund Boxing Tournament at the International Amphitheatre. Germans, Poles, Irishmen, and especially Italians were well represented at these events. A series of matches between the CYO and the national team of Ireland drew over 38,000 fans to Soldier Field. The fights continued to draw enormous crowds to the lakefront facility as well as the Chicago Stadium during the 1930s and 1940s.[106] The CYO also sponsored parish Boy Scout units, which brought hundreds of young men into contact with other nationalities.[107] Indeed, through scouting, summer schools, boxing, and numerous other activities, the CYO effectively encouraged Americanization for thousands of immigrant children. Together with the Holy Name Society, the St. Vincent de Paul Society, and the Knights of Columbus, the Catholic Youth Organization was an effective way station of Americanization.

Mundelein's own career brought Chicago Catholicism to the attention of the city as a whole. The world and Chicago knew that it could not ignore this dynamic leader after he was elevated to the cardinalate in 1924. Over one million Chicagoans greeted him on his triumphant return to the city from Rome. The *New World* reported:

> The three hour ride was with people all along the route. Banners bearing messages such as 'God bless our Cardinal,' 'Welcome Home, Our Cardinal' were frequent in the lines and American flags in places seemed a solid blaze of color. In front of St. Basil's School one little tot in white brought an armful of blossoms bigger than herself. . . . There was an ovation at 43rd St. by the

colored residents of Chicago. . . . Great large American flags fluttered and the mighty procession moved on.

When the parade finished, Mundelein spoke "of their future and that of their city, their country and their church." Five thousand dignitaries gathered in his honor at the Auditorium Theatre, where Judge Edmund Jarecki noted that "the laity particularly rejoice in your elevation, because your life is a living example of success and achievement attained by hard work and self-sacrifice." James A. Condon asked the new "prince of the church to weave the spirit of that flag in the fabric of nations." Mundelein, who was quite aware of the importance of the occasion, felt that "the attention of the world was focused on the Church," and he was its leader for the ensuing decades.[108]

Mundelein led Chicago Catholics to a fuller understanding of Americanism. When the United States entered World War I, he enthusiastically supported the American cause:

> One thing is certain, and I speak for myself, for 880 priests and 1,000,000 Catholics—the moment the president of the United States affixed his signature to the resolutions of Congress all differences of opinion ceased. We stand seriously, solidly, and loyally behind our president and his Congress. So in this hour of crisis I pledge the loyalty of our Catholic people to our flag.[109]

Mundelein, who threw his support behind the Third Liberty Loan Drive, netted $6 million from the archdiocese alone. Supporting the American Red Cross, he insisted that parishes cooperate with government directives for food, energy, and clothing. When the first Chicagoan was killed in action, Mundelein stated, "We are proud that the first hero slain on the battlefield from the citizens of this, America's largest city, was a boy of Catholic family, educated in our Catholic schools. . . . His heroic death is a conspicuous proof of the loyalty and patriotism of the children of those of our people who have come from other lands and who form such a large and such a desirable element in the citizenship of this city."[110] The future cardinal consistently maintained the loyalty of the foreign-born to the American cause.

> The year has brought forth a spirit of willingness to make sacrifice for our country and its cause that shows a deeply rooted patriotism on the part of a united people formed out of varied elements, a loyalty not only on the part of the native, but just as much on the part of the foreign-born, that gives splendid promise for the future of this republic. The year has brought with it a growth

of better understanding among all of our people, a truer estimate of the devotion of our Catholic people to this land of their birth or adoption.[111]

Indeed, Mundelein led Chicago's ethnics to a greater understanding of American patriotism.

But Mundelein also brought Catholicism to America. He represented the church's interests to politicians and businessmen. Chicago's archbishop became world famous in 1937 for his anti-Nazi speeches. Addressing five hundred archdiocesan priests at St. Mary of the Lake Seminary, he asked, "How is it possible that a nation of sixty million intelligent people let themselves be held in fear and slavery by a foreigner, an Austrian paperhanger . . . and a few henchmen like Goebbels and Goering, who prescribe every step in the life of the people?" When Germany threatened the Vatican with a break in diplomatic relations, Cardinal Eugenio Pacelli, the secretary of state, simply said that Mundelein was only exercising his right of free speech as a "prominent American citizen."[112]

Chicago's ethnics were highly enthusiastic when Mundelein became Chicago's third archbishop. The *Catholic Herald* stated: "When he came from Brooklyn to Chicago, the Poles, Italians, Germans, Irish, Bohemians and other racial groups . . . lauded him to the skies for his wisdom and energy and the sympathetic attitude he maintained towards each and all of them." [113] And yet the new archbishop would eventually disappoint his immigrant flock, although he was willing to maintain existing national parishes, for he was not as compassionate toward them as his immediate predecessor. Although he was willing to maintain existing national parishes, during his twenty-year tenure in Chicago, Mundelein established only one new German parish, St. William's, at 2600 North Sayre Avenue, in 1915; and only one new Italian parish, St. Calistus, at 2167 West Bowler, in 1919. He stated: "My purpose in the formation of these new parishes is to make them largely territorial, i.e., to give them certain limits." In 1916, he refused to see a delegation of Poles who were pressing him to establish a new Polish parish in Summit, Illinois. He wrote the following note: "I advise you therefore that you allow the matter to rest where it properly belongs, in the judgment of the Archbishop, who has his own reasons for action."[114] Slovaks also pressured the archbishop for parishes of their own, but Mundelein adamantly refused to established them. In 1927 he was still "as much opposed to the making of a Slovak bishop to look after the interests of the Slovaks resident here as I was to the making of a Polish bishop or a German bishop for the same reason."[115] Lithuanians, who had fought for control of church property under Quigley, continued to trouble Mundelein through the first four decades of the century. They opposed all attempts to introduce English into their churches and schools. A group of hard-line nationalists, who were distributing anti-English pamphlets outside the doors of Lithuanian churches in 1925, urged parishioners to resist any attempt at Americanization. The Catholic newspaper *Draugus* observed: "Our Lithuanian Church is the only stronghold for our Lithuanian nationality in America. Let us defend it from Americanization. Away with the English sermons from Lithuanian churches, and, you traitors, and Americanizing priests, get out from our Lithuanian parishes."[116]

Although Mundelein disassociated himself from his own Germanic background, he did not entirely forget it. The Federation of German Roman Catholic Societies of Brooklyn expressed "joy and satisfaction that an offspring of Germanic stock" had been raised to the archepiscopacy.[117] They urged Mundelein to continue the work of social reform he had initiated in Brooklyn and to help the Chicago Ketteler Study House (a German Catholic organization) grow and multiply. Mundelein, who supported the Chicago Lokal-Verband, urged its members to join the Volksverein. In 1933, Chicago's archbishop attended the centennial celebration of the parish where he was born, St. Nicholas in Brooklyn. Mundelein remembered how his great-grandfather and a small group of German Catholics organized the parish.

> I think that without fear of contradiction I can say that more than any other people who have come here, these early German Catholic settlers are responsible for the splendid Catholic parochial school system in this country... wherever they went they planted the parish school; the fine church could wait, their school came first.[118]

German Catholics were prominent throughout Mundelein's episcopacy, and even though he did not directly associate himself with them they continued to honor him as a fellow German.[119]

George Cardinal Mundelein died at St. Mary of the Lake Seminary on October 2, 1939. The Chicago archdiocese numbered over 1,400,000 Catholics at the time of his death. With 1,836 priests to guide them, Mundelein had supervised the establishment or continuance of 422 parishes, 388 elementary schools, 85 high schools and academies, 23 hospitals, 13 seminaries, 8 universities and colleges, 7 orphanages, and 36 other institutions.[120] A brilliant financier and fund raiser, he did not erect any building without a feasibility study and the money to support it. He converted many nonsupporting parishes to devotional centers (like the old French parish of Notre Dame), as well as turned over several Italian parishes to religious orders who guided them as territorial rather than national communities. Running a tight ship, Mundelein often made night visits to rectories to check on his priests. Often criticized for running the diocese like a "German meat market," he was sarcastically called "the Dutch cleanser."[121] And yet, despite these personal limitations, George Cardinal Mundelein left a strong and financially sound archdiocese. He was the right man for his time, worthy to be called the "First Cardinal of the West."[122]

TWO

The German and Italian City

Chicago has always been an ethnic city. The earliest census (1843) distinguished between the native and foreign-born of the city. Of 7,580 inhabitants, Chicago numbered 4,726 natives and 2,256 foreigners; of these, 816 were Germans (and Norwegians) and 773 Irish. By 1850, there were 6,096 foreign-born Irish, and 5,035 foreign-born Germans in Chicago. These two groups dominated Chicago's ethnic life through the last half of the nineteenth century. The 1900 census enumerated 170,738 foreign-born Germans and 73,192 foreign-born Irish in the city. Although both groups remained large, newer immigrants soon took their place. Poles, who began to arrive in the late 1870s, numbered 125,604 by 1910, while Italians grew to 45,160 the same year. By the end of World War I, Chicago was the third most foreign city in the United States. By 1920, 72 percent of its population was foreign stock. Poles were the leading foreign group, with 137,611 foreign-born, followed by Germans with 112,288 and Italians with 59,215. By 1930, Chicago was the largest Scandinavian, Polish, Czech, Serbo-Croatian, and Lithuanian city in the United States; it was the second largest German, Greek, Slovak, and Jewish city; and it was the third largest Italian metropolis. Sixty-seven percent of its people were foreign-born (2,174,430 out of a total population of 3,376,848). Poles remained the leading foreign group, with 149,622 inhabitants; they were closely followed by Germans with 111,366; Russians with 78,462; Swedes with 75,178, and Italians with 73,960.[1] These groups, which kept their dominance through 1940, made Chicago the most ethnic city in America.

The Irish

The Irish played a prominent role in the early history of Chicago.[2] The first Irish came to work on the railroads and canals that made Chicago the hub of the nation. Catholicism and Irish ethnicity fused into an almost indivisible unity. As Thomas Brown noted, there is a difficulty "of differentiating between the specifically Irish and specifically Catholic aspects of their lives. They had emerged into the modern world from a past in which Catholicism had played a stronger role than among any other people of Western Europe."[3] It is no wonder that one of the principal institutions the Irish established was the ethnic parish.[4] One of the first Catholic communities in Chicago was St. Patrick's at 718 West Adams Street. As families moved southwest along Archer Avenue, the city's earliest bishops established more and more Hibernian parishes: St. Bridget's, at 2928 South Archer Avenue; St. John's (address unknown); and St. James, at 2942 South Wabash Street. New parishes sprang from older ones, as Irish families moved farther and farther north and south of their original settlements. Bishop Van de Velde established St. Jarlath's and St. Columbkille's for families who had moved north of St. Patrick's; he also organized St. Thomas the Apostle and St. Anne's as missions of St. James in the mid-1860s. The South Side attracted the largest number of Irish, as the Union Stock Yards at Twenty-second and State streets provided work and security for thousands. Between 1880 and 1890, Archbishop Feehan established eleven new parishes for the Irish of the city. The Twenty-ninth, Thirtieth, and Thirty-second wards were particularly Irish, with more than 100,000 inhabitants living the area directly east of Ashland and south of Thirty-ninth Street. Six Irish parishes were established in this area between 1880 and 1886.[5]

But since the Irish were English-speaking, their parishes were open to anyone. The most susceptible to change, they quickly became "American" parishes. The history of Holy Rosary Parish clearly demonstrates this tendency.[6] Holy Rosary, at 351 East 113th Street, was first settled by Irishmen who worked at the huge Pullman works on the Southeast Side. When the strikes of 1894 forced many of the original settlers to move, French, Germans, Dutch, and Italians moved in. The parish declined from 157 baptisms in 1888, to 77 baptisms in 1895. Newer national parishes, which were carved out of Holy Rosary's original territory, left the community a mere shell of its original glory. By 1900, Holy Rosary was no longer an Irish parish, but a small collection of Italians and Lake Shore elite. St. Columbkille's on the North Side also underwent similar changes. Originally an Irish parish, St. Columbkille's reached a peak in 1905, when 1,234 students attended its school; but "an influx of strangers made its way into the district, and the people of the parish, always desirous of pleasant home surroundings, resented this, and many of the parishioners 'packed up and left for parts unknown.'"[7]

The Irish gained a deep sense of political involvement from their struggles in Ireland to gain representation in Parliament. These efforts, which were often clandestine and secretive, made them ideal politicians—men who were sensitive to the faults and frailties of mankind, but who often skipped the formalities of bureaucracy and protocol. By 1892, 10 percent of Chicago's registered voters were Irish-born; by 1896, the St. Patrick's Day Parade was a civic event.[8]

While the Irish represented the largest English-speaking minority in the city, the Germans were the most significant non-English-speaking group. Statistics indicate their numerical superiority to all other immigrant groups until 1920. Representing the most important northern European nationality to come to America, the Germans and their descendants numbered 1,282,618 by 1910.[9] The Italians remained one of Chicago's five largest ethnic groups through the 1970s. They also present an intriguing contrast to their stoic neighbors from the north. While the Germans came to America with a distinct sense of being German, Italians had to discover their nationality in America. Joseph Lopreato notes that "there is a certain irony in the fact that many southern Italians had come to the United States *to feel Italian*. The unappreciative way in which they were received forced them for a while to have a national identification, and thus *Italianized* them."[10] World War I did not traumatize the Italians as it did the Germans, since Italians did not identify with the Italian nation as closely as Germans did with theirs. Indeed, it was Fascist Italy that first unified Italians as a distinct nationality. Taken together, Chicago's Germans and Italians make up a most informative complex.

Chicago's Germans, 1820-1880

Germans played a significant part in Chicago's population as early as 1820.[11] They came better off than their Irish contemporaries, possessing some capital and trade skills to set up small shops and businesses. Economic considerations were paramount in their decision to come to America. The Chicago *Abendpost* noted that "those immigrants whose alleged preference for America is the result of political and religious suppression constitute a mere minority; the majority came in prospect of better opportunities for a livelihood."[12] Books such as Gottfried Duden's *Report on a Trip to the Western States of North America* (1829) and Traugott Bronne's *Missouri and Illinois—A Handbook for Immigrants* (1835) encouraged many Germans to make the trip abroad. Immigration agents in America and Germany tried to lure these northerners westward by promising to pay their way. Real estate men like Francis A. Hoffman (1822-1903) also encouraged their compatriots to immigrate. Hired by the Illinois Central Railroad in 1862, Hoffman populated the area between Mattoon and Effingham, Illinois, with thousands of Germans.

The earliest German settlements in Illinois evolved during the late 1820s and early 1830s.[13] Alton, an early German town, was the most important commercial center in the state until Chicago superceded it by 1850. Vandalia, Peoria, Quincy, Springfield, and Peru all had German origins. Mathias Meyer and John Wellmacher, two of the earliest Germans in Chicago, settled at Dunkel's Grove in 1831; Friedrich Mattern and Louis Malzacher later became aldermen. When the city was incorporated in 1837, there were twenty-nine Germans who voted in the first mayoral election. There were enough Germans by 1839 to elect the first German alderman, Clement C. Stose, for the Second Ward.[14] Wilhelms Haas and Lill opened Chicago's first brewery in 1840; it grew to be the largest brewery west of Cincinnati by 1857.[15]

German immigration first peaked in the two decades preceding the Civil War (1840-1860). Up to 1850, Irish immigrants exceeded Germans by 18.1 percent. From 1850 to 1860, Germans pulled ahead of them and all other ethnic groups, until Slavic and Italian newcomers superseded them in the 1890s. Between 1841 and 1850, 434,626 Germans arrived in the United States; between 1851 and 1860, 951,667 arrived.[16] They came for many reasons—overpopulation, crop failure (a potato famine in southwest Germany and a wine failure in Württemberg)—but most of all for better economic opportunities, as newer methods of production forced many farmers out of business. Many of these immigrants came to the boomtowns of Illinois. The 1843 census recorded 816 Germans (and Norwegians) in Chicago. By 1844, there were enough Germans in the city to call a public meeting against nativist influences. By 1846, they were so numerous that six out of twenty-six boot- and shoemakers, five out of fifteen merchants, and one of out three confectioners were German.[17]

The 1848 revolutions brought many liberal Germans to Illinois and Chicago.[18] Frederick Hecker, leader of a small revolt in Baden, brought a group of settlers to Belleville. George Schneider, who led an unsuccessful revolt in Bavaria, settled in Chicago in 1851 as editor of the *Illinois Staats-Zeitung*. Doctor Ernst Schmidt, a former professor at Wurzburg University, became a rabid abolitionist in Chicago. Caspar Butz, a Westphalian German, edited *Die Monatshefte*, a popular scientific and literary monthly from 1864 to 1865. A critic of Lincoln during the Civil War, he later became a member of the State Legislature, clerk of the Superior Court, and a member of the Board of Penitentiary Commissioners. All of these men were professionals, representing the highest strata of German society. They established the majority of German-speaking newspapers in America.

By 1850, Chicago, a small town of 29,375, numbered 5,035 Germans. The most significant German settlement centered around Kinzie, Ohio, Clark, and Franklin streets. Some middle-class Americans and a few northern Italians also lived in the neighborhood, but the area was by and large German. The center of German life was the Deutsches Haus (German House), a tall building at the southeast corner of India and Wells streets. The largest and most influential societies met there, as well as operatic and theatrical organizations. The first German athletic club was the Chicago Turnverein, established on October 3, 1852, "still the largest, wealthiest and most influential of all the Turnvereins of this city." Chicago's first singing society was the Männergesangverein (Men's Singing Club), founded as part of the Turverein in 1853. The Freimanner-Verein (Freeman's Club), organized in 1854, reached three hundred members its first year.[19] The growth of these early societies demonstrates the vitality and strength of Chicago's early German community. Indeed, Germans had a peculiar propensity for establishing *Vereine* as quickly as they arrived.

But not everyone was enamored with these northern Europeans. The first serous clash between Germans and native-born came in March 1855. Mayor Levi Boone precipitated the clash when he vowed to enforce Sunday closing laws. On March 7, he told all tavern owners that the law would take effect the next day; police arrested scores of Germans for breaking the law, while leaving American tavern owners untouched. The City Council then raised liquor licenses from $50 to $300; when German saloon keepers refused to pay, the police arrested over two hundred. Thousands protested, leaving one dead. The law was eventually rescinded, but not until a large amount of animosity grew up between native and German-born.[20]

There were considerable numbers of German Catholics among these first Germans.[21] Some 50,000 came to the United States during the 1830s, a number that tripled in the 1840s. By 1842, Cincinnati had 20,000 German Catholics; New York, 18,000, and Philadelphia, 12,000.[22] Chicago's community grew to such an extent that the city needed two German parishes by 1846: St. Joseph's and St. Peter's. These Catholics, proud of their Catholicity and Germanity, feared the liberal Forty-eighters who denied the authority of the Bible and the church. German Catholics also had to defend themselves against Know-Nothings and nativists, who attacked them vehemently during the 1840s. But they were not exempt from fighting among themselves. In rural northern Ohio, Germans from Alsace fought Hessen-Darmstadters over which hymn to sing in church; the discussion heated up to the point that one group burned down the church! At St. Michael's in Chicago, the trustees refused to accept six pastors between 1852 and 1860; they even locked the church doors against Bishop Duggan when he tried to hand the church over to the Redemptorists.[23]

The shape of German Catholicism was largely formed by midcentury. The ethnic parish stood at the heart of daily life.

> For the Germans, as for most other Catholic immigrant groups, the national parish was the most important ethnic institution, not only because it met their deepest religious needs but also because it furnished the social nucleus around which any voluntary associations clustered.[24]

The German parish emerged from the laity itself, since it was the laity who usually took the initiative in asking bishops for ethnic parishes. Most of the priests who serviced these parishes were German-born and belonged to such German orders as the Redemptorists or Franciscans. The people admired and respected their priests, as huge crowds attended first masses and pastoral funerals. Germans built beautiful Gothic edifices throughout the country. Taking pride in ceremonies and pageantry, they filled their churches with *lustige Gesang*. The parish mission was a central event in German Catholic life, as German missionaries stressed baptism, confession, and a return to the sacraments. One of the most important characteristics of the parish was the *Vereinswesen*, or societal life that grew up around the parish. While the Irish fostered societies outside the parish, Germans tended to gather their associations within it. These voluntary groups were either devotional or mutual-aid societies, the former devoted to local devotions and pious works, the latter acting as insurance agents for the newly arrived immigrant. German Catholic life was already flourishing on the eve of the Civil War, with five national parishes in Chicago alone.[25]

As the country girded itself for war, Germans poured into Chicago. Of 109,260 inhabitants in 1860, 22,230 were German-born.[26] Those from Prussia, Hesse, and Nassau were predominantly Protestant, while those from Austria, Bavaria, Baden, and Württemburg were Catholic. As war divided the North and South, Chicago's Germans fought for the abolition of slavery and the preservation of the Union.[27] At a mass meeting in North Market Hall on November 10, 1861, Germans chided Lincoln for not acting on the slavery question and eventually swung their support to John C. Fremont. German regiments formed throughout the city—the Hecker Jaeger Regiment became the Eighty-second. After the Emancipation Proclamation, Chicago's Germans swung their support to Lincoln, although their vote remained divided in the 1864 election. By the end of the war, Germans had sent 178,817 to war, with 18,140 from Illinois.[28]

Germans moved northwest and southwest of their original settlements during the Civil War decade. Townsend, Sedgwick, Bremer, and Larrabee streets, the heart of the German settlement, remained ethnic until the fire of 1871. The district between Oak, Chicago, State, and the Lake, which was called New Buffalo, remained a large German settlement through the Civil War.[29] Protestant churches spread to the South Side, as Lutherans established parishes at Twenty-first and Archer, Fourteenth and Union, and Seventeenth and Peoria, during the prefire decade. By 1870, the city numbered 52,318 German-born, or 18 percent of the total population.[30]

Although some Germans took an active interest in Germany, the majority—whether Catholic or Lutheran—preferred to leave politics and social reform to others. The *Illinois Staats-Zeitung* was the most vocal commentator of the day. In 1864, it condemned Prussia and Austria for refusing to allow Schleswig-Holstein (an independent German state) to hold a plebiscite. At the outbreak of the Franco-Prussian War in 1870, the *Staats-Zeitung* wholeheartedly supported Germany. German pride was so demonstrative that a ten-mile parade highlighted the end of the war in 1871. The *Chicago Evening Post* described it as "the longest and most impressive Chicago has ever seen." But most native Chicagoans resented this show of strength. Inscriptions on walls read "Denmark mourns with France," while Irish fought and killed two Germans in 1872.[31] But most Germans who were not Forty-eighters simply lived out their lives as newcomers to America. Gradually forgetting the old *Deutschland*, they set up a new life in *Amerika*.

Germans immigrated to America in record numbers after the Civil War. Small landowners and artisans, who could not adjust to a military-industrial

Germany, rushed to America's shores between 1866 and 1880. Some 718,182 came between 1871 and 1880. Friedrich Munch, a journalist of the period, noted that "they are mostly of the working class, with far better schooling than the same class of 30 years before."[32] Although immigration waned from 1873 to 1880, it swelled between 1880 and 1885.[33] Between 1881 and 1890, 1,452,970 Germans came to America. This was the last great migration of northern Europeans to the United States, as eastern and southern Europeans soon began to take their place. Chicago benefited from the large influx of Germans, as 75,205 settled in Chicago by 1880; counting second-generation sons and daughters, this figure easily reached 25 percent of the total population. By 1890, there were 161,039 German-born in the city (15 percent of the total population). Counting the second generation, Chicago was 30 percent German, with 352, 662 claiming German ancestry. By the end of the century, Chicago was 25 percent German, with 428,201 claiming German parentage.

Chicago's Italians, 1833-1900

As Germans immigrated to America in record numbers, Italians from southern Europe began to challenge their numerical superiority. Very few came before 1880—the largest number being 8,757 in 1873. But between 1880 and 1900, 971,556 Italians left their native land for an uncertain future in America.[34] Although a few northern Italians settled in Chicago in the late 1840s, migration remained small until the second half of the century.[35] But by 1870, 552 Italians resided in nineteen of Chicago's twenty wards.[36] There were three principal settlements. The first was just north of the Chicago River, on Illinois Street, a few blocks west of the northern German community, between Franklin and Orleans Avenue. These northern Italians founded Assumption Parish, at Illinois Street in 1886. The second settlement extended west of the Chicago River to Halsted Street, between Kenzie Avenue on the north and Van Buren Street on the south; the area declined rapidly, as small factories, warehouses, and retail businesses forced families to move north and south. The largest Italian concentration existed in the present-day Loop, between Randolph and Harrison. High land costs—$3,000 per square foot on State Street by 1883—forced most to leave by the 1890s. In addition, the Dearborn Station at Polk and Dearborn was the primary depot for eastern trains, the place where most Italians arrived in Chicago; they naturally tended to settle in this area. As Italians moved up the economic ladder, they moved out of the community to better housing and neighborhoods. And yet, between 1889 and 1920, only a few sections of the city were exclusively Italian, for these newcomers preferred to spread out throughout the entire city to small pockets, with no single area entirely "Italian."[37]

By 1884, southern Italians from Campobasso, Avellino, Potenza, Cosenza, Reggio, Catanzaro, Bari, and Sicily replaced the earlier Tuscans, Genovese, and Piedmontese from northern Italy. While the northerners usually came with their families and some education, the southerners came alone, with little education. The largest settlement in 1884 was now south of the Loop, between Harrison and Twelfth Street, and State Street and the south branch of the river (1,025 inhabitants). Other settlements existed between Ohio and Kinzie streets, and Franklin Street and the river (455 residents); between Thirtieth and Thirty-third streets, and Stewart and Halsted (317 Italians); between Van Buren and Twelfth streets and Halsted and the river (172 Italians, which became the largest settlement by 1898); between Fourteenth and Sixteenth streets and Morgan and Centre (130); and scattered areas around Ohio and Western and Fullerton and Pulaski (Crawford). No district was distinctly Italian, as other ethnic groups continued to live side by side with newer neighbors from the south of Europe. For example, in the area between Clark and State, and Taylor and Twelfth streets, there were 453 Italians, 362 Germans, and 99 Irish.[38]

By 1890, Chicago numbered 5,685 Italians. Life was harsh—poor living conditions and lack of proper sanitation worked against the Italian family. Studies by government agencies, private associations, social workers, and scholars all point out the deplorable effects such living conditions had on human life. A 1901 survey by the City Homes Association found filth and vermin everywhere. Rheumatism, bronchitis, pneumonia, and pleurisy were common; the infant mortality rate was high, and those who did live often developed rickets, tuberculosis, pneumonia, and even cholera.[39]

Catholicism struggled to deal with these new immigrants. Its first steps were faltering and often misled. At the Third Plenary Council of Baltimore in 1884, James Cardinal Gibbons simplistically said that "there is very little to be said about the Italians, and its study involves very little labor."[40] He and most bishops felt that Italians could be cared for by ordinary means. But it was soon obvious that these immigrants could not be treated like the Irish and Germans before them. The "Italian problem," as it came to be called, was a combination of three factors: Italians were considered poorly educated in matters of faith and religion; there were few Italian priests to care for them; and there were few churches to accept and provide for their peculiar style of Catholicism.[41] The first attempt to deal with the problem was the duplex parish, which allowed Italians to celebrate their own liturgies at existing parishes. Although a few such institutions were established in Chicago, Philadelphia, and New York, they were largely unsuccessful because native Catholics could not understand or tolerate Italian ways.[42] Irish priests complained that Italians failed to support the church, while the vast majority of men simply stayed away from Mass altogether.

There were several attempts to deal with this problem by Italians themselves. Bishop Giovanni Battista Scalabrini of Piacenza, Italy, founded the Society of St. Charles Borromeo in 1891 for the explicit purpose of aiding Italians abroad.[43] The society soon established eleven missions in North America, with three parishes in Chicago—Santa Maria Incoronata, Santa Maria Addolorata, and St. Michael's. Italica Gens, an immigrant aid society, helped Italians find jobs, wrote letters for them, and offered free legal advice. The Servite Fathers, another Italian order, administered Assumption and St. Philip Benizi parishes on the North Side, St. Anthony of Padua parish in Roseland, and Our Lady of Pompeii and St. Callistus parishes on the Near West Side.[44] These and other religious communities helped Chicago's Italians adjust to American life.

As in the case of the Germans before them, the Italians made the ethnic parish the center of their day-to-day life. It kept their ethnic traditions alive, while slowly adapting them to the American way of life. Silvano Tomasi wrote that the ethnic parish "embodied the ideals in which the people believed and united them structurally through strong group ritual and social functions . . . the apparently highly-organized, separate community, which the ethnic Catholic Church provided made the Italians another functioning group in the American mosaic, a position for which the immigrants opted as soon as they realized they had their best opportunity in staying rather than going back."[45] Graham Taylor, founder of Chicago Commons and an observer of the times, noted that Italians were "mystical and devout . . . they identify their homes and neighborhood with their church, and yet all within it and its rites is supernatural and mysterious." Indeed, it was not the ordinary functions that kept them within Catholicism, but the extraordinary ones. The church was the place for baptisms, weddings, and funerals. These were often accompanied by lavish banquets—"They are tendered on all occasions, opportune and inopportune, for marriages, baptisms, to celebrate the feast of the patron saint, for the departure of a barber . . . for funerals one spends fabulous sums." Taylor noticed that Italian funerals were "extravagant and way beyond the means of most parishioners; but the casket and gravestones were important symbols of family pride and loyalty."[46]

The most significant parish event was the *festa*, or festival in honor of a local saint. Each parish had its own particular saint, which usually corresponded to the village in Italy where the saint originated. As Joseph Lopreato notes, "This lighthearted expression of godliness *was* religion for the masses."[47] These *feste* were numerous and varied in Chicago. At Our Lady of Mt. Carmel in West Englewood, the feasts in honor of San Rocco and Our Lady of Mt. Carmel lasted eight days—bands played through the streets, money was attached to the Madonna as it circled the parish blocks, and children hung over the streets on clotheslines to greet the statue as it passed under their feet. Graham Taylor vividly recalled these festivals at the turn of the century:

> While the occasion is unhappily commercialized by granting concessions to sell refreshments and other articles, yet many tokens of religious feeling attest the sincerity of participants. With bands of music, banners bearing the name of the patron saint, and boys carrying the lighted candles, the members of the society in their regalia, followed by a multitude of men, women and children, parade through the streets of the neighborhood. Across the street a cable is strung from the second-story windows of tenement houses. From each window on either side a little girl with cherub wings is drawn as though flying. Hovering over the middle of the street until the image of the saint passes under them, they drop their flowers upon the figure. From the throngs of onlookers, as well as from the ranks of paraders, hundreds of devotees step out to pin upon the robes of the saint's image their offerings of one and five dollar bills.[48]

These celebrations, which united the Italian people to their churches, provided a focus for traditional village and provincial loyalties. They sustained the Italian through decades of poverty and discrimination. They were nowhere nearly as successful as their northern neighbors from the *Rhein* and *Donau* regions of Europe.

Chicago's Germans, 1880-1914

Chicago's Germans, who quickly moved up the economic ladder, became the backbone of late-nineteenth-century Chicago. Those from Prussia and

Saxony included such prominent citizens as the Rehms, Seipps, Nackers, and Kranzes; while those from Bavaria and the Rhineland were butchers, bakers, and laborers. Both lived on the Near North Side, the former attending Harmann Lutheran Church at Ohio and LaSalle, while the latter went to St. Joseph's or St. Michael's Catholic Church. German Jews, who also lived in the community, ran businesses on North Clark Street. Schwabian-Hungarians also lived in the community along Fullerton Avenue from Wells Street to the lake. An Irishman recalled that when he "was a boy all the district around the Water Tower was called 'Little Buffalo' for there were so many Germans there."[49] Another *Gemeinde* centered around LaSalle and Dearborn streets, north of Division. This group remained on the Near North Side until 1918, when they disappeared into the northern communities of the city. Lower-class Germans lived north of Fullerton, near Clark and Wells, while the higher class lived along Clark Street as far east as the lake.

Many Germans moved to North Center in the late 1870s and 1880s. The community, which lay directly west of Lakeview, extended as far west as the Chicago River. Bounded on the north by Montrose Avenue and on the south by Diversey Parkway, North Center extended as far east as Ravenswood Avenue and the Chicago and Northwestern Railroad.[50] The area began to develop in the late 1870s, as German families moved north of their original settlements on the Near North Side. At that time there was no water or improved streets, only still ponds where wild ducks peacefully swam. Saxons and Thuringians, who came first, soon organized clubs for "improving rifle practice among its members." The Krieger Verein quickly erected rifle ranges, "and the old-world German style of a good time was had by all."[51]

North Center retained its German flavor through the last decades of the nineteenth century. In 1891 there was only one Irish and one German family west of Western Avenue; by 1898, there were ten saloons between Irving Park and Montrose Avenue. One old German recalled that "the story goes that when a German comes to America he looks for just three things—a saloon, a church, and a singing society." Indeed, saloons and beer drinking were a part of German life. But singing was just as popular. Thirty Germans started a North Center *Sängerbund* (singing society), which became the North End Men's Choir in 1898. These societies provided *Gemeinde und Gemütlichkeit* (community and pleasure) for Chicago's early German pioneers. These early societies kept Chicago's north side community strong and cohesive.[52]

While some Germans moved north, others turned south. A few families moved into the Near South Side as early as 1850. Peter Stump, who lived at

Twenty-ninth and Cottage Grove, made fire hats for the Chicago Fire Department, and another German was a surveyor for the city. Many came to work in the breweries that spread across the city in the 1800s. An old-time resident recalled that "there were some of the best Irish and German families here, a good many of them attended St. James Church [Twenty-ninth and Wabash], so we felt right at home."[53] But by the early 1880s, the Near North Side became less and less desirable, as major vice areas moved into the area. The Levee, as it was known, grew up in this community on State Street, south of Harrison Avenue. A small community of blacks resided between Cermak Road and Thirty-first Street, just west of State, while South Michigan remained in a white residential area.

Germans seeking better living conditions began to move west into Armour Square as early as 1883. The community, which lay directly west of the Near South Side, extended to Eighteenth Street and Pershing Road on the north and south, and Federal Street and Canal and Stewart on the east and west. The area developed as a buffer zone between Bridgeport, Douglas, and the Near South Side; Archer Road, which crossed through its midsection, was an old Indian trail. The area between Thirty-fifth and Thirty-ninth streets, and Wallace and Halsted, was predominantly German. Peter Guier and one hundred other families from Hamburg settled in the area in the early 1870s. They worked in the lumber mills and salt docks in the summer, and the packing houses along the river in the winter. Catholic Germans founded St. George's Parish at Thirty-ninth and Wentworth (1884) and St. Anthony's at Twenty-fifth and Canal (1873). The community reached residential maturity in 1895, as railroads and streetcars crept into the area. But by 1900, commercial and business concerns forced many Germans to move farther south. When the Chicago White Sox built a ballpark at Pershing and Wentworth (later Thirty-fifth and Shields), the new stadium eliminated many houses in the southern sector of the community. The development of the Central Manufacturing District just west of Armour Square contributed to the residential decline of the neighborhood, and as the Germans moved out, Italians moved in.[54]

A few Germans moved southeast of Armour Square to Grand Boulevard. A black contemporary recalled that when his family moved to Fifty-first and Dearborn after the fire, everything east of State Street was white. He noted, "Our family participated in the neighborhood life along with all the other folks, in these early days. There was a German Beer Garden near the corner of Fifty-first and State where Sunday afternoon concerts and picnics were held.

Our family was always welcome at these occasions.... The houses in this part were small frame cottages housing Germans and Irish working men of the Stockyards and the railroad shops." A black colony grew up on Fifty-first Street, between State and the New York Central Railroad tracks; whites who lived north of Forty-seventh and west of State divided the two black districts in half.[55]

German families also moved to the far East Side during the last two decades of the century. The area lay along the Calumet River and stretched as far south as the Indiana dunes. The community—wild and marshy—was inhabited by only an adventurous few during the first decades of its development. Some Germans established a Lutheran church at 103rd Street and Avenue H, "which provided all the recreation and there was little of that as we took our religion seriously." They built schools and taught lessons in German. By 1885, Germans had moved as far south as Avenue L and Ewing. The community was a melting pot of various nationalities, each of which kept its distinctive flavor. A lifelong resident recalled that "it was common for each of the many nationalities represented here to celebrate their various holidays in Old World Fashion. The Scotch often would appear in their kilts playing bagpipes. It was a great spectacle. The Irish, Bohemians, Italians and Austrians all carried out their functions unmolested. . . . But the racial and nationality lines were broken down to a considerable degree during the war."[56] Austrians, who settled on the East Side in the latter part of the nineteenth century, were German-speaking nationals with customs of their own. An early pioneer recalled that "these people were called Austrians by those in the community who knew little about them and consequently had to stand the brunt of the rebuffs from the Germans. The Czechs liked the Austrians even less than the Germans. . . . I do not think there was a real Austrian, a Magyr [Hungarian], ever in the East Side."[57] Most of the Austrians, who were Catholic, built St. George's Church at Ninety-sixth and Ewing in the late 1890s. There was a great deal of animosity between the Austrians and German Lutherans, and "it caused quite a little stir" when St. George's was built. The Germans, who felt superior to the Austrians, Hungarians, and Czechs, often referred to their fellow Europeans as foreigners. A lower-class German community settled along the Calumet River and 107th Street at the turn of the century, but "these people were from a different class in Germany and rather poor. They spoke a dialect, so we thought, which put them out of our group." The community remained partly German through the first decade of the twentieth century. But as Yugoslavs moved into the area between 1919 and 1925, the Germans and

Swedes moved out, as far south as Indiana. By 1928, an observer of the East Side noted that "few of the people that come from Europe to this locality now come from the district of the Danube Valley from which my grandfather came. They now come from further east and few of them can even read or write the Austrian language."[58]

By the late 1800s, Chicago was a distinctly German city. And it was the church that united most Germans to their local community. Approximately 35 percent of the entire German population who came to America were Catholic.[59] The 1800s were crucial decades, as Germans struggled to preserve a *Deutschtum* that had taken years to establish. For German Catholics, the ethnic parish was the primary institution for this purpose. It preserved religion, language, and nationality. Loss of language meant loss of faith, for it was *die deutsche Sprache* that held Catholicism and German tradition together. The German did not claim that his language was *the* language of faith, but he did stress that faith could best be kept through that language. A letter from Friedrich von Held to the director of the Ludwigsmissionverein illustrates this point:

> The erection of new missions for German Catholics becomes more urgent and pressing each day. German immigration will increase each day, yes, considerably every night and every week. Thus the problem is for the Germans to preserve German, and this can only come about if they are snatched from the pernicious influence of American morals and habit of life through religious unity under the direction of German priests. Unfortunately, experience teaches only too well that where there is no German priest, the German parents preserve only very poorly those good civil and religious qualities which, in a more pious German fatherland, they sucked in with their mother's milk. The children in every respect are lost, and soon, without Catholic German services and schools, they necessarily succumb to the American spirit.[60]

Leading German Catholics spoke out for the preservation of German culture, customs, and language under the slogan, "Language saves Faith." King Ludwig I of Bavaria exhorted his fellow Bavarians: "I shall not forget you, but stay, German, German! Do not become English."[61]

Closely allied to the question of language was the parochial school. The Germans were so concerned for the establishment of such schools that they usually built them before their churches. It was particularly important that religious subjects be taught in German. In 1853, the parochial schools of New York adopted this method of instruction. The question of Americanization was apparent as early as 1860, when schoolchildren began to sing hymns in

English, while the German nuns led the parents in German. German parochial schools flourished through the nineteenth century, as over 95 percent of German parishes had such institutions by 1914. But by the outbreak of World War I, English had become the medium of instruction for most traditional subjects, and German was relegated to religion and other private devotions. For many children, German was already a foreign language.[62]

The densest area of German Catholic population were the counties between Cincinnati, Milwaukee, and St. Louis. Chicago was the largest metropolitan area within this district. Patrick A. Feehan, Chicago's first archbishop, actively supported German parishes and activities. Establishing eighteen national parishes, he enthusiastically supported the use of German in church services and schools. The St. Raphael's Society, an immigrant organization founded in the early 1800s, received his blessing and support. He also established various German institutions during his twenty-three year episcopate. The Poor Handmaids of Christ, who came to Chicago from Dernbach in 1875, opened the city's first day nursery in 1879, founded St. Elizabeth's Hospital in 1887, and built St. Anne's Tuberculosis Hospital at Forty-ninth and Thomas Street in 1903. The Alexian brothers, who came to Chicago from Aachen, established a hospital on North Avenue in 1869. The German Franciscans opened St. Agnes Hospital, at 693 South Halsted, in 1896.[63] Germans also established Angel Guardian Orphanage, at 401 Devon Street, as a home for parentless German Catholic children. The institution, which grew steadily, added several new buildings in 1929, and had a gross income of $174,903. At the same time, the Ketteler German Manual Training School trained 531 young men, while the Catherine Kasper Industrial School took care of 429 German girls.[64] Meanwhile, older German parishes declined. For example, St. Peter's Parish had 1,200 families in 1870, but declined to 30 families by 1890 with advancing railroads and changing neighborhoods. The school became ethnically mixed, with Irish, Italians, Arabs, and blacks attending.[65] Parishes farther north, such as St. Boniface, St. Aloysius, and St. Alphonsus, began to flourish. By the turn of the century, Chicago's Catholic *Deutschtum* was strong.

The strength of German Chicago during the last decades of the nineteenth century is mirrored in the history of the German language in the public school system. German was first introduced into the curriculum through the efforts of Lorenz Brentano, president of the school board from 1863 to 1867. By 1865, five elementary schools were teaching German, with over 700 pupils learning *Deutsch* by 1866. The history of German in the public schools fluctuated with the strength of Chicago's Germanity. The *Chicago Times*, which attacked German in 1871, severely curtailed the teaching of the language in the ensuing years. But it soon increased in popularity, and the language enjoyed a renaissance during the 1880s and 1890s. From 1890 to 1891, 44,270 students studied German with 242 German teachers. But despite this numerical strength, nativist elements continued to attack the language as a foreign influence. The *Chicago Tribune* stated on February 18, 1893: "Everyone knows that the attempt to teach German in the primary grades is absurd, that it is a waste of time and a nuisance." By 1912, 53 schools offered German, with a total enrollment of 7,806; by 1915, enrollment increased to 18,140 students in 112 schools. But anti-German feeling during World War I forced the Illinois State Legislature to ban German in public elementary schools and severely curtailed its teaching in the city's high schools. After the Supreme Court overruled this bill, Chicago's public schools again offered German as part of the curriculum. By 1929, Crane Technical Institute had 852 German students.[66]

As the United States entered the twentieth century, German Americans were in a strong position. They numbered 8,282,618 in 1910 (foreign-born and children of foreign-born). Chicago was the second largest German city at the turn of the century, with 170,738 foreign-born, and 416,729 born of German parentage.[67] They were the most preferred nationality; a Pennsylvania steel mill superintendent noted that "Germans and Irish, Swedes and young American country boys, judiciously mixed, make the most effective and tractable force you can find."[68] And the American counsel at Nuremberg recalled that, "They [the Germans] can all read and write, are good-natured, and, in my opinion, their diligence and ability can only add to the general prosperity of the United States."[69] Richard O'Connor summarized the situation:

> German-Americans had every reason to be serenely confident of their place in the national life. They had made good, they considered themselves esteemed above all other peoples which had migrated to America from Europe. . . . It impelled the German-Americans to believe that they could decisively influence the national will; that they could prevail against the Anglo-Saxon majority and most of the other minorities in keeping America out of the war.[70]

German Catholicism also retained its relative strength in the years before World War I. Between 1901 and 1910, 36,500 German Catholics immigrated to America; and between 1911 and 1920, 10,000 immigrants came to these shores. Their were still 2,000 German Catholic groups who either used German exclusively or in part as late as 1906. Twenty dioceses had fifty or more German-speaking priests; fourteen of these fell within the "German triangle" between Ohio, Minnesota, and Missouri.[71] Archbishop Quigley of Chicago, carrying on the legacy of Feehan, supported German parishes whenever possible. But older communities soon gave way to Polish and Italian immigrants. Andrew Jacke Townsend states that the decrease in German national parishes during Quigley's episcopate was due to the fact that, "The German Catholics were more Catholic than German and found that they could worship well in English-speaking churches."[72]

Chicago's Italians, 1900-1917

While Chicago's Germans entered the new century strong and vigorous, Italians struggled to find a place in American society. By 1898, the area around Dearborn Station had 1,068 Italians; there were only sixteen American-born residents in the area. It remained the heaviest concentration of Italians through the first decade of the new century. By 1912, the block surrounded by Dearborn Station, Plymouth Court, Taylor, and Polk numbered 118 families; it remained the most concentrated block of Italians until the postwar business boom forced the majority to move south and west. The original Near North Side community gradually moved north, as the area around Grand and Clark was converted to industrial use. Italians soon secured the district between Chicago and Division, Gault Court and Milton Avenue.[73] Between 1900 and 1920, they pushed across Division Street to North Avenue, between Wells and Halsted. The area soon became known as Little Italy, as Sicilians from Baglieria and Alto Villa founded St. Philip Benizi Parish, at Oak and Cambridge, in 1904. It was the second largest Italian settlement at the beginning of the century.

The largest Italian community was the Near West Side, centered around Hull House at Polk and Halsted. Italians, who were forced to move west of Halsted as early as 1905, reached Morgan and Racine streets by 1910. By 1918, they were buying single-family homes on Leavitt, Jakley, and Western.[74] Conditions on the Near West Side were intolerable, as a survey conducted by Edith Abbot and Sophonisba Breckinridge at the beginning of the century demonstrated. Coming ten years after a similar study by the City Homes Association, they found only one improvement, "the removal of the noxious privy vault." Otherwise, "we still find the same overcrowded areas, alleys, tenements, dilapidated houses, oppressive density of population, families in outlawed cellar apartments, in dark and gloomy rooms, and in conditions of overcrowding which violates all standards of decency and health." Grace Norton reported that, "The Italian is paying a comparatively high rent for dilapidated unhealthful quarters. He is living in illegally overcrowded rooms, in damp and gloomy apartments, and under conditions which . . . are acknowledged to be dangerous and demoralizing." Natalie Walker wrote in 1915 that the West Side settlement was still overcrowded and demoralizing—of 4,564 bedrooms, 1,636 were overcrowded and filthy.[75] John R. Commons observed that, "The dangerous effects of city life on immigrants and the children of immigrant cannot be too strongly emphasized . . . they are dragged down by the parasitic and dependent conditions which the cities foster among the immigrant element."[76]

The Near South Side, which had been German until the late 1880s, turned Italian during the following two decades. The Columbian Exposition increased land values, as did the building of the el into the area. The rich moved out of their palatial homes on Prairie Avenue to Grand and Drexel boulevards, or the Near North Side. By the turn of the century, wholesale establishments and warehouses took over much of the residential district. Italians moved to Dearborn and Federal streets, just south of Archer Avenue. But prostitution forced the majority to move farther south as real estate agents "could get more rent from them [the prostitution rings] than they could from the Italians." The newcomers were welcomed by some of the original settlers, as they helped eliminate vice and prostitution.[77] By 1920, there were 4,800 foreign-born Italians in a twenty-seven-block area; the heart of the community lay between Twenty-second and Twenty-fifth streets. Two thousand of these immigrants founded Santa Maria Incoronata Parish, at Eighteenth and Clark, in 1899.

Italians, who moved into Armour Square at the beginning of the century, took over the frame cottages and brick two- and three-flats vacated by the Germans, Irish, and Swedes. Italian life, which centered around the family, was close-knit and patriarchial. Some Italians entered ward politics, while others formed societies and fraternal organizations for mutual protection. As Chinatown emerged along Cermak Road and Wentworth, Italians moved south to Thirty-second and Shields, where they bought one-story frame cottages or rented apartments. By 1927, most Italians living south of Thirty-fifth were from the south, while those who remained near Chinatown were largely Sicilian.[78]

The Sicilians, who continued to move south toward Greater Grand Crossing (and even Calumet Park outside the city), replaced the older German settlers on the east side of the community. Archbishop Quigley established St. Francis de Paula Parish, at 7822 South Dobson, for their needs in 1911. The archdiocesan archives note that the parish remained Italian throughout World War I. "In spite of the international flavor of its people, the Italian flavor was very much in evidence, since Italian predominated. The annual *Festa* to Our Lady was the major parish social event of the year, complete with outdoor processions, a fiesta, and bazaar."[79] But the community gradually Americanized as other nationalities moved into the area. The Sicilians gradually moved west, where "they mingle with their Bohemian neighbors on the basis of religious interests, to some extent, but even more on the grounds of economic status, which fairly compensates for the lack of uniformity in language, customs and traditions."[80] By 1930, there were only 733 foreign-born Italians in Greater Grand Crossing; the majority had moved farther south or west to other communities.

A small Italian colony, mostly Sicilians and Calabrese, arose on the East Side around Commercial Street, from Ninety-fourth to 100th streets, in 1895. As Yugoslavs moved into the area between 1910 and 1925, Italians moved farther south to Ewing Avenue and Avenue J, where they forced the earlier Swedes and Germans to emigrate. By 1930, there were only 605 foreign-born Italians living on the East Side. A larger Italian community arose in West Englewood, a community bounded by Garfield Boulevard and the Chicago and Western Indiana Railroad on the north and south, and Racine Avenue and the Pennsylvania Railroad on the east and west. The area, which was originally called South Lynne, was incorporated into the city in 1880. Settled by Italians from lower Italy and Sicily in the 1890s, West Englewood had a large Italian colony at Sixty-fifth and Wood streets in 1900. The community grew as Italians from Greater Grand Crossing moved west in 1905. By 1907, there were fifty or more families between Sixty-ninth and Seventy-first streets, and Wood and Ashland avenues; by 1909, Italians had pushed to Seventy-fourth Street, where a third settlement arose at Wood and Lincoln. Most were unskilled laborers who gradually rose to factory workers and real estate brokers. One group founded Our Lady of Mount Carmel Church, at 6722 South Hermitage Street, in 1892.[81]

The largest Italian ward in 1910 was the Nineteenth, with 14,649 foreign-born Italians. Often called "the Bloody Nineteenth" because of its gang wars and Black Hand activities, it remained the largest Italian ward through 1920, with 15,199 inhabitants. The ward lay directly west of the Chicago River between Van Buren and Twelfth streets, in the Near West Side community. The Twenty-second Ward, which also overlapped the Near West Side, lay east of the river, between North Avenue and Division Street; despite a change in ward boundaries in 1911, the relative number of Italians remained the same (see Table 2). Besides the Nineteenth and Twenty-second wards, the Ninth Ward on the Far South Side (between Seventy-fifth and 138th streets, and Stony Island and Halsted), the Fourteenth Ward (between Chicago Avenue and Washington Boulevard, and Ashland and Crawford) and the Twenty-first Ward, in Lincoln Park (between Fullerton and the main branch of the river), all had significant Italian pockets by 1920.

Before, Germans and Italians came to Chicago for economic reasons. But while the northern Europeans quickly adjusted to American life, Italians remained on the lowest range of the economic ladder until after World War I. The earliest Italians were laborers, who worked at building and maintaining the various public and private works in Chicago. They found jobs on the railroads, in excavation and street cleaning, boot blacking, and factory labor. They often worked as scabs or strikebreakers during the labor unrest of the 1880s and 1890s. But these southerners gradually worked their way into heavy and light industry, as many found jobs in the steel mills of South Chicago, the foundries of Cicero, or the factories of McCormick. Some opened restaurants and barber shops; others entered the tailoring business for Hart, Schaffner and Marx. By 1895, Italians were involved as pavers, saloon keepers, hod carriers, mosaic layers, teamsters, and carpenters. Italian women entered the teaching field by the end of the century; between 1898 and 1899, eleven Italians were Chicago public schoolteachers; by 1921, there were forty-two Italians in the city's schools.[82]

Italians gradually recognized the importance of education for their economic betterment. *L'Italia* urged parents to send their children to the public schools, since "to become good American citizens you must know how to speak, read and write English" (October 29, 1892). Again, "citizens of the Italian colony ... are not cooperating with the Board of Education in sending their children to school ... this ignoble characteristic lowers our social position in Chicago ... in comparison with Americans. We should send our children to school, and make them good American citizens" (September 16, 1893).[83] Jane Addams recognized that "Italian parents count upon the fact that their children learn the English language and American customs before they themselves do, and act not only as interpreters of the language about them,

TABLE 2

Principal Italian Wards, 1910-1920

1910		1920	
Ward	Foreign-Born	Ward	Foreign-Born
1	3,045	1	3,913
4	1,892	4	1,766
14	1,652	8	1,059
17	4,910	9	3,100
19	15,649	11	1,311
22	8,216	13	1,548
33	2,963	14	3,540
		17	5,199
		18	2,611
		19	15,199
		20	1,217
		21	2,604
		22	6,183
		29	1,499
		33	1,301

SOURCE: Puzzo, "The Italians in Chicago, 1890-1930," pp. 26, 47.

but as buffers between them and Chicago, and this results in a certain, almost pathetic dependence of the family upon the child."[84] There was a constant conflict between the ideals of education and the realities of life. Many parents preferred parochial schools, but could not understand why they had to pay for them. Only 1,937 children attended Catholic elementary schools in 1915,[85] but these statistics gradually improved after World War I.

Both Germans and Italians agreed that Chicago's political life was not for them. Charles E. Merriam noted that Germans preferred to work through voluntary associations rather than political bureaucracy. As he stated in his classic work on Chicago politics: "The tradition of efficient public school service, the thrift of the small home owner and taxpayer, the emergence of prominent fixtures in the cultural world and the interest in independent civic action all characterized the German in Chicago's political life."[86] Italians also disdained politics, but for a different reason. Edward Corsi observed that "the Italian . . . is too poetic for the 'game.' He prefers loftier pastimes. While the Irishman is organizing the ward and the Jew listens to the platitudes of the soapbox orator . . . the Italian is at home, enjoying the rapturous strains of 'O Sole Mio.' "[87] As late as 1910, only 6,408 of 22,668 foreign-born Italians were naturalized American citizens; although this figure rose to 11,097 by 1920, Italians remained one of the lowest naturalized groups in Chicago. Italian newspapers stressed self-help over political activity. It is not surprising that the Bloody Nineteenth was ruled by the notorious Johnny Powers for twenty-eight years. Personally responsible for granting utility franchises to Charles Yerkes, Chicago's utility magnet, Powers, the Prince of Boodlers, ran his ward like a king. But Italians saw him as a friend, a man who fed them when they were hungry, released them from jail, sponsored community dances, and mourned their dead. Powers himself said that "I am what my people like, and neither Hull House nor all the reformers in town can turn them against me."[88] All attempts to reform the Nineteenth failed in the face of Powers's affability and the Italians' need for local help.[89]

No area is more associated with Chicago's Italians than crime. But in fact only a small minority turned to illegal means to better their life. In the 1880s, some officials believed that all Italians were criminals. The United States Immigration Commission advocated stronger immigration laws, since "certain kinds of criminality are inherent in the Italian race."[90] Mob violence escalated as native Americans vented their disappointments with the industrial age on the Italians. The murder of a New Orleans police chief on October 15, 1890, created a violent reaction against all Italian Americans. Chicago's community, which paid the defense for the nine accused men (all Italians), viewed the incident as a general pattern of anti-Italian feeling.

Prior to 1890, Italian crime was largely limited to child labor abuse and family-style vendettas. But after the New Orleans episode, the term "Mafia" was first used for organized Italian crime. *L'Italia* and other Italian-language newspapers declared that "this fable of the Mafia is an unreasonable stupidity, an imbecility pure and simple. Every small quarrel between Italians gives rise to the cry of 'Mafia.' This organization does not now and never did exist . . . to make a long story short, the Mafia exists neither in Chicago nor in Italy" (October 8, 1892). To counteract this term, Italian newspapers began to refer to Italian crime as the "Black Hand." But whatever the term, Italians vehemently denied its existence, declaring it "a myth, insofar as the phrase conveys the impression that an organization of Italian criminals exists in America." A few native-born Americans agreed with this assessment. Congressman William S. Bennet (N.Y.) felt that "Italy does not impose its criminals upon us; the idea that Black Handers are bred exclusively in Italy to slip into this country through lax immigration precautions is a myth fostered by police officers anxious to shift responsibility."[91]

But crime was a significant problem in Chicago during the first decades of the new century. Quack doctors, shyster lawyers, and shrewd businessmen often cheated the southerner of his life savings. Small-time punks extorted money from newcomers who were unable to fight back. Prostitution, arson, counterfeiting, election fraud, and embezzlement were pastimes of petty criminals. But it was the old-fashioned vendetta (the *lex talionis*) that caused the most anxiety among Chicago's Italians. The press bitterly denounced these ancient rivalries, though little could be done to stop them. *L'Italia* noted that, "Day after day, week after week, more and more crimes are being committed, the perpetrators of which are invariably Italians."[92] There is no doubt that the political and social situation in Chicago made crime a lucrative step to economic success. When local politicians and police cooperated with criminals, it only furthered the belief that the means did justify the end. Black Hand activities continued through the 1910s, but quickly disappeared when large-scale syndicate crime took its place in the 1920s. It is important to remember, however, that the vast majority of Italian *contadini* were simply trying to make a new start in a new land.[93]

Ethnic Institutions, the Foreign-Language Press, and Immigrant Societies

One of the most significant forces in immigrant life was the foreign-language press. It was particularly strong among Chicago's Germans.[94] One of the earliest German newspapers was the *Chicago Volksfreund*, established by Robert B. Hoeffgen in 1845. The *Illinois Staats-Zeitung*, which began publication in 1848, became a daily by 1851. Although consistently supporting German causes through the nineteenth and twentieth centuries, it lost readership during World War I to the more moderate *Abendpost* established in 1889. The latter newspaper, which was more American than German, published a German daily through 1979. But the total number of German newspapers declined through the first two decades of the century, until there were only seven dailies in Chicago, with a total circulation of 255,645 in 1917.[95] The numbers continued to decrease during the twenties and thirties, as more and more Germans turned to Chicago's English-language newspapers for their news.

The Italian press did much better than the German in holding the immigrant's attention.[96] The first Italian-language newspaper in Chicago was the short-lived *L'Unione Italiana*, founded in 1867. One of the most significant immigrant newspapers was *L'Italia*, founded by Oscar Durante and Carlo Gentile in 1886. By 1889, it had the largest circulation of any Italian newspaper in the United States. By 1892, it has 17,500 readers in all parts of the Midwest. Taking a decidedly Republican stand during the 1890s, *L'Italia* called the GOP "the champion of public schools and free education."[97] *La Tribuna Italiana Transatlantica*, founded by Alessandro Mastrovalerio and Giuseppe Ronga in 1898, was the second most important Italian-language newspaper in Chicago.[98] Its format was flashy and nationalistic; its heroes were Mazzini and Garibaldi. It carried on a continuous feud with the Catholic *New World*, although neither Mastrovalerio nor Ronga appreciated the function of politics. By 1921 *La Tribuna* had a circulation of 25,000, but it ceased publication when Mastrovalerio returned to Italy in 1935.[99]

But it was not only newspapers that furthered ethnic culture—immigrant societies did so as well. Of all the nationalities that came to America, the Germans were the most adept at establishing *Vereine* for the perpetuation of their own unique culture.[100] The earliest societies were founded on the basis of occupation, sex, and interest. The Wagner Verein (Coachmakers' Association) and the Schreiner-Verein (Carpenters' Association) were founded in the 1850s, while the Junge Männer Verein was established the same decade for the young German men of Chicago. The oldest women's club in Chicago was the Columbia Damen-Klub, founded in 1893. Many clubs were mutual-interest societies, the most important being the Verein für Künst und Wissenschaft (Association of Art and Science), which was directly responsible for the erection of the Deutsches Haus, the focal point of German society until 1871. The Masons, Sons of Herman, Knights of Pythias, and the Catholic Order of Foresters all started as German fraternal organizations.[101] Singing societies (*Sängerbund*) were particularly popular among Germans, as hundreds of small groups formed in parishes and local communities throughout the 1800s. The Chicago Symphony was a direct descendant of one of these early *Sängerbund*.[102]

The earliest and most numerous *Vereine* were *Unterstüzungsvereine* (insurance unions), which collected dues and paid out benefits on deceased members. For example, the Bismarck-Bund (or Gegenseitiger Unterstützungsverein von Chicago), which began as a mutual-help society in 1868, grew to 897 members by 1871. Although its membership declined during World War I, it quickly rebounded and numbered 5,666 by 1930. Indeed, "the Mutual Aid Society played a prominent role in the societal life of Chicago . . . it is certain that our Association has raised the appearance of Germans in the eyes of so-called Americans."[103] The Germania Club, which grew out of the Germania Mannerchor, became "the most important club of Chicago's German element" after the fire. Its members established the German-American Historical Society, which published the *Deutsch-Amerikanische Geschichtsblatter* from 1900 to 1937. Its constituency, which steadily climbed to 1,100 by 1940, consistently supported Chicago's Germanity through six decades of acculturation and change.[104]

Both Catholic and Protestant Germans established numerous societies to counteract the influence of the liberal *Vereine* founded by Forty-eighters. Most of these societies, which centered around the parish, federated into larger associations and groupings. The German Catholic Union of Illinois (Deutscher Katholischer Vereins-Bund von Illinois) began as a lobby group in Springfield for German-American causes. The union, which was established in 1893, opposed free textbooks and public school transportation.[105] The Chicago Distrikt-Verband, a German Catholic organization, joined forces with the Catholic Order of Foresters to form an employment bureau for out-of-work Catholics. Archbishop Mundelein, who supported this work, said, "I am going to leave it the care of the jobless to the care of the German societies. It is a good work for the common good."[106] The Ketteler Club, a Catholic lay society, organized a German-Austrian Relief Committee in 1919 to aid the suffering in Austria and Germany. The Rt. Rev. R. A. Rempe of St. Gregory's and William J. Dettmer of St. Benedict's were chairman and secretary, respectively, of the committee.[107] But it is important to realize that the German parish was the focus of these activities. It organized, supported, and maintained scores of *Vereine* for over one hundred years. Indeed, the German parish was one of the principal institutions furthering German culture in Chicago.

Italians also fostered ethnic societies, although they were not as numerous or strong as their German counterparts. They did serve to preserve ethnic ties while helping the immigrant adjust to American society. The earliest Italian society in Chicago was the Società di Union e Fratellanza Italiana, established in 1866. Other associations soon followed as Italians began to pour into the city: The Humberto I Society (1881), the Core Assunta No. 50 (1886), the Re d'Italia (1887), and the Fratellanza Siciliana (1892). Many societies were linked to local societies, such as the Società S. Cristoforo di Ricigliano and the Società S. Stefano di Castellone. The early societies were *"di mutuo soccorso"* (mutual aid), which often failed due to unsound actuarial practices. Many of these societies joined larger fraternal groups, which gave them financial stability and larger membership. By 1919, there were 110 such societies in Chicago alone. When the state of Illinois passed new mutual benefit laws in 1927, the majority of these Italian organizations joined other fraternal insurance groups.[108]

Italian societies were also based on mutual interest or profession. The Bersaglieri di Savoia, the Bersaglieri e Carbinieri, and the Reali Carabinieri were military clubs that celebrated national holidays and military events. The Lincoln Italian Republican Workers' Club, the McKinley Italian Club, and the Italian Political Club were prominent Republican organizations, while the Italian Progressive Democratic League of Cook County represented the minority party in Chicago.[109] Other *società* were purely social, such as the Maria Adelaide Club, the Italian Pleasure Club, and Nuova Lega dei Trampi (1902). These societies, which advertised their meetings and social events in immigrant newspapers, fought against immigration restrictions, celebrated Italian holidays, and built monuments to Italian heroes. A number of societies joined forces to erect a statue to Garibaldi in Lincoln Park in 1901. But this emphasis on statue raising often overlooked neighborhood and civic improvement. And since the state supplied public education, Italians were not as concerned about parochial education as their German contemporaries.

The two most significant Italian societies in Chicago were the Unione Siciliana and the Sons of Italy.[110] The former, which was established in Chicago in 1895, gathered scores of village societies into one all-encompassing group. Numbering 800 members by 1910, the unione changed its name to the Italo-American National Union in 1925, a sign that America's Italians now considered themselves a distinct ethnic group. The Order of Sons of Italy, a national group established in New York City in 1905, was an effective instrument of Americanization through five decades of war and peace. Its stated goals were "to promote civic education among its members; to uphold the concept of Americanism, and to encourage the active participation of our membership in the political, social, and civic life of our communities."[111] Chicago's societies, which organized themselves under the United Italian Societies in 1906, numbered 6,000 members by the late 1920s. All these societies fostered a sense of Italianness among people who first considered themselves Salerni, Riciglianesi, or Siciliani. Humbert Nelli notes that "through these activities [i.e., the societies] the immigrants first developed some knowledge of things Italian, a concept which had little meaning before their arrival in America. In America, the immigrant widened his horizon beyond his village and province, and began to think of himself as an Italian, with heroes linking them to the past."[112]

There were various institutions that furthered ethnic culture. Two of the most important were the foreign-language press and the immigrant society. While Italians clung to their newspapers longer than Germans, Germans developed a societal system that was far more extensive than the Italian. But both groups relied on these important institutions to further ethnic information, provide news from abroad, and supply needed money at a time when large-scale insurance companies did not exist. While most newspapers were secularly founded, immigrant societies were often religiously oriented. But whatever the source, immigrant newspapers and societies were valuable way stations of ethnicity and Americanization.

Ethnic Provincialism

One of the most striking parallels between Chicago's Germans and Italians was a deeply embedded sense of provincialism, which ran through most nineteenth- and twentieth-century immigrants. Both Germany and Italy were latecomers in an otherwise unified Europe—*Deutschland* was not united until

Bismarck came to power in 1871, while *L'Italia* did not unite its northern and southern provinces until 1860. Both nations lacked a sense of nationality, a sense of being German or Italian. For Germans, it was the local province that demanded loyalty, while for Italians, it was the local village.[113]

The majority of German immigrants before 1870 were northerners. Many came from Schleswig-Holstein, the northernmost German province. Religious sects like the Anabaptists, Mennonites, Quakers, Schwenkfelders, and Amish joined these earlier pioneers in settling Pennsylvania, Ohio, and Michigan, while some three hundred peasants from Württemburg founded a communistic society in Tuscawaras County, Ohio, in 1802; by 1832 it became the "separatist community of Zoar." Swabians and Prussians settled Indiana in the 1840s. A contemporary noted that "the Saxon does not like the Swabian, nor the Prussian the Bavarian, and the Westphalian would . . . devour the poor Badenser alive, and so conversely."[114]

Germans continued to arrive after Bismarck's efforts to unite their homeland in 1871. Herman Hagedorn felt that "Germans abroad felt the need of a united and powerful Germany almost more than the Germans at home . . . what was a Hanoveria, a Saxon, a citizen of the free city of Lubeck or a subject of the Grand Duke of Sachsen-Colburg-Gotha?"[115] But Germans continued to see themselves as Bavarians, Prussians, or any number of provincial loyalties. The Missouri synod (Lutheran), which kept its ties to Saxony, called itself The Evangelical Lutheran Free Church in Saxony and other States. The Saxon church sent the Missouri synod pastors, seminary candidates, and financial help; its ties were "emotional, religious, and ethnic."[116] Indeed, the history of the Missouri synod is a history of the continued provincial loyalties that influenced America's Germans through the twentieth century.

Chicago also maintained a strong sense of provincialism among its German populace. Statistical data from 1860 to 1880 classified Germans according to provincial *Länder* (see Table 3). That there did exist a sense of provinciality among Chicago's Germans is best understood in what they said about themselves. A German saloon keeper in Northcenter recalled that there were so many dialects of German heard in his area that it was difficult to sing together: "When you came from one part of Germany as some of us did you call a word differently than if you come from some other part. I speak five languages besides the different German dialects I understood, but the teacher didn't like us to be different when we sung."[117]

Protestant and Catholic Germans also maintained separate loyalties based on provinciality and religion. In the 1916 mayoral elections, Big Bill Thompson "drew to his banner thousands of sturdy Protestants from Saxony, Prussia, and the other German states more moved by Lutheran than Jesuit casuistry"; while Roman Catholics from Bavaria voted for Robert Schweizer, the Democratic candidate.[118] Mrs. Henry Hahn recalled that the neighborhood around St. Alphonsus Parish was "kind of divided up—Bavarians and people from different parts of Germany." Each provinciality had its own societies, while Bavarians delighted in the annual *Oktoberfest*. She noted that "people were still complaining" about the use of English in liturgies as late as 1935. Mrs. Hahn also remembered the numerous German societies that enlivened early twentieth-century Chicago. She particularly recalled the Swaben picnic, which featured a unique "tower of vegetables."[119]

Theresa Krutz vividly recalled the provincialism of twentieth-century Chicago as she was growing up on the northwest side of the city. Her home, a neat ranch-style house, reflected her German ancestry. Beer steins and other German collectibles filled up the living room and den. Her father came to America from a small town in Baden-Württemburg in the early 1900s. When I asked her whether there was a strong provincial sense among Germans, Mrs. Krutz emphatically answered: "Oh, my dear, yes—you better believe it. My aunt married Uncle Joe who was from the north of Germany and my father always thought that was generally what was the matter with him—the language is still so different, the dialects you can't disguise where you're from. From hearing this Schwabish dialect all my life I thought that was German. Then you hear someone give a homily in higher German or pure German—you can hardly understand it if you're from Bayern [Bavaria]. . . . As far as I'm concerned, Germany is 'Sound of Music' country—small towns and pretty hills."[120]

German provincialism was particularly evident in the numerous societies that existed and continue to exist today. Mutual-aid and recreational *Vereine* were particularly common in the nineteenth century. For example, Swabians founded a Schwabisher Unterstützungs-Verein in 1883; Berliners established a Berliner Vergenungsverein as a recreational club; and Bavarians, Rhinelanders, and Saarlanders founded a Bayern Verein, Rheinischer Verein, and Saarlander Verein, respectively. The most significant of all these societies was the Schwabenverein, since "It provides a many-sided picture of German life in Chicago, because it points out an eternally changing enterprise in politics, social life and culture throughout its history and development."[121]

TABLE 3

German Immigration to Chicago by Provinces, 1870-1880

	Percent of Foreign-Born		Percent of Total Population	
	1870	1880	1870	1880
Prussia	17.25	16.07	8.34	6.54
Bavaria	2.56	1.28	1.24	.52
Baden	2.24	1.05	1.09	.43
Mecklenburg	2.35	.94	1.13	.38
Hanover	1.71	.94	.83	.38
Saxony	1.17	.79	.56	.32
Württemberg	1.47	.69	.71	.28
Hesse	2.35	.36	1.14	.15
Hamburg	.22	.20	.11	.08
Nassau	1.4	.05	.07	.02
Oldenburg	.04	.04	.02	.02
Brusswick	.06	.02	.03	.01
Weimar	.03	.006	.01	.002
Lübeck	.008	.004	.004	.001
Not specified	4.54	14.28	2.21	5.81

SOURCE: Pierce, *A History of Chicago*, 3: 516.

Swabians interested in carrying on Swabian traditions established the society in 1818. The society flourished through the 1890s and early 1900s. It took part in a German Day celebration at the Chicago World's Fair in 1893; it helped celebrate an elaborate Bismarck Day in Chicago in 1898, and it celebrated its twenty-fifth anniversary in 1903. Swabians commemorated the 100th anniversary of the death of Friedrich von Schiller, a prominent Swabian poet, with the publication of his complete works, compiled through the German department of Northwestern University, at a cost of $11,471. The society continued to flourish through World War I, as it participated in the German and Austrian-Hungarian Relief Association (Deutsch und Österreichisch-ungarischen Hilfsverein), which was established in 1914 for war-stricken Europe. Swabians also supported the rebuilding of Germany by buying milk cows for the destitute, contributing to the Ausland Institute in Stuttgart, and helping university students in Württemberg. By 1918, the Schwabenverein numbered 1,361 members.

One of the most important festivals of the society was the Kanstadter Volksfest, named after the Roman settlement of Cann in southwestern Germany. The first Chicago celebration was held at Ogdens Grove (Milwaukee near Armitage) in 1877. The proceeds went to various German causes: in 1879 the society donated $500 for a statue to Schiller; in 1914 it gave $10,000 to the German and Austrian-Hungarian Relief Association, and in 1920 the society donated the entire proceeds of the festival ($15,000), to war-torn Germany and Austria. Forty-eight such festivals netted $442,748,00. The society celebrated the 100th anniversary of the Kanstadter Volksfest at Buffalo Grove, Illinois, in 1977. The history of the Schwabenverein is a history of the continued presence of provinciality in twentieth-century Chicago. It demonstrates that Chicago's *Deutschtum* was alive and well through World War I.[122]

Italians also fostered a sense of provincialism, but it was more local than regional. Italy was divided for centuries into a variety of kingdoms and principalities, governed by such foreign powers as France and England. Southern Italy remained an area of peasant villages and poor *contadini*. Between 1876 and 1930, approximately 80 percent of the 5,058,776 Italians who came to America were southerners. The following list clearly demonstrates the numerical superiority of the *mezzogiorno* during these fifty-five years.[123]

Campania (Napoli)	1,105,802	(27.4%)
Abruzzi and Molise	652,972	(16.2%)
Apulia	300,152	(7.4%)
Basilicata	232,389	(5.8%)
Calabria	522,442	(13.0%)
Sicily	1,205,788	(29.9%)
Sardinia	14,699	(0.4%)

The first Italians who came to America considered themselves immigrants from a particular town or village; they even referred to those who lived a few miles away as *forestieri* (forest dwellers).[124] While northerners could point with pride to Columbus, Dante, and Rossini, southerners had few heroes to look up to. Most immigrants were aware of the provincial differences between them. Rosa, an Italian immigrant in New York, recalled these differences at the turn of the century. "The people of Toscana they're not good like the people from Lombardia. But they're not bad like the people from Sicilia. I should say no people from Piemonte are a little more bad than the people from Lombardia, but they come next. Lombardia is the last in the world to do bad things."[125] An Italian doctor from Chicago recalled that his father, who was Genoese, settled in a predominantly Genoese district along Kinzie, Franklin, Illinois, and Kingsbury streets in 1852. As he stated: "The Genoese dialect is very different from Italian and I do not like it. I'm reading Dante in Genoese and I laugh and laugh some evenings because Dante translated into Genoese is very funny." Even as late as 1928, the doctor noted that "they [i.e., the southern Italians] seem to me to be of an entirely different race, and we do not even speak the same language."[126]

Italian provincialism is illustrated in the history of our Lady of Pompeii Parish. Mr. and Mrs. Anthony Serritella vividly recalled the history of the parish. I met them in their modest apartment off Racine Avenue. The block where they lived is lined with neat two-flats, while the parish church gracefully adorns the far end of the block. A grassy mall four blocks long borders the southern side of the street, with Mother Cabrini Hospital on the far east side acting as a buffer to the outside world. Indeed, the area was a small piazza, an "enclave where all the people from a certain town would stay." The Serritellas recalled that Our Lady of Pompeii was originally founded by *contadini* from Ricigliano, near Salerno, in southern Italy. As other villagers moved in, they founded their own village societies. "There's one Riciglianesi Alleanza—then there's St. Vito of Ricigliano—people from Abruzzo had their own societies, they called it Santo Croce." Although parishioners came from various regions of Southern Italy—Naples, Calabria, and Abruzzi—"everybody went to the same church, they weren't separated—as far as living, everyone lived just where they wanted to."[127] And it was the parish church that united all these separate loyalties into one Italian-American population.

Provincialism remained a strong factor in Chicago life through the first decades of the twentieth century. Germans continued to be divided along regional and religious lines—while Saxony and other northern provinces remained fiercely Protestant, Bavaria and Austria clung tenaciously to their Catholicism. Italians were also divided along geographic lines, although their strongest attachment remained the local village (*campanelismo*). Both Germans and Italians founded provincial societies to further this regionalism. While gradual Americanization erased many of these provincial differences, some regional societies continue to exist as a legacy of Chicago's immigrant past.

World War I

As the world prepared for war in 1914, Chicago's German and Italian communities remained worlds apart. While Chicago's *Deutschtum* was strong and flourishing, with numerous societies and newspapers to nourish ethnic life, Italians were struggling to find a place in Chicago life. By the eve of the war, German Catholics had established over thirty ethnic parishes within seventy years. They had dotted the city with Gothic edifices. Meanwhile, within the Italian community, clergy struggled to keep the immigrants' loyalty, as the parish fought the secular forces of the immigrant newspaper and Protestant proselytizing. Fettered with a long tradition of anticlericalism and government support for Catholicism, Italians could not understand why they had to support the church. While German Catholics had established an extensively parochial school system, to such an extent that they built schools before churches, Italians had founded only one parochial school by 1914. But paradoxically, as the world was plunged into war, it was the German community that suffered the most. While Chicago's *Deutschtum* was shaken to its very foundations by the war, Italians scarcely noticed it, and entered the twenties with a new sense of Italianness.

Many Americans were openly anti-German during the war.[128] Theodore Roosevelt said that "our bitter experience should teach us for a generation . . . to crush under our heel every movement that smacks in the smallest degree of playing the German game."[129] William K. Skaggs's *German Conspiracies in America* (1915) found a wide audience in the United States. The German language disappeared from schools and universities, while German books vanished from public libraries. Orchestras even banned Beethoven and Bach from their repertoire. Chicago's newspapers, which were generally anti-German, lashed out at "the disloyal Dachshund," while publishing inflammatory articles against all German Americans.[130] Aliens suspected of sympathizing with the enemy were summarily interred and their property confiscated. For example, Peter Schoenhofen, a prominent Chicago breweryman, was arrested for pro-German tendencies, and members of the Chicago Symphony Orchestra were warned to show no disloyalty to America. Even Chicago streets lost their Teutonic origins, as Berlin, Hamburg, Frankfurt, Coblenz, and Rhine streets disappeared from the city map forever; only Goethe and Schiller streets remained as a remainder of Chicago's once proud *Deutschtum*.[131]

German Americans themselves were decidedly against the war when it broke out in 1914. A few joined pan-Germanic societies, although this movement never attracted many followers.[132] Advertisements in Rudolph Cronau's *German Achievements in America* (New York, 1916) pictured England as "The Giant Octopus," a "Destroyer of Nations"; it asked "German Militarism or British Navalism—which is the Menace?" Germans even joined Irishmen in forming an Irish-German-American League, dedicated to keeping America out of the war.[133]

Chicago also had its German sympathizers. Max Annenberg, founder of the *Chicago Tribune*, described France and Belgium as "corrupt and immoral nations," while Germany was "in the full bloom of health and power." His cousin, Joseph Patterson, who also supported Germany, observed that "the German idea cannot be beaten in war."[134] The Catholic *New World*, although officially neutral, described events in Germany with such articles as "Germany is Little Disturbed," "Germany's Case Stated," and "Letters of a German Chaplain." As it stated in 1915, "Germany's greatest concern today is to preserve for itself the ideals and institutions that she has erected in the Fatherland during the long years of peace." And a few months later it observed that "feelings of mistrust began to separate the English from the Germans, who, by all the laws of nature, should stand side by side in this world . . . to advance the sum total of civilization."[135] The German-American Alliance held a mass rally at the Auditorium Theater on August 5, 1915, with sixty German societies and over ten thousand German Americans attending.

The alliance also sponsored a Bismarck celebration to support Germany and prepare for the battles ahead. Congressman Henry Vollmer stated that, "A slanderous and venomous battle is being waged against us. Whatever we may say or do, it will be misconstrued. . . . I find that a spiritual and physical campaign against Germany and Austria, and in favor of England and her allies, has started in the United States."[136]

German sympathies continued to play a prominent role in Chicago life as the war entered its second year. When Germans sank the *Lusitania* on May 8, 1915, the *Illinois Staats-Zeitung*, Chicago's leading German daily, declared that the American government had "a secret agreement with England to force a break with Germany . . . we hope Germany will not blame the people for the present government's action." Several German pacificists founded the Friends of Peace at the Sherman Hotel in late summer 1915 and asked the federal government to control the manufacture of firearms, to convene a conference of neutral nations to mediate the warring parties, and to ensure freedom of the seas. A national meeting, which was held in Chicago during the first week of September, declared itself against militarism and navalism, the manufacture of arms for profit, and the use of the Federal Reserve Bank to finance munitions for England. The *Tribune* called the society a pro-German organization, since eleven of its fifteen executive members were German-born. The Teutonic Sons of America, which was organized shortly thereafter, appealed to working-class Germans; it numbered two million members by September 1915.[137]

After continued attacks by German submarines, the United States declared war on Germany on April 6, 1917.[138] From that moment on, everything German was anathema. The *Tribune* declared: "Never was patriotism so feverish, so mindless, so nakedly jealous of the slightest qualification or mildest questioning." Sauerkraut became liberty cabbage, while the frankfurter became the hot dog. Germans could do nothing but declare their loyalty to the United States. As William O'Connor observed:

> Within the hours it took to bring the United States into the war, German Americanism disappeared forever. It could no longer exist. In those febrile times, the German-American had to make his decision to be either German or American. With startling few exceptions, the choice was made instantly for Americanism.[139]

Chicago's Germans also joined the cause. German Methodist ministers swore "unwavering loyalty to the United States." Chicago's Lutherans declared themselves loyal citizens as soon as the war began. Their schoolteachers, who met in December 1917, declared that "Americanism undefiled" would be taught in their schools and the national anthem played before and after school. The *Tribune* noted that Germans "want to let Chicago know that they are for America, and they intend to start with the third Liberty Loan." Charles H. Wacker and Levy Mayer, two prominent Chicago Germans, were members of the Illinois Defense Council. Oscar Knopf, another well-known German, criticized those who were lukewarm toward America in her time of need.[140] The full effect of the war on German Americans was devastating, for "it made everything German suspect. It put all German Americans on the defensive and reduced their influence. It speeded the dissolution of their organizations and press, and eroded their cultural identity. After 1917, German Americans found themselves on an irreversible downward course as a cultural force in American life."[141] After 1918, German Americans had to prove their loyalty again and again. They focused their postwar efforts on relief work to Germany and Austria. America's *Deutschtum* was never the same, for although remnants remained through the twenties and thirties, German America never never regained the vitality it had had before 1914.

While Germans were severely shaken by the war, Italians scarcely noticed it. They had no intense loyalty to Italy, for their allegiances were to local villages and towns, rather than an entire nation. Except for a few socialist newspapers, the Italian press solidly supported the American effort. When war broke out in 1917, *L'Italia* declared: "Long Live America! Long Live Wilson! Long Live Democracy! Down with Prussianism!"[142] Most Italians were reluctant to buy Italian war bonds, and few went back to Italy to fight for their country. When the war ended, hostilities immediately broke out between Italy and Yugoslavia. Italian papers, which unanimously supported Italy's claims, denounced Yugoslavia's betrayal. *L'Italia* proclaimed that "the Italy that will emerge from this war will not be the humble servant of the past, but, enlarged and suffused with a new breath of life, will inspire awe in the concert of nations, and will attract a great new respect to her sons scattered throughout the world."[143] Indeed, while the war marked an end to things German, it marked a beginning for Italian Americans. As the country moved into the prosperous twenties, Italians gained a new perspective on themselves and their native homeland. Italians broke out of their narrow *companalismo*, which isolated them from the rest of society, and began to see themselves as Italian Americans.

Postwar Ethnicity, 1918-1930

With the dawn of a new decade, America entered a period of prosperity that lasted until a gloomy October Thursday in 1929 shattered all its myths. America's Germanity, downtrodden but not beaten, reawakened in the 1920s. Between 1921 and 1930, 412,202 Germans immigrated to America. They remained the leading foreign-stock in Illinois, Indiana, Ohio, Wisconsin, Iowa, Missouri, South Dakota, Nebraska, Kansas, Kentucky, Arkansas, Oklahoma, and Oregon. Second-generation Germans were prominent in Wisconsin, Minnesota, and Nebraska.[144] The New York City schools reopened their curricula to German clubs. German celebrations also revived as German Americans honored General von Steuben, a revolutionary war hero, and Franz Sigel, a prominent German civil war general.[145] German celebrations also revived in Chicago. By 1923, the German Day Festival attracted 100,000 Chicagoans to Navy Pier. The *Abendpost* exclaimed: "The German oak tree is still alive despite some devastating storms." The German Theatre, which performed even during the war years, continued to thrive. The Victoria Theatre, at Sheffield and Belmont, presented German operettas and plays throughout the 1920s, while several Chicago theaters presented German films during the same period.[146]

Chicago's German-born community, which numbered 112,611 by 1920, was 4 percent of the total population (2,701,705) at the beginning of the decade. German stock numbered 421,443, or 16 percent of the whole. The majority lived on the North Side, with many communities partially German. The Near North Side with 83,936 inhabitants in 1920, had a large concentration of German foreign-born, while Lincoln Park, with 94,247 inhabitants, was almost as large; as the German community moved northward, other community areas became predominantly German. Northcenter and Lakeview had significant German populations by 1920. Rogers Park at the city's northernmost boundary, with 26,857 inhabitants, also had a large number of Germans by 1920. Other Chicago communities that had a strong percentage of Germans included West Ridge (7,490), Albany Park (26,076), Avandale (38,192), Logan Square (108,685), and Humboldt Park (65,095). South Side Teutonic communities included Gage Park (13,692), Beverly (not available), and Washington Heights (8,024).[147]

Meanwhile, during the same decade, Chicago's Italians overran the Near West Side. The community, which numbered 59,215 foreign-born Italians in 1920, remained an Italian stronghold through the ensuing decade.[148]

Although the area between Halsted and Racine declined during the 1920s, Italians continued to move west between Kinzie and Chicago, and northwest between Ashland and Leavitt. The communities of Austin and East Garfield Park grew considerably during this decade, while the Near North Side declined in favor of Mexican and black arrivals. On the Far South Side, Our Lady of Mt. Carmel Parish declined as more and more Italians moved south of the original community. Many, who left for the suburbs, filled up the subdivisions of Oak Park, Melrose Park, Kenilworth, and River Forest. In 1928, a Chicago Italian American observed that the Italian settlements "are fast disappearing because there are so few emigrating to the United States now, and partly because as the Italian makes money he moves into better neighborhoods, and doing this he no longer remains in concentrated groups."[149]

As Italians steadily improved their lot, they left the low-paying jobs they had before the war. While 50 percent of all Italians were laborers in 1916, only 31 percent remained on that level by 1931. Marriage certificates in New York City indicate that more and more Italians were electricians, painters, plumbers, contractors, foremen, and small businessmen. But it was Mussolini who gave Italians a real sense of pride in their culture and nationality. A young Chicago Italian said: "You've got to admit one thing; he [Mussolini] has enabled four million Italians in America to hold up their heads, and that is something. If you had been branded as undesirable by a quota law, you would understand how much that means." The 1920s were the high point in America's flirtations with Il Duce, as neo-Fascist organizations arose in America to support the new Italy. Eighty of the 129 Italian-language newspapers in the United States supported Mussolini, while the main opposition came from labor leaders, radical partisans, and a few liberal intellectuals. The Vatican's rapprochement with Mussolini only furthered Italy's esteem among Italian Americans. It was only after the invasion of Albania in 1939 and the formation of the Axis powers in 1940, that Italian Americans dissassociated themselves from this enigmatic leader.[150]

As the second generation came to maturity, more and more Italians saw themselves as Americans. Stefano Miele observed this process: "There is a change in the second generation, change that is too frequently not for the better . . . the majority of Italian immigrants come from the rural districts of Italy . . . they are not prepared to meet the situation presented in the big industrial centers and in the streets of the crowded tenement districts the children see graft, pocket-picking, streetwalking, easy money here, easy money there." Edward Corsi observed that "America's doors are fast closing and the tide of a new civilization which is not Anglo-Saxon or Latin or Slav, but 'American' is setting in." The generation gap widened to such an extent that many parents could not speak to their own children. A young Italian remembered this struggle in New York City:

> I am nervous when I bring friends to my house; the place looks so Italian. Here hangs a picture of Victor Emmanuel, and over there is one of the cathedral of Milan, and next to it, one of St. Peter's, and on the buffet stands a wine-pitcher of medieval design . . . these things are heirlooms belonging to my father, and no matter who may come to our house, he likes to stand under them and brag. So I begin to shout to him. I tell him to cut out being a Wop and be an American once in awhile. Immediately he gets his razor-strap and whales the hell out of me . . . a Wop! That's why my father is! Nowhere is there an American father who beats his son this way.[151]

Indeed, it was in the daily life of Italians such as these that the struggle to become American took place.

Meanwhile, as Italians discovered their heritage, Germans lost a good deal of what they had had. Much of the vitality that characterized German life before the war disappeared after 1918. By 1930, there were only 172 German-language newspapers in the United States. The German-American Alliance, chartered by Congress in 1899, dissolved itself in April 1918. Most German-American organizations, which were politically active before the war, waned during the twenties and thirties. Only a few progressive *Bunds* (associations), like the Deutsch-Amerikanische Reform Bund and the Deutsch-Amerikanische Burger Bund, remained active.[152] Most Germans simply stayed neutral during the twenties, which explains their lack of support for the Nazi Party in America.

But Chicago's *Deutschtum* continued to function despite nationwide losses. The *Abendpost* noted that Germans still had the most significant number of active clubs of any ethnic group. Even new societies were established. For example, the Steuben Society was founded in 1919, "to thoroughly Americanize whatever Germanism remained, without, at the same time, foreswearing any pride in the pre-World past of the German Americans."[153] These goals were later expanded "to protect citizens of German stock from insults, misrepresentations and discrimination." The *Abendpost* continued to report the activities of hundreds of German societies throughout the twenties and thirties. It noted that there were at least 452 active clubs in Chicago by 1935: 13 compatriotic clubs, 59 male and 23 female *Sängerbund*, 25

Turnvereine, 100 *Unterstatzüngsvereine*, 73 lodges, 2 professional clubs (the German Medical Association and the German Press Association), plus hundreds of other *Vereine* and associations.[154]

The Schwabenverein, which continued to function during this period, is a prime example of Chicago's *Deutschtum* in the 1920s. Increasing its enrollment to 1,277 by 1927, the Schwabenverein continued to thrive despite national losses.[155] Theresa Krutz recalled that the "Schwabs they were all in this area of the parish [St. Alphonsus]—the Schwabs had a building on Clark Street—a really big building where they had their meetings—where the kids rehearsed for their plays, where they kept their records—where they did their business. They had the Schwabenverein which was purely a social group—the Schwabischer Singerbund was a choral society. And then there was the Schwabischerunterstutzungsverein which is insurance—naturally, you belonged to all three, even if you weren't an active singer and didn't go to the *Singstunde* singing hour every Friday night. You got your tickets for the concerts and paid your dues—they had an active and passive membership."[156] Indeed, throughout the 1920s, the Schwabenverein held *Volksfests*, raised money for war-torn Germany and Austria, and significantly contributed to Chicago's German life.

German Catholicism also flourished at this time. In 1920, Cardinal Gibbons addressed a group of German delegates:

> I admire the German Catholic element in this country. Although as loyal Americans we had to fight the German government, we never had any ill feelings against the German people. The German Catholics have always been a loyal and conservative element of the Church in America, especially in enthusiastically establishing everywhere Catholic schools. . . .
>
> We have, of course, properly speaking, no German Catholics, no Polish Catholics, no English Catholics in this country. We are all American Catholics. But we are all indebted to the German element for their great service.[157]

The National Catholic Women's Union (Der Nationale Katholische Frauenbund), which began as a women's arm of the Central Verein in 1916, increased its membership to 56,000 by 1930. It distributed food and clothing to the poor of Germany after World War I, and operated several settlements in New York, Wisconsin, and Missouri. German communities in Wisconsin, California, and Massachusetts continued to encourage German art and worship throughout this decade.[158]

Although Cardinal Mundelein discouraged new German parishes, the clergy and laity of Chicago often demanded them. When the Reverend Martin F. Schmidt began a new parish in a German area of the city, Mundelein insisted it be national and territorial. But when the Germans, Austrians, and Luxemburgers of the area protested, Schmidt secretly introduced German prayers after Mass.[159] Hugo Stobba recalled that there was a strong sense of Germanity in Chicago between the world wars—a sense of "Deutschland über alles." Mr. Stobba first attended German services at St. Augustine's from 1923 to 1927, then enrolled at St. Raphael's Parish until 1937. Masses were conducted in German at 8:00 A.M., with announcements and Gospel in German. Mr. Stobba also belonged to the Kolping Society, a Catholic lay organization established in 1849. Visiting Germany in 1931, he observed Catholic pilgrimages and processions, which were still popular despite the rise of Nazism. But even after moving to St. Rita's Parish on the southwest side, Mr. Stobba continued to attend German services at St. Alphonsus Parish as late as 1950.[160] Indeed, though the German city was shaken and feeble, it lived on in the Catholic parish.

Ethnics have always been part of Chicago's history, from the French who first settled on the banks of the "Chicagou," to the Spanish-speaking refugees of more recent times. While the native-born often disdained these newcomers, the city eventually absorbed them into the larger mosaic. Various institutions supported and nourished immigrant ways, from the mutual-aid societies of local parishes to the immigrant newspapers of the more liberal element. But of all the institutions that supported ethnic ways, it was the Catholic parish that did so most successfully and that endured the longest.

THREE

The German Parish

German parochial life flowed north and south from its two mother churches, St. Peter's on the South Side and St. Joseph's on the North. St. Peter's, which was established in 1846, grew to 1,200 families by 1870. But the advancing Loop soon forced most settlers to move south, as the downtown slowly emerged during the last decades of the nineteenth century. As Germans moved away from St. Peter's, they established St. Anthony of Padua Parish, at 518 West Twenty-eighth Street; St. Paul's Church, at 2127 West Twenty-second Place; and St. Augustine's, at 5049 South Laflin. The Reverend Peter Fischer, of Neuenkirken, Germany, who founded St. Anthony's in 1873, nurtured German life there for five decades. The parish remained German for sixty years, after which "what had once been a strong, almost insular, settlement of German immigrants and their descendants clustering around the Church, dwindled during the years."[1] Rome finally combined St. Anthony's with All Saints' Parish in 1968, with St. Anthony's the principal place of worship.

Bishop Thomas Foley established St. Paul's Church in 1876. Henry J. Schlacks, a noted church architect, designed the impressive medieval church, which became known as the "church without a nail," since it was built entirely with cement. The German Benedictines from St. Vincent's Abbey in Pennsylvania guided the parish from 1904 to 1966. St. Benedict's also remained German through the 1930s, as devotions and prayers continued *auf Deutsch* through World War II.[2]

As German settlers moved southeast and southwest of St. Anthony's through the 1870s and 1880s, they established new ethnic parishes along the way. One group, who moved south to New City, formed the nucleus of St. Augustine's Parish. Most were West Prussians, Rhinelanders, East Prussians, and Alsatians, who were later joined by Austrians and German-Hungarians.[3] The area was sparse and uninviting, with only a few houses breaking the monotony of the flat prairies. Miniature lakes formed when it rained heavily, and crab holes abounded in the area. The roads, which were often impassable, ended at Fifty-first and Justine. The Glick Brothers Fertilizer Factory befouled the air with flies and mosquitoes. And yet, amid all of this, St. Augustine's grew as the most important South Side German parish.

The German Franciscans took charge of the parish in 1886. Coming to the United States from the Saxon province of Warendorf in the 1850s, they established a motherhouse in Teutopolis, Illinois, in 1858. The Reverend Kilian Scholesser, O.F.M., pastor of St. Peter's, discussed the possibility of a second Franciscan parish with his provincial:

> Fr. ex-provincial Vincent for years entertained the wish that the Most Rev. Archbishop would offer us a second German parish in the city, since St. Peter's is continually declining instead of growing. . . . I went with Fr. Anselm [Peutz] to look over the place. We found three Sisters in the school. They were overjoyed to hear that the Most Rev. Archbishop had offered us St. Augustine's Parish. They at once notified three of the trustees of our coming, and we found that the good people were willing to do everything agreeable to the Fathers. . . . The parish, which now has 160 families, would double in that number in a few years, because most of the Germans were now settling in the southern part of the city.

Although the provincial first declined the parish, he reconsidered and accepted it for the province. Father Kilian felt that "it is the cream of the pick. The people are all steady working people and are earning good wages. They are of good Catholic stock, as good or even better than you will find elsewhere."[4] Growing steadily during the 1890s and early 1900s, the parish numbered 1,400 families by 1911. Fostering German traditions through World War II, St. Augustine's continued to maintain its German character through the 1950s. Indeed, it was the most significant German parish on Chicago's South Side. But there were other parishes as well.

Some Germans, moving southwest along the Illinois and Michigan Canal, established Immaculate Conception Parish, at 3111 South Aberdeen Street, in 1883; while another group, moving farther south, established St. Maurice Parish, at 3515 South Hoyne, in 1890. A small group of Austrian Hungarians, moving south toward Indiana, founded St. George's Parish, at 3515 South Wentworth Avenue, in 1890. The parish received German pastors for eighty years, until physical and demographic changes forced its closing in 1969.[5] Another group of Germans, moving farther southeast along the Calumet River, established Sts. Peter and Paul Parish, at 9041 South Exchange Avenue, in 1881. The parish prospered from 1903 to 1913, but attracted few Germans after World War I, as Poles, Yugoslavians, and other eastern Europeans moved into the area to work in the steel mills of the East Side.[6]

St. Martin's Parish, at 5842 South Princeton Avenue, began when Michael Reich donated five lots of land on Fifty-ninth Street in 1885. The community flourished through the first decades of the new century, as 2,435 children were baptized in 1911 alone. When Father J. Schikowski became pastor in 1908, St. Martin's was "one of the most important German parishes in the city."[7] Despite pressure from American Catholics, Mundelein refused to change St. Martin's to a territorial parish. During Father Schikowski's long pastorate (1908-1941), St. Martin's gradually changed to an English-speaking parish. The golden jubilee booklet of 1936 noted that "the second and third generation came to maturity, completely assimilated into 'the American Way of life.' . . . Gradually, the use of German in sermons, pulpit announcements, and the 'Parish Post' was discontinued."[8]

St. Paul's, St. Anthony of Padua, St. Augustine's, and St. Martin's all represent significant South Side German parishes. The mere establishment of ten such parishes south of Madison Street indicates the strength of German Catholicism on Chicago's South Side. But this does not belie the fact that the heart of Chicago's German community was the North Side. St. Joseph's Parish, at Cass and Orleans streets, was the mother church for all North Side German parishes. Founded by Bishop Quarter in 1846, St. Joseph's became a Benedictine parish in 1860. When fire destroyed the parish in 1871, parishioners rebuilt it at 1107 North Orleans Street. But many parishioners moved north, as better homes and neighborhoods beckoned in Lincoln Park and Lakeview.[9] One group established St. Michael's Parish, at 1633 West Cleveland Street, in 1852, at the border between the Near North Side and Lincoln Park. The parish began when a group of Germans petitioned Bishop Oliver Van de Velde for a new parish to alleviate crowding at St. Joseph's. Michael Diversey deeded a lot at North Avenue and Church Street for a new church, which was dedicated on October 17, 1852. The centennial history of the parish points out that "under the wise leadership of the Redemptorists . . . St. Michael's Parish became one of the largest and most admired Catholic parishes in the City of Chicago . . . the history of St. Michael's Parish is one of progress and growth. It is interesting to note that through the years, step by step, it developed to the point where it enjoyed the distinction of being the largest parish in the City of Chicago serving Catholics of German ancestry."[10]

But Germans also settled north of St. Michael's, as they sought better quarters in Lakeview. The township was organized in 1857, incorporated as a town in 1861, and finally annexed to Chicago in 1887. The original settlers—Germans and Swedes—built small frame houses around Diversey and Clark. In the beginning, "these new settlers were Catholics . . . they returned to the church of the district from which they had moved [St. Michael's], not only for the sake of their religion but for social events. A sense of unity was dearly developed in these first German settlers because of their religious interest."[11] But a new parish was clearly needed. Archbishop Feehan established St. Alphonsus Parish, at 1429 West Wellington Street, for these Germans in 1882. Although the area was already subdivided, it remained sparsely populated until the 1890s, when newer immigrants filled up its empty blocks. The parish soon took off as a major German community. Feehan dedicated a Gothic church on October 3, 1897; a new school opened on Wellington Avenue in 1903; and an atheneum began operations in 1911. The area around Lincoln and Belmont was the "hub of the north side," as people came from Bowmanville, Morton Grove, and Niles Center to do their shopping in the shadows of St. Alphonsus.[12] Most were Bavarians or Tyrolians from southern Germany and Austria.

Lakeview and St. Alphonsus remained a German community through the 1920s. A University of Chicago community report noted that the Germans "are the oldest settlers of the north side and really form the backbone of the community. . . . St. Alphonsus German Catholic Church situated one-half mile north of Lincoln Avenue and Wellington is the social center of the neighborhood." But the community began to lose its German flavor at the end of the decade. An old German resident noted that "the Germans in this neighborhood are about half Catholic and half Lutheran. South of us are Polish people. Until recently [1928] about 90 percent of the people going to St. Alphonsus were German and Luxemberger, but there are so many Austrians, Hungarians, and Italians coming in the district that it could not be true any more." Another woman, whose father ran a saloon in the district, remembered that "this whole district has always been mostly German but now there is every nationality around here. There are some Italians, Hungarians, Swedes—the Italians are getting into business on the main business streets—the Germans are moving out but I don't know where they are moving to."[13] By 1930, German foreign-born were 28.3 percent of the total foreign-born population (9,383).[14]

The area between St. Alphonsus and St. Michael's gradually filled up with Germans during the 1890s and early 1900s. As parishioners from St. Michael's moved farther north into Lincoln Park, they founded St. Theresa's and St. Clement's parishes. A group of 325 German families established St. Theresa's, at 1037 West Armitage Street, in 1889. Archbishop Quigley established St. Clement's, at 624 West Deming Street, in 1905.[15] Father Francis Rempe, the pastor of St. Clement's, represented Chicago's German clergy in Europe after World War I and directed relief services to Germany and Austria during the postwar years. Lincoln Park, as the community was known, retained much of its German flavor through the twenties and thirties. There were 11,418 foreign-born Germans in the community by 1930, with 2,043 Austrians adding to their number. Although the German population decreased during the following decade, there were still 7,283 foreign-born within the community in 1940.[16]

St. Boniface Parish, at 921 North Noble Street, offers a glimpse of the ethnic parish as it really was. As one of Chicago's leading German parishes, St. Boniface's history is an epitome of all German parishes.[17] The area that encompassed St. Boniface was swampy; sidewalks rose and dipped with the elevation and floods covered the primitive streets with annoying regularity. A group of German laymen who lived in the community met with the pastor of St. Joseph's and Bishop Duggan to discuss the possibility of a new parish west of the Chicago River. The Reverend Ferdinand Kalvelage, pastor of St. Francis of Assisi, investigated the possibility and recommended the establishment of St. Boniface. The Benedictine Fathers, who had guided a primitive mission as early as 1862, relinquished the parish to diocesan clergy in 1865.[18] Bishop James Duggan appointed the Reverend Philip Albrecht as St. Boniface's first pastor. There were only twenty-five families in the parish at the time, with seventy-two baptisms and nine weddings recorded the first year.[19] When Albrecht was transferred to another parish in 1867, Bishop Duggan appointed the Reverend James Marschall St. Boniface's second pastor. Although he spoke German, English, and Polish fluently, Marschall could not adapt to the needs of his parishioners. Duggan was forced to appoint a new pastor.

The Reverend Clement Venn, born in Westphalia, Germany, guided St. Boniface to the end of the century.[20] Father Venn served at various parishes in McHenry County, Illinois, before coming to St. Boniface. He then founded the St. Boniface Fraternal Society (St. Bonifacius Liebesbund) to counteract the Unterstützungs-Verein's influence. A battle ensued over which society would prevail in the parish, a conflict that reached a dramatic conclusion when a member of the mutual-aid society knocked Father Venn down in the middle of the church. This altercation marked the end of the *Verein*'s influence. Joseph Reisel, a prominent member of the Liebesbund, told a defeated Unterstutzung member that he would die miserably, for "he had stepped on an ordained minister behind his back."[21] Father Venn soon consolidated his position, and led St. Boniface to the dawn of a new century. During his long tenure as St. Boniface's third pastor, Father Venn established numerous parish societies, founded St. Boniface Cemetery on the Far North Side, and left the parish $4,000 when he died in 1895. St. Boniface had grown to be the largest German parish in the city at the time of his death.[22]

Archbishop Feehan appointed Father Albert Evers as Venn's successor. Born in Warburg, Germany, in 1863, Evers served in Aurora and Kankakee, Illinois, before becoming St. Boniface's fourth pastor. By this time the parish was growing rapidly. Father Evers built a new school in 1896 (including twelve classrooms, an auditorium, a small meeting hall, a kitchen, and a bowling alley) and a new church in 1903. Indeed, the highlight of Father Evers's career was the consecration of St. Boniface's church. The *Pfarrbote* commented: "The Church is a magnificent structure. Large, stately, and imposing, it compares in architectural beauty with the finest churches in the West."[23] The *Chicago Examiner* noted that "through the crowded streets decorated with flags, banners, evergreens, 30,000 men marched yesterday at the dedication of St. Boniface. . . . It was one of the most impressive spectacles in the history of Chicago."[24]

Father Evers's pastorate was not altogether happy, for he saw his beloved parish change from a predominantly German parish to a community of Poles, Slovaks, and other eastern Europeans. He did what he could to stop this process. The *Pfarrbote* continually exhorted its parishioners to stay within the parish: "It is important for our community that those who live within the parish stay there. Don't leave your mother church, don't leave the holy St. Boniface parish." And again, "it is wise and smart for every good German Catholic to maintain a home in the neighborhood, to buy goods in the shadow of the old and worthy St. Boniface Church."[25] The parish, acting as a real estate agency, even listed good homes for sale and encouraged parishioners to sell to Germans alone. The *Pfarrbote* remained optimistic through 1907, despite the appearance of "foreign elements." It was optimistic because the parish had grown to 750 families, Poles were joining the parish, and the new church seemed to strengthen the devotion of the old German members. But Father Evers was not so optimistic, for he could not accept the

Poles and Slovaks who were weakening his parish. He called St. Boniface a "hut in a wine garden" and a "wasted city." Many parts of Chicago "which stood earlier in highest bloom, in this way have been robbed of their best supports and their most beautiful jewels." Evers, who intensely disliked these newcomers, urged his parishioners to stay in the parish and keep "the dirty and unsightly elements far from our homes."[26]

St. Boniface did decline during Father Evers's pastorate (see Table 4). The school decreased from 1,200 children in 1901, to 20 children in 1916 (half of whom were Slovaks from another parish). Jews began to move into the neighborhood from 1913 to 1915. Father Evers decided to turn the church over to a German order, but a group of laity became so incensed that they forged a number of signatures on a letter to Archbishop Mundelein and insisted that there were enough Germans to keep it a national parish.[27] The aging pastor, who could not keep up with the strain of a changing neighborhood, resigned his pastorate on June 16, 1916.

Father Charles A. Rempe took charge of St. Boniface in July 1916. Born in Aurora, Illinois, he studied at Teutopolis, Illinois, and St. Francis Seminary, Milwaukee, Wisconsin.[28] Ordained on June 9, 1906, Rempe served at St. Clement's Parish in Chicago and at Cathedral College as a professor before coming to St. Boniface. He faced monumental difficulties, since the average Sunday attendance was only four hundred and the average collection $55.81. The parish debt stood at $128,392. The centennial history of the parish noted that "Fr. Rempe soon realized that it would be impossible for him to be pastor of a German parish in the old tradition."[29] Since he spoke Polish, he tried to attract the unchurched people of this newer immigrant group. Father F. L. Kalvelage summarized the situation:

> But while the census proved the insufficiency of the German element, it also showed that a large percentage of the Polish population was not affiliated with any parish. Some of them had made their First Communion, either in St. Boniface Church or some other non-Polish parish in the neighborhood . . . others had never been to confession or communion. There are literally thousands of these in our neighborhood. Most of them were born and raised in this country, scarcely understanding Polish. Others though born abroad have become lax in the performance of their religious duties; among these are generally the parents of the children who make their First Holy Communion in our Church. Here was indeed a large and legitimate field of labor and recruits for St. Boniface Parish. And it is from these that the Parish has grown.[30]

But the growth did not take place overnight. A year after he came, Father Rempe complained to Archbishop Mundelein that the obstacles he met at St. Boniface were insurmountable. Mundelein insisted that Rempe continue his work, since "all that matter was gone over and thoroughly considered when St. Boniface was permitted to conserve its character as a German-speaking parish."[31]

St. Boniface gradually revived, but it lost most of its German flavor. Rempe sought new parishioners from the Poles directly north of St. Boniface, a move that angered both Germans and Poles. The Germans who remained in the parish were indignant about the new Polish members, while the Polish clergy accused the new pastor of stealing their parishioners. But the parish continued to attract new members from this unchurched group. Rempe started First Communion classes for public schoolchildren in 1916, classes that averaged four hundred a year by 1917. Mass attendance rose from 400 a Sunday in 1916, to 1,400 a Sunday in 1926.[32] Parishioners reduced the parish debt to $105,806 by 1920. As America entered the twenties, St. Boniface was once again a flourishing parish. But it was no longer a strictly German parish, for many of its parishioners were now Poles or Slovaks from eastern Europe. But the parish did not die, for it continued to serve other immigrant groups through World War I and beyond. It functions today as an important Hispanic parish on the Near West Side.

As parishioners moved north of St. Boniface in the 1880s, they developed new communities in Humboldt Park. Archbishop Feehan established St. Aloysius Parish, at 2300 West Lemoyne Street, in 1884, for these Germans.[33] Catholics began to drift into this area as early as 1870, when Chicago's western boundaries were Western Avenue north of North Avenue and Kedzie Avenue south of it. Humboldt Park lay outside of Chicago at the time, as the settlements of Holstein, Almira, and Hermosa testify to its German character. Most German Catholics considered St. Boniface their home parish until St. Aloysius was built to care for their needs. Father Aloysius J. Thiele guided the parish from its founding until 1932; he received the support of Archbishop Feehan in making the parish a complete German community. Archbishop Quigley entrusted him with the appointment of German priests and made him a spokesman for the German clergy of the archdiocese. For example, he defended the German Sisters of Christian Charity during World War I, when they were required to register as aliens. He complained to Mundelein "of the fear and dread which they feel when looking forward to the registration of

TABLE 4

Decline of St. Boniface's Parish, 1901-1914

Year	Families	Baptisms	Marriages	Funerals	School-children
1901	825	208	28	107	961
1904	830	186	51	no stats	902
1905	800	189	42	91	865
1906	750	205	42	93	798
1911	700	225	65	113	620
1912	600	235	65	99	498
1913	400	220	54	103	413
1914	300	192	52	78	380

SOURCE: St. Boniface parish baptismal records, 921 North Noble Street, Chicago, Illinois; Kalvelage, *Annals St. Boniface*, pp. 156-160.

their foreign-born Sisters. It is not so much the registration itself, as the embarrassing publicity of it."[34] When Thiele died in 1935, his parish had already lost its German flavor. His successor, Fr. Bernard Laukemper, continued to be active in several German societies, but the parish itself was no longer German. The old-timers moved west to St. Philomena Parish, at 1921 North Kedvale Avenue, while a few continued to the northwest boundary of Chicago and St. William's Parish, at 2600 North Sayre Avenue, the only German parish established by Cardinal Mundelein.[35]

St. Philomena began as a mission of St. Aloysius in 1888. The area known as Hermosa lay outside the city of Chicago until its annexation in 1889. Times were difficult, as the area was sparsely populated and "it is said that a sidewalk was a rarity as late as 1897." Most of the population was Scottish, Scandinavian, and German. St. Philomena, which remained a mission of St. Aloysius until 1890, became a self-sustaining parish in 1895. The parish grew rapidly, but its German character faded after World War I, as "anti-German feeling compelled Church and School to limit German language and cultural activities to a bare minimum." An Irish secretary, recalling the days when Poles and Irish moved in the neighborhood, noted that the parish limited German culture to a few plays and bulletin articles after the War.[36]

St. Francis Xavier Parish, at 2840 West Nelson Avenue, also began as a mission of St. Aloysius in 1888.[37] But it had no financial credit until 1898, when the parish finally began to attract parishioners. The Reverend Edward T. Goldschmitt, who headed the parish from 1890 to 1930, championed German causes as editor of the *St. Aloysius Banner* and president of the Katholischer Gesellenverein. His successor, the Reverend John Liebreich, guided the parish until his retirement in 1960.

St. Matthias Parish, at 2310 West Ainslie Street, began as a distinct German community in the early 1880s. The area known as Bowmanville was originally outside the city, with German truck farmers forming the predominate ethnic group. Archbishop Feehan established the parish for German Catholics living between St. Henry Parish (6335 North Hoyne) on the north, and St. Alphonsus Parish (1429 West Wellington) on the south. Feehan dedicated the first church in 1890, while the School Sisters of St. Francis established a school by 1900.[38] As parishioners moved north at the end of the century, they established St. Gregory's Parish, at 1634 West Gregory Street, in 1904. The community known as Summerdale was "a sprawling area of truck gardens with an occasional house. The streets laid out were paved with macadam . . . there were even sidewalks, many of them concrete. But there was no gas, no electricity." Parishioners erected a combination church-school in 1904. Other institutions soon followed, such as a German singing society in 1904 and the German Western Catholic Union in 1910. St. Gregory's grew steadily during the next two decades, from four hundred families in 1910, to five hundred in 1924. As two-flats and bungalows spread throughout the community, the parish prospered and grew. The parochial school numbered 478 pupils by 1929, with 56,643 First Communions the same year. But the German character gradually diminished, as Irish moved into the neighborhood.

> Old customs were gradually being converted to the new conditions, and so too St. Gregory's was fast losing its reputations as a German parish . . . naturally the German services gradually became fewer and fewer. The impact of the World War I hurried the process along . . . the great influx of our Celtic parishioners was the finishing blow of course, and the old wars were swept away by the new. . . . More and more new families poured into our boundaries changing a predominantly German parish into a truly cosmopolitan American parish almost before our old timers realized it.[39]

But Chicago's *Deutschtum* lived on in Lakeview. St. Benedict Parish, at 2215 West Irving Park Boulevard, has been called "the last Catholic parish that could be called 'German.' "[40] Begun as a mission of St. Matthias Parish in 1886, St. Benedict's drew its parishioners from St. Boniface and St. Aloysius parishes to the south. Lakeview began to fill up after 1910, as vacant lots became cottages and apartment buildings for Teutons. The Reverend Joseph Zimmerman, who became St. Benedict's first pastor in 1904, guided the parish through World War I. St. Benedict's remained German through these decades: "I wish to inform you that I have you [i.e., St. Benedict's] in mind for a priest that I can spare . . . I would advise that you make some temporary arrangement in the meantime, as I hope to have a young priest at my disposal *who speaks German* probably within a month's time."[41]

St. Benedict's continued to grow as a German parish under the pastorate of Father William H. Dettmer (1918-1938). The parish expanded from 90 families in 1919 to 1,000 families in 1938. German Catholics dominated the parish for the duration of Dettmer's pastorate. One group outside the parish petitioned Archbishop Mundelein to be included with St. Benedict's boundaries, even though they were juridically within St. Francis Xavier Parish: "it is necessary to ride on three different car lines to get to St. Francis and we still have three blocks to go to St. Francis Xavier School, whereas attending St. Benedict's school, many children would be within a half mile and most would be within a mile."[42] St. Benedict's continued to function as a German parish during the ensuing decades. Indeed, St. Benedict's carried on Chicago's *Deutschtum* long after other parishes had abandoned it.

Chicago's German parishes flowed outward from St. Joseph's on the North Side to St. Peter's on the South. They slowly ebbed their way away from the Loop; from St. Gregory's in Uptown to Sts. Peter and Paul on the East Side. The history of St. Boniface Parish indicates a continued German presence in Chicago through seven decades of war and change. But the parish was not a mere spectator to events—it was an active initiator. It encouraged ethnicity through a variety of institutions and organizations.

German priests and lay leaders were active supporters of German tradition at all levels of parish activity. A group of Germans of St. Boniface petitioned Archbishop Mundelein to carry on the activities of the K.G.A., a German lay organization, which would help keep St. Boniface a German parish. Mundelein replied:

> A committee from the old-time K.G.A. called on me the other day and presented me with a copy of their Constitution and by-laws. On that occasion, I told them I would appoint the Rector of St. Boniface Church as their Spiritual Director and likewise attach them as a body to St. Boniface Church. I also suggested that they revive again the old uniform they used to wear, and when all of the members are properly accoutred they could be used on solemn occasions . . . it goes without saying, that I have made this suggestion to them in order that they might be helpful to you in the reviving of the old German parish of St. Boniface.[43]

Many parishioners returned to St. Boniface for marriages or burials, even though they had already moved to other German parishes. A couple petitioned the chancery to be married at St. Boniface, since "for sentimental reasons we would be happy if it would be permissible for us to have the ceremony performed at St. Boniface Church as our parents were married there and the prospective bride's parents were members of the parish for many years."[44]

German pastors were often appointed for life, and it was not unusual for a pastor to head a parish for over forty years. They were strong-willed and stubborn men, but were needed to build up an often-hated church in a bustling, growing city. Father Aloysius J. Thiele was one of these pastors.[45] He became pastor of St. Aloysius Parish in 1884. The voice of the German clergy for some forty years, he took an active interest in Guardian Angel German Orphanage, established the German cemetery of St. Joseph in River

Grove, Illinois, and brought the German Sisters of Christian Charity to teach in his own school. When Thiele died at the age of eighty-seven in 1935, he was succeeded by the Reverend Bernard Laukemper of Westphalia, Germany. Father Laukemper, a liturgical innovator, was active in the Kolping Society, a German lay organization, through the 1940s. He continued to take an interest in German affairs, although St. Aloysius lost much of its German flavor during his lengthy pastorate (1932-1949).

St. Benedict's Parish was guided by a succession of German pastors who actively supported German causes. The Reverend Joseph Zimmerman, a former assistant at St. Joseph's, guided the parish from 1902 to 1918. He established numerous German societies for the perpetuation of German culture.[46] His successor, the Reverend William H. Dettmer, supervised the German festivities of the Eucharistic Congress and hosted hundreds of dignitaries at his own parish in 1926. The Reverend Walter L. Fasnacht, who became St. Benedict's third pastor in 1938, served on the Board of Trustees of Angel Guardian Orphanage, was spiritual adviser for the German Catholic Union of Illinois (Deutscher Katholischer Verein Bund von Illinois), and was a member of the Board of Governors of Josephinum College in Worthington, Ohio. Monsignor Fasnacht continued St. Benedict's German traditions through World War II. He invited Cardinal Otto von Preysing of Berlin to visit St. Benedict's during the war, even though von Preysing himself was anathema to Hitler's Third Reich for denouncing its anti-Semitic theories.[47] Indeed, the entire history of St. Benedict's illustrates the practice of sending German pastors to German parishes. Priests continued to speak of the "German circuit" as late as 1960; and when Albert Cardinal Meyer died in 1965, they asked "would the new man be Irish or German?"

German religious orders also played a prominent role in fostering German ethnicity. The Redemptorist Fathers established St. Michael's Parish in the early history of the city. Mrs. Henry Hahn recalled that St. Michael's pastor was "as German as they came." In fact, he mysteriously disappeared during World War I, and was either interned in a concentration camp or returned to Germany.[48] The Redemptorists also operated St. Alphonsus in Lakeview. Theresa Krutz recalled that "the parish was *definitely*, definitely a real center" [of German culture]. The priests only spoke German, which "was probably the cohesive thing in a parish—the language was there—the knowledge and background the same. I am amazed at how much it means to older people to speak German."[49]

The Franciscans of St. Augustine's also nurtured German ethnicity through a variety of institutions. Forced to immigrate from Saxony in the early 1850s, the Franciscans set up an American province in Teutopolis, Illinois. These early Germanizers fostered ethnic traditions throughout the history of St. Augustine's. Father Symphorian Forstmann, the first pastor, established several societies for the perpetuation of German culture. He urged the construction of a German hospital, and began a German library that grew to 5,500 volumes by 1934. The Franciscans continually reminded their parishioners that "all German families, who live within our boundaries, rightfully belong to St. Augustine's Parish, and we priests are always ready to serve such families."[50] The parish also supported Angel Guardian Orphanage.[51]

Ethnic parishes also built up a following through *Pfarrbote*, which disseminated information about parish happenings. Although they were usually written by laymen, they reflected the thoughts and ideals of the clergy itself. Publishing articles exclusively in German through 1916, and bilingual thereafter, St. Boniface's *Pfarrbote* relayed news from Germany, told what was happening among Chicago's Germans, and was an advertiser for German products and businesses. It strongly resisted the introduction of English into parish life, as "it was no blessing or grace for religion." It encouraged younger Germans to join local *Vereien* and read German newspapers. The bulletin also urged its readers to attend meetings of the Federation of German Catholic Societies, "to demonstrate that the German Catholic citizens are firmly united . . . and that they endeavor to further the Catholic cause."[52]

But the *Pfarrbote* also interpreted America for the German immigrant. St. Boniface's monthly bulletin deplored the loss of esteem felt for church, school, and society. It felt that family life was threatened and that juvenile delinquency was a growing problem (August 1919). The *Pfarrbote* also decried the growing tendency of young people to delay marriage, for it "has caused a young man to be spendthrift, it has caused many a noble and worthy young woman to spend all her life in a lonesome and companionless existence, and it has increased the horde of unfortunate women in the resorts . . . the trouble with people of today is that they are suffering from too much luxury" (December 1914). The bulletin accordingly published "10 Rules to live peacefully with one's family," which included avoiding gossip, paying loans back quickly, and warning children not to steal (August 1904). There was also concern for the dress of the day, "the shamelessness of attire, the unbecoming freedom of manner and conversation" (January 1914). Contemporary dances were also occasions of sin, as "no self-respecting woman should parade her physical form around a ballroom in a scanty decollete sheath gown." Articles reported "22 Wedding Guests Wounded by the Tango," and "The Modern Dances Unhealthy" (October 1914). The theaters were also dangerous, since there were dangerous companions there; hence, "no believing Christian businessman would hire an employee because he is a theatre friend to the employer" (October 1914).

Ethnic parishes also used leaflets and other printed material to instruct their parishioners. St. Boniface started to distribute the *Sunday Visitor* in 1914. Father C. A. Rempe relied on printed leaflets of his Sunday sermons to publicize his views. Most of his letters concerned traditional Catholic themes. He reminded his flock what it meant to be Catholic: "There are many Catholics who do not realize how very generous God has been to them. . . . Having this faith we are members of the true Church established by our Lord Jesus Christ. This Church is the Holy Roman Catholic Church" (December 1919). It was important for every Catholic to belong to a parish, for this was the source of all grace and divine benefits.

> The whole world is divided into parishes. A Catholic, no matter where he lives, must belong to one of them. Only in his own parish can he receive the sacraments; only the priests of his own parish are bound to render him service . . . otherwise a Catholic cannot have his children baptized in any church; in case of sickness he cannot get a priest from anywhere; in case of death he cannot be buried from any Catholic cemetery; in case he wishes to be married no Catholic priest is allowed to perform the ceremony. (November 1925)

Rather Rempe emphasized the importance of attending Mass and contributing to the support of the church. He sent out several letters in which he wanted "first, to make you realize the enormity of the sin of missing Mass on Sundays, and secondly, to make you realize your duty as far as financial support of your parish is concerned." He called some parishioners "cheapskates": "I am convinced that we must earn God's gifts, and that the best way to do this is to properly contribute to his Church. Some never give God a chance to reward them."[53] Father Rempe's letters were published simultaneously in German, English, and Polish, in order to reach all of St. Boniface's multicultured parishioners.

But it was the liturgies themselves that held the people together as Germans. Most services were conducted *auf Deutsch* through World War I. The Franciscans of St. Augustine's preached and held evening devotions in German though the 1930s, and the Redemptorists of St. Alphonsus continued to say High Mass in German as late as 1935. Besides the normal Sunday services, ethnic parishes also held special devotions and celebrations that cemented their people together. Parish missions brought in outstanding German clergy, who preached the Word and revived the faith. At St. Boniface, the Precious Blood Fathers held a mission in 1912 to attain "luck and peace" for all; they conducted masses every hour from 5:00 a.m. to 9:00 a.m., and held confessions in German for the duration of the mission. The Franciscan Fathers later conducted a similar mission in English and German for the young people of the parish.[54] Father Rempe worked diligently to maintain the dignity of German Catholicism, even after the wreckage of World War I. Feeling that many Americans equated German-Americanism with Protestantism, Rempe believed that German Catholics had to publicize their heritage and culture. He encouraged all parishioners, both past and present, to take part in an annual St. Boniface Day celebration (*St.-Bonifacius-Tag*); he called the festival "a modest beginning towards the regaining of our self-respect" (June 1917). The 1919 celebration began with the national anthem, followed by two plays in German—*Der Hausschlussel* and *Viel Lärm um Nichts* (Shakespeare's *Much Ado About Nothing*). Speaking in German, Rempe urged his parishioners to attend Mass and receive Communion "for our hard-beset countrymen and fellow-believers" (June 1919). This and other celebrations made St. Boniface one of the principal German shrines of the city.

> A list of German Catholics who have attained prominence in the social, political, and commercial life of our city and the State of Illinois sounds like the roster of St. Boniface. Almost all the German Catholic families of Chicago have at one time or other worshipped there . . . it is this fond association with the great past that has made St. Boniface so dear to all the German Catholics of Chicago.
>
> St. Boniface is a shrine to which pilgrims come from every part of our great city . . . they come from so far, they say, because they always feel like praying in St. Boniface. Perhaps it is because the church where so many generations have prayed is so redolent with prayer.[55]

Parish anniversaries were special occasions when national customs could be fully displayed. At St. Benedict's silver jubilee in 1927, Cardinal Mundelein dedicated two German shrines to Ss. Benedict and Scholastica. As the choir sang several German hymns the entire congregation rose in song. When the church was redecorated in 1940, it included statues to the Emperor Henry and St. Boniface, the apostle of Germany. St. Michael's celebrated its golden anniversary with "the world-famous Thomas Orchestra," playing Mozart and

Haydn.[56] St. Augustine's celebrated its fiftieth anniversary in 1936 with German songs and a traditional rathskeller. The Franciscan Sacred Heart Province celebrated its own golden anniversary with two plays in German.[57]

Of all the nationalities that came to America, Germans were the most prolific in establishing local societies to perpetuate their own culture. Germans developed their associational life around the parish, which provided a focus for their personal, religious, and ethnic needs, The earliest societies were mutual-aid organizations; others were devotional. These societies appealed to young and old alike, as Table 5 illustrates. Many of these societies joined together to form the Federation of German Catholic Societies of Illinois, which tried "to interest the members in the study of the social question . . . with a vow to advancing the interests of the laboring class."[58] Members often clashed with clergy over goals and methods, although much of this friction diminished in the twentieth century. The *Pfarrbote* of St. Boniface noted that "we see in that the dawn of a better time, a better understanding between priest and societies."[59]

Many societies sponsored community plays, which provided relief from the tedium of daily life. St. Augustine's established a dramatic club (Deutsche Dramatische Gesellschaft) in 1904 to promote German literature, drama, and entertainment. The society also assisted the School Sisters with childrens' plays, as well as providing music and song for other parish affairs. Through all these activities, German *Vereine* furthered the ethnic ties of their early German members.

The ethnic parish also functioned as a focus of traditional German customs. Christmas was a special time for all Germans, as families gathered to celebrate their traditions. Theresa Krutz fondly remembers these customs. Christmas celebrations began with St. Nicholas Day, on December 6. It was a time for children, as "all the good kids got apples and oranges and nuts. The bad kids got coal. And we always hung up our stockings for as long as we can remember."[60] Easter was celebrated with Teutonic seriousness. Mrs. Krutz recalled "baking Easter lambs," a tradition common to many Europeans.

Germans also celebrated traditional Catholic feasts. Southern Germans brought the feast of the Ascension (*Christi Himmelfahrt*) to the United States in the early 1800s. Bavarians, who introduced the feast of Corpus Christi (*Fronleichnamsfest*) in the late eighteenth century, brought the traditional processions to American parishioners. St. Augustine's *Pfarrbote* noted that, "It is a feast right for the German spirit, because it came from a German heart and German soil, and first took hold in German land." The cities of Cologne,

Wurzburg, and Augsburg popularized the processions; as the *Pfarrbote* reported, "The Corpus Christi processions, which take place in spring under the clear-blue sky and in front of flower-bedecked homes, are such a rich experience to nature-loving Germans that whoever participates once—in a spirit of faith and prayer—never want to miss them again."[61]

The ethnic parish also provided the milieu around which the rituals of life and death took place. Funerals were social occasions for most Germans, as they were for Irish and other immigrant groups. Mrs. Krutz recalled that it was common at St. Aloysius to hold funerals in the home. A wreath of black crape was put in front of the house, furniture was placed in the living room, and the coffin put in front of a window. "That was common practice—I don't know when it happened that people started going more to chapels—at that time—the neighbors would all provide food—it was just more community than it is now."[62]

German parishes were active centers of German ethnicity for more than seventy years. German religious orders like the Redemptorists and Franciscans nurtured Chicago's *Deutschtum* through local celebrations, parish *Vereien*, and numerous publications and sermons. Parish *Pfarrbote* encouraged the retention of German on the family level, reported on happenings in Germany, and advertised German products and services. Parish anniversaries brought out the most noted German clergy of the day, while German *Vereien* carried on such traditional Teutonic concerns as singing, drama, and *Gemütlichkeit*. But the parish was more than this—it was the focus of the family, a place where members gathered for the important celebrations of life. It was even a way station for the primordial rituals of life and death.

But the ethnic parish was not only a way station of ethnicity—it was also a focus of Americanization. Through a variety of institutions and organizations, the parish actively encouraged this difficult process. Some of the primary institutions that furthered Americanization were the same *Vereien* which encouraged ethnicity. German priests established local societies that directly or indirectly encouraged contact with other nationalities. St. Augustine's organized a Young Men's Society in 1887 to promote "the moral, physical, and social welfare of its members." It provided space for recreational reading, bowling, pool, and gymnastics, as well as operating a library and baseball team. Through these facilities and activities, the Young Men's Society promoted contact with other young men in Chicago. The parish also founded a Young Ladies Society in 1891 for the same purposes. The members helped America's soldiers during World War I by knitting socks and sweaters for the

TABLE 5

St. Boniface *Vereine*, 1904

Men	Women	Children
St. Bonifacius Unterstützung Verein	Mutter-Gottes Verein	St. Ralphael Junglings Verein
St. Bonifacius Liebesbund	Rosenkranz Verein	Jungfrauensodalität
St. Bonifacius-Zweig der Katholisch Garde von Amerika	St. Bonifacius-Fosterinnen-Hof	Mädchenschutzengel-Verein
St. Antonius-Zweig der Katholische Garde von Amerika		
St. Bonifacius-Fosterhof	Arme Seelen-Verein	
St. Hubertus-Fosterhof	Herz-Jesu-Gebets-Apostolat	
Christopher Columbus Fosterhof		
St. Vincenz-Armen-Verein		
United States Junior Cadets		

SOURCE: *St. Boniface Pfarrbote*, June 1904, p. 29.

"boys over there." They also introduced English plays during the 1920s, which further expanded their neighbors' horizons. Both groups contributed significantly to the support of the parish.[63]

But German parishes did not act alone. They cooperated with archdiocesan organizations that actively encouraged Americanization. The Holy Name Society became the leading men's society in every parish in the 1920s. At St. Augustine's and other parishes the society dedicated itself to the care of delinquent boys (the Big Brother movement). But the society had to adapt to German ways, for St. Augustine's and many parishes refused to change the official language of the society to English. When Father Charles Schlueter tried to attract more members by doing just that, a vast majority left the society with hurt feelings. Schlueter quickly returned the meetings to German, but he founded an English branch of the society to meet the growing needs of a younger English-speaking community. The St. Vincent de Paul Society, which also joined immigrants to a wider Catholic organization, was active at many German parishes. St. Augustine's, which affiliated itself with the South Side Council of the Archdiocese in 1920, was particularly effective during the Depression. Acting as an arm of the Illinois Emergency Relief Commission, St. Augustine's St. Vincent de Paul Society took in $90,611.81 from 1929 to 1936, which was spent on food, housing, and shelter for the depressed of the 1930s.[64]

The Catholic Youth Organization was the most important Catholic society in Chicago during the 1930s. It actively encouraged young men and women to become better citizens and better Catholics. St. Augustine's gym became the center of CYO activities after 1929, "one of the most outstanding recreational centers of Chicago's South Side." Used night after night from 5:00 to midnight, it was chosen CYO Divisional Headquarters in 1934. The CYO also sponsored numerous scouting activities, which also promoted Americanization. St. Augustine's troop, which began operation in 1920, participated in many citywide activities. They won the *Chicago Tribune* Musical Festival in 1934, presented English-language plays, and guarded street crossings before and after school.[65] These and other activities encouraged young men to enter American society with a sense of enthusiasm and confidence.

German parishes also nurtured lesser-known societies to encourage Americanization. The Altar and Rosary Society, as well as the Legion of Mary, brought many parishioners into larger archdiocesan organizations. St. Augustine's sponsored the Catholic Knights of America, which prompted American ways as a mutual-aid society. Its charter read: "We are Catholic in word and deed; we are Knights as of old, ready to help our fellow man at all times, we are Americans true to our colors, red, white, and blue."[66] St. Aloysius established a Booster Club that organized dances, parties, and social evenings for the young people of the parish. It also organized an athletic group (the Starlights), which played other teams throughout the city. Established in 1923, the Starlights separated from the parish in 1934 to expand its schedule to other Chicago teams—a move that indicates that it had grown from a parochial (and German) activity to a citywide (and American) organization.[67]

Through local and archdiocesan-wide organizations, Chicago's German parishes actively supported American customs and morals. They even participated in politics.[68] But it was the parochial school more than any other institution that firmly planted German Catholics on American soil. The parochial school was a microcosm of the parish as a whole—while it nurtured German ethnicity, it also fostered Americanization.

Education was always important to German Americans; it was Germans, for example, who first introduced the kindergarten system to America in 1855. American high schools were modeled after similar institutions in Prussia; and German universities were the basis of the American graduate school system. German educators devoted their lives to improving the quality (and quantity) of education in the United States. A number of secular German institutes arose in the middle of the nineteenth century—the German-English Academy in Milwaukee, the German-English Institute in Baltimore, and numerous other institutions throughout the Midwest. These schools nurtured German culture through the mid-1800s, and declined only when public schools introduced German into their ordinary curricula. The Milwaukee public schools introduced German in 1867, while a bilingual (German-English) public school was established in Baltimore in 1873. By 1900, there were six such bilingual schools in the United States, with 7,000 students in enrollment.[69]

Chicago's German Catholics were particularly interested in education, and they established a vast network of parochial schools (see Table 6).[70] These schools nurtured German traditions and encouraged assimilation for six decades. First staffed by German laity, the parochial schools soon hired German sisters to train their children—the School Sisters of Notre Dame, Franciscans, Benedictines, and Holy Cross congregation were all German branches of their respective congregations. German schools often rose next to Irish ones, as both immigrant groups settled in the same community. Germans established St. Francis of Assisi and Holy Trinity schools on the Near West

Side, while Chicago's Irish established five schools in Holy Family Parish at the same time; there were only 900 students in both German schools in 1890, while there were over 5,000 students in Holy Family's five schools the same year.[71] The situation was reversed on the North Side, where German schools outnumbered Irish two to one.

Parish bulletins continuously stressed the need for German parochial schools.

> Children not only learn religion, but also reading, writing, arithmetic, history, and geography; in short, all those things which are necessary to succeed in this world. . . . In the German parish school, the children also learn their German mother tongue next to the language of the country—which is important not only for daily conversation but also for business and religious life.[72]

German schools encouraged ethnicity through the continued use of German in the classroom. Mrs. Henry Hahn recalled that all the subjects at St. Michael's high schools were taught in German (except English grammar), while students presented German plays through the 1920s. As she recalled, "The nuns would insist that students only speak German during recess; if someone started to speak English, they would tell them 'Du musst Deutsch sprechen' ['You must speak German']."[73] Theresa Krutz remembered her days at St. Alphonsus, where "until I was in third grade we had German readers. I think everybody in the school knew the Christmas chorales in German. We read and talked German—not on a regular basis, there were just some people who went to this special class."[74] The school set aside special hours for German reading (in Gothic print!) and German literature. Through all these activities, German schools nourished a sense of German ethnicity in their young immigrant pupils.

But German schools also prepared their students for Chicago life. St. Augustine's introduced English-language curricula as early as 1912. Other parishes established commercial schools in early 1910, to prepare young women for the business world. At St. Alphonsus, "hundreds of graduates of St. Alphonsus Grammar School learned business skills which enabled them to obtain jobs in downtown Loop offices." St. Martin's commercial program, which continued through World War II to 1950, prepared scores of young women for secretarial work.[75] German parishes also established high schools, which became commonplace in the United States by 1930. St. Michael's set up separate boys' and girls' high schools in the early teens, and expanded its facilities to two separate school buildings by 1929. St. Augustine's, St. Gre-

TABLE 6

Growth of German Parochial School System, 1903-1940

SCHOOL	PUPILS 1903	1910	1920	1930	1940
St. Joseph	402	300	260	231	130
St. Peter	182	243	268	56	50
St. Henry	333	435	434	387	485
St. Michael	1804	1695	1475	1592	1398
St. Francis Assisi	413	385	548	352	300
St. Boniface	971	684	323	483	350
St. Anthony	670	166	458	557	339
St. Paul	780	748	446	289	231
St. Augustine	1056	1172	1100	1076	1037
Sts. Peter and Paul	200	173	123	225	430
St. Alphonsus	1680	1700	1528	1796	1345
Immaculate Conception	391	427	255	330	305
St. Aloysius	634	632	464	446	509
St. George	285	300	285	340	320
Holy Trinity	257	241	154	197	171
St. Martin	340	416	457	534	556
St. Francis Xavier	270	347	329	380	402
St. Maurice	125	180	197	278	360
St. Matthias	226	312	285	563	600
St. Teresa	405	360	380	400	398
St. Nicholas	120	250	321	258	236
Sacred Heart	200	267	380	675	600
St. Clara	123	140	340	291	310
St. Philomena	206	442	675	925	996
Holy Ghost	80	112	195	170	130
Our Lady of Perpetual Help	200	285	125	——	——
St. Raphael	105	187	374	380	367
St. Benedict	——	458	586	869	807
St. Gregory	——	315	360	446	594
St. Clement	——	224	373	540	505
St. William	——	——	——	803	585

SOURCE: *The Official Catholic Directory.*

gory's, and St. Benedict's also erected high schools in the 1920s.[76] Many parishes introduced auxiliary courses, which further prepared their children for daily life. St. Augustine's parish souvenir reflected the success of these programs:

> The pastors of St. Augustine's Parish left no stone unturned or overlooked an opportunity to promise the standard of education in as far as the demand of the parish warranted. This is seen in their manifold efforts, for instance, to enlarge the school buildings, to improve the educational methods, to extend the curriculum of studies, adding grade after grade, a commercial high school, a kindergarten; by encouraging sewing classes for the girls, the music, of course, courses in hygiene and physical culture.[77]

It is clear that the ethnic school consciously encouraged Americanization through specialized courses, commercial schools, and high schools. Indeed, the ethnic school was a microcosm of the parish as a whole, a place where German immigrants could foster their own traditions while preparing to enter the larger American society.

But German parishes did not exist unto themselves. They supported nationwide organizations that nurtured German ethnicity and promoted Americanization. They also supplied the membership of these societies, while actively publicizing their efforts. One of Chicago's principal German Catholic societies was the Kolping Society, an important organization that was German and American at the same time. Fr. Adolph Kolping established the society in 1849 as a home away from home for young Germans who were forced to travel from city to city as journeymen tradesmen. He set up homes where these men could live and grow economically and spiritually. He set down his goals in the following creed: to help young men become "better Christians, better citizens . . . masters in their trades, and prepare them for marriage."[78]

The society immigrated to the United States in 1849, and Kolping established his first house in St. Louis in 1856. By 1914, there were seven societies in Chicago, New York, Dayton, St. Paul, Kansas City, and Racine. The Kolping Society was proud of its German heritage and strove to maintain it through a long and varied history. It was difficult to maintain this heritage during World War I, as "the ravaging storm of anti-Germanism shook and rattled the Kolping tree, and it could not grow at all." But the society revived during the 1920s and it pledged itself "to serve the Church and Germanity through preserving the German language and German culture." By 1923, the Kolping Society had grown to 300 members, 2 houses, and 2 *Vereine*; by

1936, it numbered 1,500 members, 11 houses, and 15 *Vereine* from New York to Los Angeles.[79] Despite the ravages of a war, the Kolping Society persevered and flourished during the postwar decades.

The society actively encouraged ethnicity through a variety of activities. It provided rooms for singing and music, theater and gymnastics, as well as sports and chess. The theater section brought German works to the public, while members decorated the recreational areas with German handwork. Libraries and reading rooms provided intellectual enrichment; a refectory fed hungry bodies, and "it seemed as if the German food tasted as good to other nationalities as it did to the Germans." Indeed, the Kolping Society occupied a central position in German Catholic life: "There is no doubt that in many states the establishment of Kolping Societies occupy the first place among German societies. This Society occupies the first and last place among German Catholics, and is a German island in the midst of the all-encompassing process of Americanization."[80]

Chicago's Kolping Society also flourished during the twenties and thirties, providing an oasis of Germanity in the heart of Chicago. A three-story apartment building, at 811-813 Oakdale Avenue, served as the organization's headquarters from 1922 to 1968.[81] Father Hermann Weber, an assistant at St. Martin's, was chaplain of the society during the 1920s, a post Mundelein allowed him to keep as long as "it is understood that this office will in no way interfere with our duties as Assistant at St. Martin's." Father Weber defined the society as German, although "regarding the admission, all nationalities are accepted and represented."[82] A *Hausmeister* and secretary, who lived at the apartment, counseled and encouraged the occupants. The Kolping Society attracted members from all German parishes. Theresa Krutz recalled that many young men from St. Aloysius joined the society, and it was through the society that they found their future wives and lifelong friends. Indeed, members of the Kolping Society were also members of a number of parish organizations. Father Bernard Laukemper, a long-time resident of St. Aloysius (1932-1949) who was very active in the society through the 1930s and 1940s, became its president in 1946. The society continued to foster its ethnic roots throughout this period. At its ninth quadrennial convention in Chicago in 1947, the organization collected $74,000 for war-torn Germany, as well as 88,000 pounds of food for its inhabitants.

The Kolping Society continued to attract new members through the second half of the twentieth century. The organization celebrated its ninetieth anniversary with a Mass of Thanksgiving at St. Mel Church, 717 West

Eighteenth Street, on December 2, 1962. Father Matthew Fischer, director of the society since 1958, called Kolping House "more than just a home. This is where he [the German immigrant] got his start when he had nowhere else to begin."[83] For more than a century, the Kolping Society helped young Germans find a place in American society, while allowing them the space to nurture their Germanity.

National parishes and organizations were not only ethnic, they were also Catholic. Catholicism bound together the various nationalities of Chicago in one common faith. Parish bulletins and priestly sermons stressed the commonality of this faith. St. Boniface's *Pfarrbote* saw the world as a battleground, where the forces of good and evil struggled to take over humanity: "Those that stand for God and his Church, and those who deny and destroy God, Belief, and the Church" (May 1902). The parish priest was a "mediator between God and man, in which he brings to us the good deeds of God and brings our prayers to Him" (July 1907). Several articles stressed traditional tenets of faith. In the first place, the Catholic Church was the one true church; through its sacraments, the faithful are led to "union with God." Only Catholicism had confession and the Holy Eucharist (February 1913). But Catholics were also bound by strict rules, which demonstrated the strength of their faith. They were obliged to go to Mass every Sunday under penalty of sin. They were encouraged to go to Communion according to the teachings of Pius X, and finally, as true Catholics, they were bound to fast on Fridays, for "fasting is painful, but it defends us from our worse enemies, the devil and the flesh" (August 1911).

Ethnic parishes also fostered traditional Catholic devotions. Veneration to the saints was a centuries-old practice in Catholicism, and it was not absent in ethnic parishes. As the *Pfarrbote* noted, "we honor them because they are the friends of God, leaders to heaven . . . they are honored as God's servants" (January 1916). The Forty Hours offered "praise and offering to God in his wonderful sacrament, thanksgiving for all the good deeds done for body and soul and for all our sins" (October 1905). Ethnic parishes also upheld traditional Catholic mores, for "morality without religion is false, and the moral reformers seem to think that religion is unnecessary" (May 1911). Public schools were havens of immorality, for "if moral conditions are deplorable, the entire blame is to be laid at the door of false teaching on the part of the churches and schools" (May 1911). Ethnics also condemned Socialism, Freemasonry, anarchism, and nihilism, as forbidden Catholic societies that undermined faith and morality. In all these activities, ethnic parishes simply joined their fellow Catholics in upholding traditional doctrine and morality.

German Catholics were more tolerant of Protestants than their Irish and American coreligionists. While most Catholics feared Protestantism, German Catholics welcomed them as fellow Germans. Parish bulletins and sermons consistently praised Luther, Zwingli, and Calvin. But it was the lives of the parishioners themselves that exhibited an open-mindedness toward Protestants in general. Germans lived next to them for centuries and accepted them as fellow conationals. Although there are no statistics to indicate the extent of this acceptance, numerous citations in German *Pfarrbote* indicate a general tolerance of Protestants unknown among Chicago's other Catholic elements.

World War I shook the very foundation of Chicago's *Deutschtum*. After 1917, it was no longer possible to be openly German in America. It was also a critical time for Chicago's German Catholics. They were forced to choose between Germanism and Americanism. The majority chose the latter. Many parishes that were marginally German before the war became American overnight. At St. Philomena's, "with the outbreak of World War I, anti-German feeling compelled Church and School to limit German language and cultural activities to a bare minimum." At St. Clement's, the school sisters had to register their alien members with the War Bureau.[84] St. Boniface's *Pfarrbote* stressed the contributions of Catholicism to the country as a whole to ward off anti-German feelings. When two St. Boniface boys returned from the war in 1918, the bulletin stated that, "Both of these boys were among the first in the firing line. It is true that everyone of us won the war, but the doughboy most of all (July 1919). Again, "The Catholic Church Stood out on the battlefields of Europe, among other things, for this one conspicuous quality; she took care of the dying and the dead" (October 1919). At St. Aloysius, many parishioners opposed German-language parish meetings, and despite the opposition of Father Thiele, all were changed to English by 1917.

But Germanity did not die out overnight, and many parishes continued their German ways. St. Augustine's, German throughout the war, constantly berated the English "warmongers." The *Pfarrbote* noted that, "Ties of blood and religion naturally inclined the German Americans of St. Augustine's to sympathize with their relatives and friends abroad." The parish did participate in the Liberty Bond drives and War Savings Stamps program, while women sewed clothes for American doughboys. But St. Augustine's was also first in line to aid the starving and war-stricken of Germany and Austria. The Central Committee of the Red Cross thanked St. Augustine's for its participation in the various relief programs "in the name of the whole German people."[85] Monsignor Charles Rempe of St. Clement's was sent to Europe to coordinate the distribution of relief activities in Germany and Austria, and at St. Michael's "though the war caused a great change of attitude toward the use of the German language . . . St. Michael's still maintains its title of a German parish."[86] Huge rallies took place at St. Alphonsus Atheneum for Germany and Austria. Hence, despite nationwide losses, Germanity continued to function throughout the war at Chicago's German parishes.

German Catholicism also continued to function after the war. Indeed, James Cardinal Gibbons of Baltimore commended America's Germans as "a loyal and conservative element of the church in America."[87] Although Cardinal Mundelein discouraged new ethnic parishes, he allowed those already in existence to continue to function. Nowhere was Chicago's German Catholicism so evident as at the Twenty-eighth International Eucharistic Congress, held in Chicago from June 20 to June 24, 1926.[88] Of all the nationalities that participated in the congress, Germans were the most numerous and well known. American Catholicism came of age at the congress in honor of the Blessed Sacrament. Twelve cardinals, 64 archbishops, 309 bishops, and over 8,000 priests gathered to celebrate the Eucharist. It was a public display covered by the press and radio throughout the nation. Chicago and America saw the strength and vitality of Catholicism as the pomp and pageantry of the congress unfolded. John Cardinal Bonzano, the papal delegate, was joined by Patric Cardinal O'Donnell of Ireland, Louis Cardinal Dubois of France, Michael Cardinal von Faulhaber of Germany, John Cardinal Czernoch of Czechslovakia, and Gustave Cardinal Piffl of Austria. A multitude of civic and religious leaders, led by the Knights of St. Gregory, greeted the dignitaries. As they marched down Michigan Avenue to the roar of thousands, a phalanx of marchers accompanied them—mounted police, Boy Scouts, the St. Mary's Training School Band, the Knights of Columbus, and various lay and clerical groups.

Scores of ethnic parishes hosted the German delegates who came to the congress. Foreign prelates said Mass in German, while dignitaries preached to Chicagoans *auf Deutsch*. German sectional meetings drew thousands to St. Alphonsus Atheneum and the Ashland Boulevard Auditorium. Speech after speech praised the heritage of German Americans. Prelates and laity alike stressed the contributions that Germans had made to the history of the United States. They reminded their conationals that they were sons and daughters of Germany and Austria. And they gratefully thanked all German Americans who had contributed to the rebuilding of the Fatherland. Indeed, the Eucharistic Congress was a showcase of German Catholicism in America. And it showed the nation that German Americans were still a presence in the United States.

FOUR

The Italian Parish

Italian immigrants arrived in Chicago fifty years after their German counterparts. Some of the earliest settlers, who were from the province of Genoa, founded Assumption Church, at 323 West Illinois Street, in 1886. The priests of Assumption, hard-pressed to meet the needs of a growing Italian population, founded a mission church on Ewing Street in 1894. A parochial school opened at 317 West Erie Street in 1899. But the advancing Loop soon doomed the parish to a marginal existence, as the original settlers fanned out to the north and west.[1] A separate Italian colony arose on the far South Side in West Englewood. This colony founded St. Mary of Mt. Carmel Parish, at 1722 South Hermitage, in 1892. The area, formerly known as South Lynne, was incorporated into the city in 1880. A frame church arose at Seventy-second and Peoria in 1898, but a fire destroyed it in 1900. The Precious Blood Fathers (C.PP.S.) took over the parish at this time, as the colony continued to grow with the addition of Italian settlers from Grand Crossing. A large community settled at Sixty-fifth and Woods streets at the beginning of the century; it continued to be Italian through the 1920s and 1930s. The Reverend Angelo della Vecchia, C.PP.S., pastor from 1923 to 1970, opened a school in 1927 and saw it grow to 350 students by 1937.[2]

As Italians moved south of Assumption, they established Holy Guardian Angel Parish, at 869 West Cabrini Street, in 1899. The Reverend Edmund M. Dunne set up an improvised chapel, at 716 West Arthington, in 1898, and replaced it with a new church in 1899. Archbishop Feehan formally established the parish the same year, as the Servite Fathers of Assumption took control of all activities. Called the "cradle of Chicago Italians," Guardian Angel served the needs of the Italian West Side for sixty-four years. At the turn of the century the parish was strong and flourishing, with over one thousand baptisms recorded annually. A huge Sunday school developed under the leadership of Mrs. William Amberg and William Bogan, principal of Lane Technical High School; it attracted 1,400 children a week in 1900, and expanded to 2,500 students a week by 1913. When Father Dunne left the parish in 1905 to become the first bishop of Peoria, Illinois, the Scalabrini Fathers took charge of the parish. It continued to flourish through the twenties and thirties, until the new University of Illinois Circle Campus forced its closing in 1963.[3]

Another group of Italians, from Ricigliano, established Santa Maria Incoronata Parish, at 218 Alexander Street, in 1899. Begun as a mission of St. John's School at Eighteenth and Clark, the parish grew considerably during the first decades of the twentieth century. The *New World*, referring to Santa Maria as "Chicago's Melting Pot," stated that "contact with these Catholicized versions of American institutions—nursery, kindergarten, free school and mission—give the growing Italian . . . a lasting realization of the . . . words 'Mother Country' and 'Mother Church.' "[4] When construction of the Dan Ryan Expressway cut the parish in half in 1963, Santa Maria closed its doors and combined with Santa Lucia Church, at 3022 South Wells Street. The newly formed parish (Santa Maria Incoronata-Santa Lucia) continues to serve a small pocket of Italian immigrants on the outskirts of Chinatown.[5]

As Italians continued to move west, they established newer and bigger parishes. Santa Maria Addolorata, at 528 North Ada Street, began as a parish for Italians from Tuscany, Piedmont, Venice, and Sicily, in 1903. Archbishop Quigley bought an old Swedish Lutheran church for the community and appointed Father James Gambere as its first pastor. After fire destroyed the original church in 1931, the parishioners erected a new place of worship at May and Erie streets. When a school opened in 1939, the *New World* observed that "the new school will add to the entire neighborhood. This will be another contribution of Chicago's Italians to the city and its people."[6] Addolorata functioned as an an Italian parish through World War II, and eventually dedicated a new church, at 528 North Ida Street, in 1960.

St. Michael's Parish, at 2325 West Twenty-fourth Place, is one of the few "old neighborhood" churches still in existence. Established by settlers from Tuscany, it formally opened in the basement of an old Swedish Lutheran church in 1903. The parish fought with Socialist and free-thinking Italians in its earliest years. Father Caesar Molinari organized the young men of the parish into a Holy Name Society to combat these new philosophies. The Chicago police largely ignored the area during Prohibition and bootlegging went unnoticed in the immediate environs. Such well-known restaurants as Febo's, Bruna's Cafe, Toscano's, and La Fontanella started as Prohibition restaurants serving illegal wine and beer. The area continues to represent an insular community of northern Italians who have survived the ravages of

Americanization and change. As the *New World* noted in 1978: "St. Michael Parish is keeping alive the Italian traditions of the community spirit in conjunction with the heart of Chicago community spirit. We still believe that we can help the city of Chicago by maintaining our *ethnic background*."[7]

The Near North Side, one of the oldest sections of Chicago, was part of the original city when it was incorporated in 1837. The area did not develop quickly during the 1840s, since there were no bridges to connect the Loop with the northern parts of the city. Engineers finally constructed three bridges over Rush Street, Erie Street, and Grand Avenue between 1856 and 1857. This opened the area to speedy development. The Irish, who first settled the area, built homes along the river and worked as laborers in the neighboring factories, mills, railroad yards, and shops. Germans, who lived north of Chicago Avenue and east of Clark Street, ran small truck gardens and independent businesses. Swedes, who settled in the southwestern part of the community by 1860, added to the ethnic diversity of the area. But the community already showed signs of deterioration by 1864, as more affluent Irish and Germans moved northwest. When the Chicago fire destroyed the area in 1871, the community had to rebuild from the beginning. But the sturdy immigrants who settled the area were more than ready for the challenge, and a new Chicago soon arose over the ashes of the old.

The Near North Side began to live again during the 1880s and 1890s, as the Chicago and Northwestern Railroad laid its tracks along the north branch of the river. Electric surface lines, which became operational the same decade, made the area a desirable residential district. Clark Street became a rooming house neighborhood by the early 1880s, while the area west of Wells degenerated to a slum. Irish immigrants, who populated Goose Island in the middle of the river, worked the neighboring tanneries and factories. As a new century dawned, older manufacturing and business establishments pushed farther and farther north and east, where they converted residential land to commercial use. Chicago's elite left their once-affluent neighborhoods and built newer mansions on Lake Shore Drive and its adjoining streets.

Clark Street became a string of cheap hotels, secondhand stores, and dance halls. As industries enveloped the area between Clark and Grand, Italians secured the blocks between Chicago and Division streets, Gault Court, and Milton Avenue. The area soon became "one of Chicago's oldest and most colorful Italian communities," known as Little Italy to contemporaries of the Near North Side.[8]

The vast majority of these Italians belonged to St. Philip Benizi Parish, at Oak and Cambridge streets.[9] St. Philip's parishioners were Sicilians. They tended to settle with their own compatriots—to such an extent that individual streets were often occupied by Sicilians from the same small village. The Reverend Peregrine Giangrande, O.S.M., St. Philip's first pastor and prior, oversaw the building of the first church in 1904. The occasion was a typical Italian *festa*, with parades and bands adding to the joyous celebration.[10] Archbishop Quigley formally dedicated the church on December 18, 1904. When the Solemn Mass was over, Quigley preached to these newcomers in their own native tongue, forever endearing himself to his new flock. The souvenir program recalled that "the Parish of St. Philip was a 'bit of Italy' for the huge mass of Italian immigrants that came to this country from 1904."[11]

One of the most important Italian personages to live in Chicago at this time was Mother Francis X. Cabrini, who was raised to sainthood only thirty years after her death. Coming to the United States from Italy in 1889, she founded a day school and orphanage in New York City. She soon received approval for a new congregation of sisters, the Missionary Sisters of the Sacred Heart, who extended their charity work to Latin America. She arrived in New Orleans in 1905 to provide emergency relief for the Italian victims of yellow fever. Finally settling in Chicago, Mother Cabrini founded Columbus Hospital and supervised numerous charitable activities. Her sisters came to St. Philip's to teach catechism and prepare young Italians for Holy Communion and confirmation. The St. Philip Sunday School Association, a group of lay volunteers who started a Sunday School in 1910, assisted them in their work. Led by Eva Rocca and Catherine McKeon, this group of young Catholic women cared for the poor, teaching them how to work for the good of the church. Sunday School attendance rose from 200 in 1910, to 1,800 in 1914. The Mantellate Sisters, an Italian branch of the Servite Order, came to St. Philip's the same year to initiate a kindergarten and teach the older children Catholicism. Through all these early efforts, St. Philip's met the challenge of a growing immigrant flock.

When Father Giangrande died at the age of forty-nine in 1915, he was succeeded by Father Luigi Giambastiani, O.S.M., who had already been an assistant at St. Philip's for five years. A sociological study of St. Philip's in 1918 noted that "the Italians hold together with more tenacity than any other racial group in the ward. . . . With them the primary relationships are maintained, partly because of their inherent clannishness and partly because their ignorance of the English language isolates them."[12] Protestant proselytizers tried to lure them from their faith, but these attempts were largely unsuccessful because Catholicism was a way of life to most Italians. To abandon it was unthinkable. Father Luigi tried to combat these efforts by establishing an auxiliary church between Olivet Presbyterian Church and the Episcopalian St. John's. Using an old kindergarten building, Giambastiani provided a place of worship for Italian Catholics living on the fringes of the parish. He also succeeded in stopping any Protestant conversions in his parish.[13]

A University of Chicago student who observed Chicago's North Side Italian community in 1925, noted that St. Philip's was atypical of Chicago's Italian colonies. The main thoroughfares, which were poor and depressing, showed none of the old-country atmosphere of Grand Avenue or Taylor Street. The Sicilians of St. Philip's were poor; they could only afford $5.00 a month for rent. Although the Lower North Community Council tried to improve the situation, the community remained in decrepit condition through the 1920s. Only one in ten owned their own home and most public facilities were held in common. The majority of men worked as day laborers, shopkeepers, barbers, or peddlers. A German *Frau* recalled that Italian women were hardworking, "sewing pants or making lamp shades or anything that they can do in their homes."[14]

But the community slowly changed, as blacks from the Deep South moved into Chicago's old neighborhoods after World War I. It was a dramatic change, for both the native and foreign-born could not adjust to these newcomers. Blacks remained on the lowest economic and social ladder throughout the century, while other immigrants moved to better quarters. By 1928, blacks had moved between Oak and Division streets, on Sedgwick, Franklin, Wells, and Elm; they soon reached the fringes of St. Philip's parish.[15] Relations between the Sicilians and blacks remained tense for decades. Although both shared poverty and prejudice, they could not overcome their racial differences. Father Luigi, who was reluctant to welcome them, often said that blacks could not coexist with Americans or Sicilians. When blacks first moved into Cabrini Green—one of Chicago's first public housing projects built on the Near North Side—Father Luigi protested that "the Negroes might be uplifted, but the whites by the very laws of environment will be lowered. . . . The presence of Negroes in the Francis Cabrini Homes will not work for good and in time; it might frustrate the noble purpose that inspired this project and making of it a slum worse than in the past."[16] Father Giambastiani firmly

believed that blacks had destroyed St. Philip Benizi Parish, and he never changed his conviction for as long as he lived.
Italians began to move out of St. Philip's by 1928. Father Luigi recalled this transformation:

> When I first came to this colony on the lower North Side it was very much more a foreign community than it is now. At that time the emigrants from the villages around Palermo were living together closer than they do now and retained the same customs, religious ceremonies and feasts that they had had in their own country. The women seldom left their homes except to go to Mass.
> . . .
> Since the war there has been a great change and it is no longer an Italian community for there are so many nationalities who live here and so many Negroes.[17]

Time and gradual Americanization worked against Chicago's Italian parishes, as blacks and other immigrants took over their old neighborhoods. Hundreds simply moved away to newer neighborhoods on the South and West sides.

Archbishop Quigley established several Italian parishes on the Near West Side during the prewar years. Holy Rosary Parish served the needs of a growing West Side community, as Italians moved along Grand Avenue and its adjacent streets. By 1930, Holy Rosary numbered 10,000 parishioners.[18] As parishioners from Holy Guardian Angel Parish moved westward, Quigley decided to establish another Italian parish, Our Lady of Pompeii, at 1224 West Lexington Avenue, in 1911. The Reverend Peter Barabino, the first pastor, supervised the construction of a combination church-school the same year. By 1920, the parish was flourishing and the principal buildings had been erected.[19] But as Italians continued to move west, they needed newer parishes to accommodate them. Archbishop Mundelein established St. Callistus Parish, at 2167 West Bowler Street, in 1919, for this purpose. The first church—a Methodist building at 2169 DeKalb Street—served St. Callistus until parishioners completed a combination church-school in 1926. When internal discord threatened the very existence of the parish, Mundelein appointed the Scalabrini Fathers to take charge. The parish, which served the Italian community for twenty years, numbered some twenty thousand parishioners by 1937.[20]

Two isolated Italian communities arose on the Far South Side at the beginning of the century, The first was St. Anthony of Padua Parish, at 11533 South Prairie Street. Established by Quigley in 1904, St. Anthony's fostered

Italian ethnicity through the first decades of the twentieth century. When parishioners built a new church in 1936, after fire destroyed the original one, the Italian consul general expressed the desire "that the rebuilt church of St. Anthony in Kensington may become a thriving Italian center for religion as well as for patriotism. I also sincerely wish that all Italians may always gather closely around the church because it and the *fatherland*, especially abroad, represent *the two greatest directors* of our moral and material life and the source from which one can draw new strength and consolation. In other words, Italians are naturally Catholics as they are naturally Italian and naturally civilized."[21] The last Italian parish established by Quigley was St. Francis de Paula, at 7822 South Dobson Street, in 1911. The archdiocesean archives note that "the Italian flavor was very much in evidence, since Italians predominated. The annual Festa to our Lady was the major parish social event of the year, complete with outdoor processions of the Madonna, the fiesta and bazaar."[22] But the parish changed quickly as newer immigrants inundated St. Francis after World War I, and the community became bilingual (Italian-English) by 1920.

Italian parishes followed the movement of the Italian people as they moved outward from their original settlements north of the Chicago River. Sicilians, who moved northwest, founded St. Philip Benizi Parish on the edge of the Near North Side. Other southerners moved south of the river and established Holy Guardian Angel Parish on the Near West Side. Santa Maria Addolorata, Holy Rosary, and Our Lady of Pompeii soon followed as West Side institutions. Italian parishes served their people well, as they preserved ethnicity and aided Americanization at the same time. They were necessary stops on the way to full assimilation into American society. But they were stops that were never left behind, for *Italianità* was a way of life to these southern Europeans, and it was impossible simply to forget their native origins.

Italian priests actively affirmed Italian traditions throughout the twentieth century. Father Luigi Giambastiani consistently fostered Italian culture and tradition. He was a leading figure on the Near North Side for fifty years. When friction arose between the Italian Servites and those born in America, Giambastiani sided with the Italians. Father Angelico Barsi, an assistant of Father Luigi's during the early part of his pastorate, also supported a break between the two groups. He told a friend in Colorado that "the Italians want Italians . . . but the Americans do not see it."[23] The Vatican settled the dispute in 1927 by dividing the Servites into two separate groups, one under American jurisdiction and the other (including St. Philip's) under Roman law.

Giambastiani continually supported the viability of Italian parishes. Consistently troubled by jurisdictional disputes between himself and other neighboring pastors, he insisted that Italian couples attend Italian churches. He wrote Monsignor Morrison at Holy Name Cathedral to "kindly refer the Italian couples to the Italian Church so they can be married by their lawful pastor in keeping with the laudable traditions of the past," and added that "Italian families are to be given service by their own Italian priests in the Italian churches as in the past. To do otherwise means to confuse the mind of the people, to bring discord in the families, to break the unity of the parish, to lessen the authority of their pastor." Giambastiani was particularly annoyed at the pastors of St. Michael's and St. Joseph's, who stole St. Philip's parishioners for their own parish coffers.[24] These disputes continued unabated through the first half of the century.

St. Philip's dynamic pastor guided Chicago's North Side through the 1930s and beyond. Although St. Philip's changed dramatically, he continued to support it as an Italian community for five decades. He never accepted the blacks who joined St. Philip's after World War II. Although there were many similarities between blacks and Sicilians, the two groups never united for one common goal. Most Italians simply left the neighborhood for the Far North Side or suburbs. Father Luigi closed his parish to black parishioners for forty-six years. Retiring to a Servite community in Welby, Colorado, Father Luigi Giambastiani, O.S.M., the man who had guided St. Philip's and the Near North Side for half a century, died in 1976.

Italian religious orders like the Servites and Scalabrini Fathers also encouraged devotion to Italian culture. The Scalabrini Fathers of our Lady of Pompeii "ran different affairs just to bring the people together."[25] The Reverend Angelo della Vecchia, C.PP.S., of Our Lady of Mt. Carmel, led his parish as an Italian center for fifty years. The Reverend Joseph Gentili, C.PP.S., who continued this tradition through the 1970s, carried on the traditional *feste* in honor of San Rocco and Our Lady of Mt. Carmel. Some Italian clergy were so jealous of their traditions that they fought for them with non-Italian parishioners. When a small Slavic element at San Rocco Parish in Chicago Heights asked for a voice in parish affairs, the Italian clergy appealed to the archbishop to put them in their place. The ensuing conflict forced Mundelein to put the parish under the direct supervision of Rome and appoint a new pastor. A contemporary noted that the dispute was largely a personality conflict between an old pastor and other priests within the parish: "The agitation against him was not because he did not speak Italian, for he spoke it even as did his predecessor, not because he spoke German, for he was American-born, but it was against him personally . . . largely engineered by one of his own brethren in religion, an Italian Franciscan."[26] It would seem then that the conflict was personal more than ethnic, for ultimately it was a power play within the order itself for control of the parish. But the players—as seen by the priests—could only be Italian. There was no room for outsiders.

Ethnic parishioners were conscious of their Italianness. Parish bulletins and sermons repeatedly echoed this sentiment. *Il Calendario Italiano* stated: "St. Philip is a little diocese; a little Palermo if you like it, because in St. Philip you will find a group of almost every town and village of the great royal Diocese of Palermo. . . . We have copies of the saintly men that made Sicily the Island of the Saints."[27] Again and again, *Il Calendario Italiano* emphasized the need for Italian churches.[28] Father Giambastiani cajoled his parishioners to attend St. Philip Benizi: "Don't say that you live near the German, the Irish or the Polish church; friends know no distance, and besides the German church was built by and for the German people, the Irish church is built for and by the Irish people, the Polish church by and for the Polish people, the same way the Italian church of St. Philip built by and for the Italian people."[29] But the unfortunate fact was that many Italians forgot their ancestral roots when they moved to American churches. Writing "to our faraway friends" (i.e., those who had moved away from St. Philip's), Father Luigi claimed that Italian Americans remembered only the nickel they gave to him, while they threw dollars into the American basket with an air of superiority; in other words, Italian Americans forgot their ethnicity when they moved to more cosmopolitan parishes. They were ashamed of their origins and preferred to give their new-found money to American churches. Father Giambastiani repeatedly reminded his readers that "St. Philip's has *need* for your help . . . the Church of St. Philip has been made for the Italians; and it is just that Italians help it; and if they don't help it who will? . . . Italians, do not be afraid to honor your Catholicism with a sentiment of Italianness."[30]

Italian parishes also provided a focus for the liturgical events of life: baptism, marriage, and death. While the actual number of parishioners at St. Philip Benizi declined during the first half of the century, baptisms and marriages kept proportionately ahead. Between 1904 and 1929, there were 25,000 baptisms at the parish; between 1930 and 1934, there were 10,051. There were 5,000 marriages between 1904 and 1929, and 1,273 between 1930 and 1954.[31] Mrs. Anthony Serritella recalled that even when people moved out of the parish, they wanted to return to be married or buried. As she said, "you would be surprised throughout the years how the people do come back. A few years ago people came back to light the candles—you could also see the old-timers coming back to visit the church."[32]

But it was the traditional *feste* that most appropriately expressed the unique brand of Catholicism that came from Italy. Fr. Luigi Giambastiani described these festivals in an interview with the Chicago Historical Society in 1928. "In Sicily each town, which is usually located on top of a mountain, has its own festival, one town having its festival in May, the next in June, etc. This had a tendency to bring the people of Sicily together. And so it is in Chicago."[33] Father Luigi noted that St, Philip's retained the meaning of these festivals through the 1920s and 1930s, in particular, the Feast of Our Lady of Loretto. He called it the "loveliest festival" of the year, which retained "almost all of the significance and beauty which it had in Sicily,"[34]

The thousands of dollars spent at these festivals give an indication of the appeal and strength they had through the twenties and thirties. The financial records of St. Philip Benizi indicate that parish income increased considerably from 1915 to 1927—from $2,902.87 to $45,103.49. Even during the Great Depression, income totaled $30,191.01 (1937).[35] The large majority of this income came from *festa* and procession, as well as numerous carnivals and votive candles. Festival income totaled $8,150.51 as late as 1950. Father Giambastiani, who consistently stressed the religious nature of these festivals, had to remind his people to control their excesses: "Let us remember not to restrict this feast to worldly entertainment through the streets. It is necessary that religion be the predominant element of these festivities. . . . I especially recommend that all parishioners attend the sacred functions in the church."[36] He reminded the Deputazione Lauretana not to "interfere in anyway in whatever devotion or service the Fathers of St. Philip's church intend to have in connection with our Lady of Loretto."[37] But Father Luigi basically supported the festivals, and noted that "a people who in the midst of such poverty and grief are capable of such religious enthusiasm are a healthy people, a strong people, a people who can conquer the future with security."[38]

St. Philip's also fostered traditional Sicilian feasts. St. Lucy had long been a favorite Sicilian saint. St. Agatha, another Sicilian saint, was also popular among St. Philip's parishioners. Father Luigi reminded his people that "the Sicilian race should be proud of these national glories." But non-Sicilian feasts were also honored at Oak and Cambridge. The Feast of the Holy Cross—a Tuscan festival from Lucca—was also celebrated, "a traditional feast which recalls the most beautiful manifestations of faith of our beautiful country; a lucchese who does not sanctify this day is not worthy of the name."[39] Santa Maria Incoronata annually celebrated the Feast of Santa Maria Incoronata di Ricigliano, a local festival from the outskirts of Palermo. St. Mary of Mt. Carmel celebrated the feast of San Rocco every year from 1906 to 1967. And Our Lady of Pompeii solemnized its feast on October 5, with traditional processions and bands. Anthony Serritella vividly recalled this *festa* in a 1978 interview: "They put the statue on a platform, the cart was pulled, there was a band and the schoolchildren and all the societies would have their banners—Christian Mothers, Holy Name, Mothers' Guild, Sacred Heart. There were other societies outside the Church who would have their Mass. If their patron was Saint Rocco, the Society of St. Rocco would come here and have their procession and that money would go to the society."[40] Through all these *feste*, Italian parishes nurtured a love of Italy and her culture. They provided an outlet for these new immigrants. They allowed time-honored celebrations to continue in America.

St. Philip's continued to foster festivals some forty years after its founding. It joined Assumption parish in a procession to Holy Name Cathedral in 1929. After returning to Oak and Cambridge, the participants crowned Mary Queen of May, as the Italian people solemnly consecrated themselves to the Blessed Mother. They recited the Rosary in English and Italian, and they sang bilingual hymns. Father Giambastiani, who consistently upheld the right of the church to approve parish devotions, defended an Italian prayer known as the "Rosary of the Wounds of Our Lord" when the Chancery threatened to disavow it. Writing to the archbishop, Father Giambastiani emphasized that "this devotion was brought into our parish unofficially by some pious ladies. . . . I beg to submit to you that I have heard those prayers recited since I was a little boy, in more or less the same way."[41] These actions clearly demonstrate the strong loyalty that St. Philip's clergy and laity alike maintained toward Italian culture.

Father Giambastiani also supported the creation of an Italian seminary in suburban Elgin, Illinois. He wrote Bishop William V. O'Brian that the Servite churches had helped to "preserve the faith among the Italians . . . it is from this ambition to preserve the Italian people in the faith of their ancestors that sprung the idea of building a seminary for the boys of Italian parentage."[42] This idea grew into St. Joseph Seminary, which opened in October 1937. An advertisement on the back page of *Il Calendario Italiano* noted that it was meant "for the Italian-American youth who felt a vocation to the priesthood."[43]

Like their German counterparts, Italians fostered a host of societies and organizations. Most of these societies, which centered around the town from which the immigrants came, carried on a good part of their activities through the local parish. St. Philip's principal society was the Società di S.S. Lauretana di Altavilla (Society of Our Lady of Loretto from Altavilla). It sponsored the parish festival of the year, the Feast of Our Lady of Loretto, on September 5. La Madre dei Dolori was established when the parish began in 1904; the Figlie di Maria (Daughters of Mary) also began at the beginning of the century. Table 7 lists the extant societies of St. Philip's in 1937. Many of these associations were devotional, such as the Società del Crocifisso di Ciminna (Society of the Crucifix of Ciminna), which held various Masses and processions during this period. An annual banquet of all the Italian societies of the North Side attracted twenty-four societies in 1941. Parishioners soon established the Ladies of St. Philip Benizi Guild as "one of the largest group of Italian ladies (over 1,100) to support the work of the parish school."[44]

Father Angelico Barsi, an assistant at St. Philip's, supported the work of Italica Gens, which sought to support the Catholic faith of the immigrant and maintain his cultural ties through employment, the support of Italian agricultural communities, a legal committee to defend poor Italians, promotion of Italian newspapers, and continual efforts to retain the Italian language in parochial schools.[45] Although the society's activities stopped in the United States in 1923, it sent out a questionnaire to various Italian parishes to see whether Italians living in the United States should have the right to vote in Italian elections. The vast majority, who voted against this privilege, chose to become naturalized American citizens. They knew that their future lay more with America than the old country.

Italian parishes were active centers of Italian culture. Italian religious orders like the Servites and Scalabrini Fathers encouraged Italinization through local *feste*, parish societies, and numerous bulletins and sermons. The parishioners consciously supported the priests through physical participation and financial contributions. They kept their ties to the old country by encouraging the continuance of the Italian language at all levels of parish activity—*feste*, local societies, and ordinary worship. Italian officials acknowledged their presence by attending local activities and even soliciting their vote.

TABLE 7

Italian Societies, St. Philip Benizi, 1937

Soc. di Maria S.S. Lauretana di Altavilla
Soc. di Maria S.S. dell'Udienza di Sambucca
Soc. S.S. Crocifisso di Ciminna
Loggia 1.ma, Soc. Crocifisso di Ciminna
Loggia 2.da, Soc. San Giovanni
Loggia 3.za, Soc. San Vito
Loggia 4.ta, Soc. San Guiseppe
Loggia 5.ta, Soc. San Michele
Soc. di San Giuseppe di Bagheria
Soc. di Gesu Morto di Bagheria
Soc. S. Lucia di Castellano
Soc. S. Cuore di Gesù di Aragona
Soc. San Leoluca di Corleone
Soc. Maria S.S. del Rosario di Ventimiglia
Soc. di Fratellanza Morrealese
Soc. S.S. Sacramento di Ciminna
Soc. di Paina dei Greci
Soc. di M.S. Ventimiglia
Soc. Maria S.S. Addolorata di Burgetto
Soc. Unione di Vacari
Soc. Santa Fortunata
Soc. Immacolata

SOURCE: Archives St. Philip Benizi, II, V 29.

Chicago's Italians gained pride in themselves as the stature of Mussolini grew. Ethnic parishes—seeing in him the hope and vision of what Italy could be—consistently supported his activities throughout the twenties and thirties. When the Vatican concluded a concordant with Mussolini in 1927, Italian parishes rejoiced as the dawn of a new nation arose. *Il Calendario Italiano* noted that "Mussolini stands for good sense, reason, and all history and faith."[46] St. Philip's also participated in relief work to Italy, with Father Giambastiani acting as executive director for the eighteen Italian parishes of the archdiocese. Constantly promoting ethnic loyalty, Giambastiani praised the work of his parishioners in behalf of Italy: "You have done so much in behalf of a people to whom we are attached throughed the sweetest ties of *blood, culture* and *faith*."[47]

Christopher Columbus—as a man of two worlds, the old and the new—occupied a unique position among Italian Americans. For Chicago's Italians, Columbus was one of "the two great exponents of Italianness in this country."[48] He was a man of America and Italy. He would always occupy a special place in the hearts of Italian Americans.

Italians also had "an innate love of music and art and a religiously devout spirit that finds expressions all their own."[49] St. Philip's shared this musical love in many ways. Italian music played a prominent part in liturgies, *feste*, and other celebrations. Italians' love of music naturally flowed into art and architecture. Busts of Dante and Columbus adorned St. Philip's school, while Rome itself was extolled as the heart of Christianity.

> Where is the source of such enthusiasm, of such glory?—Rome! Christian Rome! . . . Italian Rome. And it is to Rome that one must go after all things to be consecrated in history. The prominent among us—gossipy, decayed, and speculating—are ashamed to call themselves Italian or profess themselves Christians. It is enough to look at these historical events to condemn these men, stuffed with money and false glory. No, Italians cannot be Italians if they are not Christians and Catholics at the same time.[50]

Reverence for national heroes, devotion to Rome, and an innate love of music and art—all these demonstrate an enduring love for *cara Italia*.

But ethnic parishes were not only way stations of ethnicity, they were also a focus of Americanization. National parishes actively encouraged this process though parish institutions and societies, bulletins and sermons, as well as constant cooperation with archdiocesan-wide activities and organizations. Fr. Luigi Giambastiani felt that the ethnic parish had done everything possible to

Americanize the immigrant. *Il Calendario Italiano* observed that "all should be Americans and there should be no distinction of nationalities . . . you can be just as good Americans at Saint Philip as in any other church German, Irish, Polish, or whatever nationality it might be."[51] Various institutions and organizations furthered Americanization. Monthly bulletins, which began English-language announcements in 1916, continued bilingual publication through the 1930s. Servite missionaries conducted English missions "for the young people of the parish." Indeed, pastors and laity, conscious of Americanization, did everything possible to further assimilation.

Americanizing efforts at St. Philip Benizi began at the lowest level, with the establishment of a kindergarten and day nursery, at 535 West Oak Street, in 1911. Founded by Father Giambastiani to counteract the influence of Protestant nurseries, it was a place where "family troubles are settled, marriages are made legal and rectified; work and employment is found in critical times, and all kinds of charitable assistance in clothing, coal, and groceries is provided for the needy."[52] The Maria SS. ma Lauretana Day Nursery and Kindergarten promoted the same activities, although it closed for lack of proper help. But St. Juliana's more than made up the loss with a vigorous Americanization program during the twenties and thirties. Cooperating with the Chicago Association of Commerce in exchanging practical information, the day nursery cared for more than 12,228 children in 1935. St. Juliana's united with other parish social programs to form the St. Philip Community Center in 1936. Besides the original kindergarten, the center sponsored three Boy Scout troops, a sewing school, a manual training course, a dramatic club, boxing facilities, and civics classes. These activities helped Chicago's Northside Italians adjust to life in America. By directly fostering such efforts, the parish became an essential institution of Americanization.[53]

Ethnic parishes also established sodalities and organizations for the betterment of the young men and women of the community.[54] St. Philip's founded two public school sodalities in the 1920s, as well as a band for girls and a Junior Holy Name for boys. Both groups, which numbered over five hundred members by 1926, adequately served the public schoolchildren of the area. The Third Order of Servites, a choral society, a sewing club, and social club also brought many young men and women together under the patronage of the parish. A mothers' club cooperated with the parish Sisters for "the *civic* and *Christian* formation of our children, the Chicago citizens of tomorrow."[55] During the 1930s, St. Philip's cooperated with the North Side Civic Center in providing all the facilities of a modern boys' club—a game room, arts and crafts equipment, and numerous sporting events. Our Lady of Pompeii also sponsored a variety of athletic teams that were supported by local politicians or tavern owners. In addition, it operated a summer camp in Wisconsin for the enjoyment of the entire parish.[56] Our Lady of Mt. Carmel established the Orchid Club, which operated a social center for the young people of the area. Open to Germans, Irish and Jews during the 1920s, the club brought Mt. Carmel's youth into contact with all nationalities and creeds.[57] Through all these activities, ethnic parishes fostered Americanization for the youth of the early twentieth century. Instead of alienating them, the national parish actively supported them and provided societies and organizations for their economic and social betterment.

Ethnic parishioners also supported naturalization efforts. Both priests and laity actively encouraged this process. Our Lady of Pompeii conducted classes where Italians learned to read and write English. Later on, "doctors and lawyers would tutor them [the immigrants] and go down and sponsor them for their papers. They helped each other out quite a bit years ago. You wouldn't hesitate to go to your doctor to ask for guidance . . . it wasn't just for medicine . . . you would go for advice in investments . . . when they had banquets they would honor these professional men. They looked up to them quite a bit." But it wasn't just the professionals who commanded respect—it was the priests as well. They were consulted for legal advice, sought after by politicians, and guided the parish as one of the principal socializers of the period. Anthony Serritella recalled that "if a person had anything to do with courts at all the priests would go along to see that they were treated right. And they would be the first ones they would call on as character witnesses. . . . They went to the priests for a lot of things. The Italian people used to get pushed around, so they got better treatment."[58]

Italian parishes also encouraged political activity. *Il Calendario Italiano*, which repeatedly supported Italian candidates, exclaimed that "Italian voters are reminded to vote for our compatriots and to recognize their name and all their friends."

Father Luigi Giambastiani was a shrewd politician himself. At a 1926 banquet in honor of Big Bill Thompson, Father Luigi invoked the blessing before the meal, as Mayor Thompson praised the ideals and hopes of the Italian people. The bulletin reported: "The evening was completely Italian, the music was Italian . . . the food and drink were also Italian."[59] Always a political realist, Father Luigi sought the interest of his people through persuasion and personal intervention. He did not hesitate to use his position as pastor of one of the most influential Italian parishes to better the lives of his parishioners.

But ethnic parishes did not function as entities unto themselves. Archbishop George Mundelein encouraged Americanization through archdiocesean organizations and societies. By participating in such societies, immigrants gradually came to know other immigrant groups, were exposed to American ways, and brought to a fuller realization of the catholicity of their church. Mundelein actively fostered the establishment of the Holy Name Society in all ethnic parishes.[60] This society became a laymen's militia for the sanctification of its members. St. Philip Benizi, which established numerous bilingual societies during the twenties and thirties, tried to encourage the development of the Holy Name on the parish level. Although some parishioners objected to the society as denigrating ethnic associations, most parishes allowed members to join both societies. As *Il Calendario Italiano* stated in 1924: "If you join the Holy Name Society it doesn't mean that you cease to be a member of the club you now belong to. No, quite the contrary. We want to avoid all this rivalry by having a society made up of many members and clubs and troups."[61]

The Catholic Youth Organization also acted within the parish to Americanize the Italian immigrant. A nationwide organization, the CYO appealed to young people at the parish level through summer activities, arts and crafts, and numerous sporting events. Having as its motto "For God and Country," the Chicago-based organization was the most influential Catholic group in the United States during the 1930s. St. Philip's promoted the society with great enthusiasm. As the parish bulletin noted:

> Eager boys are joining this organization because they realize the *physical, moral*, and *spiritual* benefits that are to be had. We must remember that *the youths of today are the citizens of tomorrow*, and that we must prepare them to fight life's battle with good will, sportsmanship, courage, honor and self-sacrifice. *We must uplift the human race.*[62]

The Mantellate Sisters supervised a CYO summer vacation school at Stanton Park, just north of Division Street at Larrabee. It provided a variety of activities to keep Italians physically and mentally alert. Boys learned woodcraft, while girls took up art and needlework. Boxing was especially popular among Italian *ragazzi*, as hundreds looked forward to the Saturday-night boxing programs by the CYO. The organization also financed numerous scouting activities (for boys and girls) through the 1930s. St. Philip's troops, which were reorganized in 1932, participated in a variety of citywide activities, including an enormous Scout rally on Lake Shore Drive in 1933. These activities encouraged Italian boys and girls to meet other ethnic groups on a common ground. But it was the parish that brought all these activities together and molded them into one cohesive force of Americanization.[63]

Italian parishes were not only way stations of ethnicity, they were also stops on the way to full participation in American life. The national parish actively established and encouraged institutions that fostered a broad acceptance of American society. Day nurseries allowed young women to find jobs and support their families. Social clubs encouraged youth of all nationalities to meet and know one another. Sporting teams brought thousands of young men and women into contact with the rest of Chicago. Parish priests encouraged naturalization, gave legal advice, and even went to court for their flock. Although there was a strong tradition of anticlericalism among Italians, this tradition softened in the American environment. The priest became one of the few educated men who could guide and lead an uneducated and disliked minority. But the parish did not act alone. Through participation in such organizations as the Holy Name Society and CYO, the Italian immigrant came to know the multiethnic church that Catholicism really was. He also came to know the multiethnic city that was Chicago.

But the Italian parish was not only ethnic and American, it was also Catholic—and it was Catholicism that linked it to the rest of Chicago. Father Michael O'Hearn, pastor of St. Edward's Church, 4350 West Sunnyside Avenue, complained to Father Giambastiani of deficiencies: "*I do object* to these Italian people not going to *Mass* . . . I do object to them being *married by a judge* and living that way. I do object to these people never *receiving the Blessed Sacrament.*"[64] Italian clergymen tried to arouse their flock through parish bulletins, weekly sermons, and personal admonition. Fr. Giambastiani noted that, "The Italian people in the great cities of America are guilty of two great religious and social faults at the same time: the profanation of the Lord's Day and a failure to contribute to the support of the Church." *Il Calendario Italiano* listed a series of "don'ts" for its parishioners: "Don't be late for Mass. . . don't go to Mass without a prayer book or rosary . . . don't talk . . . don't leave the church until the priest has left . . . don't forget to bend the knee." It reminded its readers that American Catholics went to Mass every Sunday.[65] They portrayed Al Smith as a model Catholic, a man who went to Mass every day of the week. By emphasizing these points, the ethnic parish fostered a strong sense of Catholicism among its Italian parishioners. It then linked itself to all Chicago Catholics in a bond that stretched to Rome itself.[66]

Closely allied to Catholicism was a strong fear of Protestant proselytizing. Presbyterians and Methodists were particularly militant in trying to win converts from Italian districts. Immigrant priests were vigilant in resisting their efforts. Father Luigi expressed the sentiments of many in a letter to his parishioners:

> The Methodists, Presbyterians, 7th Day of Adventists, and Episcopalians are all trying to win over the Italians, through large parishes and renegaded Italian priests. Also socialists and atheists. . . . How can I fight all these religious enemies without a school or encouragement of any kind? I am thoroughly convinced that you people do not build the school because you do not realize the absolute necessity of it. . . . I have been here for seven years doing my utmost for this wrecked people and all the fruit of the past is a large crowd of young people growing round the church that don't care neither for Church nor God.[67]

Giambastiani was afraid that "unauthorized ministers" would steal his uneducated flock. The solution to the problem was a parochial school, which would provide a place for moral and religious training against Protestant inroads. Italians generally feared public schools, since they "did not set a high value on the child's moral training, which is, in reality, immeasurably more important than secular knowledge." Protestant efforts eventually failed, since "the church the Italians love is the Church of their Fathers, the Church of their native Sicily, the Holy Roman Catholic Church."[68]

Like the Germans who lived north of them, Chicago's Italians also participated in the 1926 Eucharistic Congress. This celebration was ethnic as well as Catholic, with scores of nationalities participating in the five-day extravaganza. The congress was a showcase of American Catholicism, for it showed Chicago and America what the Catholic Church had become in two hundred years, and Italian Chicago was part of this church—a nationality that kept its ethnicity while belonging to a worldwide organization.

The Italian parochial school was a microcosm of the parish as a whole. While it encouraged Italian ethnicity at all levels of education, it also functioned as a primary source of Americanization. Italian parochial education grew slowly during the early part of the century, but improved enormously after World War I (see Table 8). The archdiocese did not take affirmative action on the Italian school question until Archbishop Quigley took a more active interest in the Italian himself. Quigley established ten national parishes within Chicago by 1910. But the parochial school system did not grow as fast; the *New World* reported that, "The Italian parochial school is still lost in the land of the future." Monsignor Aloysius Pozzi, a vocal Italian cleric, urged the establishment of "an association that will take up the work of establishing something like adequate Catholic primary school education."[69] But the schools did not attract students until 1920, when 3,753 students enrolled.[70] They grew considerably during the 1920s and 1930s, with St. Philip's and Our Lady of Pompeii the largest educational institutions.

Archbishop Quigley first proposed a school for St. Philip's in 1914, but the project remained unfilled until 1919, when Father Luigi Giambastiani strongly supported the idea. A twelve-room building costing 80,000 was finally completed in 1920 and dedicated by Archbishop Mundelein the same year. The school had three primary purposes: the spiritual development of its children, the continuance of Italian as a language and a culture, and the Americanization of its pupils. The parish bulletin stressed the spiritual aspects of the school:

> The school built for the spiritual and moral dedication of your sons.
> The school where they have the opportunity to learn and to know how to fear the Lord.
> The school in which the Commandments of God are the base of the education of the young.
> The school where your sons learn to be respectful and obedient to their parents.[71]

Beginning with 160 students in 1920, St. Philip's grew to 610 students by 1940; it remained the largest Italian parochial school in Chicago for over two decades.

Like the parish as a whole, St. Philip's parochial school functioned as a way station of Italian culture and tradition for more than twenty years. The parish bulletin noted in 1925:

> It is the school where your children learn that there does exist in this world a land called Italy, mother of every present civilization and center of Christianity.
> It is the school where they will learn not to be ashamed of being known as Italians, offspring of saints and heroes.
> It is the school where they will learn to speak the language of Dante, the sweet and beautiful Italian language.[72]

TABLE 8

Growth of Italian Parochial School System, 1920-1940

	1920	1930	1940
Assumption	503	225	84
Our Lady of Mt. Carmel	——	333	380
Holy Guardian Angel	——	320	300
Santa Maria Incoronata	352	425	400
Santa Maria Addolorata	170	——	250
St. Michael	——	——	——
St. Philip	160	560	610
St. Anthony	310	225	360
Holy Rosary	410	407	352
Our Lady of Pompeii	500	564	355
San Callisto	——	184	300

SOURCE: *The Official Catholic Directory.*

Special emphasis was put on learning Italian. The school established a separate Department of Italian for this purpose. Suor Lucilla, O.S.M., the "maestra di Italiano," felt that her students could use Italian in everyday life, since many American businesses needed Italian translators. Over 600 schoolchildren took Italian by 1929, an enrollment that did not decrease during the ensuing decade.[73]

St. Philip's maintained a Department of Music to provide proper entertainment for *feste* and other celebrations. At Our Lady of Pompeii, opera singers gave benefit concerts and performed oratorios.[74] Through all these activities, the Italian parish fostered a devotion to Italian culture.

But the ethnic school was also a center of Americanization. It prepared its children for life in twentieth-century America. *Il Calendario Italiano* expressed this mission:

> Our parochial school students are universally grounded in penmanship. . . . English expression and arithmetic. . . . Far from being the menace to our American institutions . . . our Catholic educational institutions are daily proving them selves the *real bulwarks of our national life, the best conservators of our American ideals, the foundations sources where our future American citizens* receive the most thorough preparation for the fulfillment of their religious and civic responsibilities. (Italics mine.)[75]

Fr. Giambastiani pleaded with parents to send their children to St. Philip's, since "they need this kind of discipline to help to cope with the ever-increasing demands made on the young people by all businessmen." By attending a Catholic elementary school, "Italians have all the ammunition they need to completely conquer the American way of life in the near future." St. Philip's stressed such virtues as "earnestness" and "stick-to-it-iveness," it emphasized correct English, and it stressed the need for cleanliness.[76] By emphasizing practical studies, St. Philip's prepared its children for success in American life.

The parochial school also encouraged a broader vision of the world through a variety of organizations and activities. The Catholic Grammar School League in baseball and basketball brought young Italians into contact with other ethnic children. School concerts featured a variety of ethnic cultures—Norwegian dances, Irish tunes, as well as Hungarian and Spanish folk dances. School assemblies and bulletins constantly praised American culture. Sam Spinale, a 1926 graduate, wrote the class elegy:

What we always love and respect is our *Flag*. It stands for Washington and the patient brave struggle he made for our country. It stands for the soldiers of Valley Forge whose bare feet left marks of blood on the snow. It stands for the fathers who toiled uncomplainingly to earn food and clothes and a chance for an education for their children, and mothers who cook and sew, sacrifice that their children, may be *true Americans*. So we leave for you of the next class, the emblem of the brave the Flag and liberty which represents all the true men and women, boys and girls who now live in the United States or have ever lived in the United States.[77]

Father Luigi even encouraged his children to go to high school at a time when such an achievement was rare among Italians.[78] It is clear that St. Philip's purposely nurtured a broad view of America. While it allowed space for Italian language and music, it also encouraged contact with other national groups. It fostered patriotism and loyalty to the country that gave its children refuge.

While the ethnic parish supported ethnicity and Americanization through a number of institutions and activities, it also encouraged other Italian-American organizations to do the same. The settlement house movement was one of these organizations. The settlement impulse maintained that social and economic reasons played a primary role in the formation of poverty. Settlement work was linked with the humanitarianism implied in Christianity. As Jane Addams stated in her autobiography on Hull House: "I believe there is a distinct turning among many young men and women toward this simple acceptance of Christ's message. . . . The Settlement movement is only one manifestation of that wider humanitarian movement which throughout Christendom . . . is endeavoring to embody itself, not in a sect, but in society itself."[79] It is not surprising that over 88 percent of all social workers in America and England were Christians.

Settlements were basically intended for the foreign-born. They nurtured the customs and traditions of each foreign-born group, while acclimatizing them to their new culture in America. Allen F. Davis maintains that "the settlement's greatest contribution lay not in its teaching history or English, but in its insisting that immigrants preserve the customs and traditions of the old country, assuring immigrants that it was not necessary to reject the past to become an American."[80] The settlements preserved ethnicity through folk festivals, handcraft exhibits, and other native displays. But they also Americanized through English classes, civics lessons, and support for the nascent labor movement. They introduced child-care centers and kindergartens, as well as classes in homemaking, sewing, cooking, and shopping. The public schools later adopted these techniques in home economics curricula. These early experiments in progressive education paved the way for the Chicago public school system.

Chicago was the most important settlement town in the United States through the first two decades of the twentieth century. Hull House was founded in 1889; the Northwestern University Settlement in 1891; and Chicago Commons in 1894. By 1911, there were thirty-two settlements in Chicago alone. But it was Hull House that made Chicago and Jane Addams famous. Located at Polk and Halsted, Hull House tried to close the gap between the educated and the poor through classes, lectures, and discussions. John Dewey, Frank Lloyd Wright, and Sinclair Lewis were frequent visitors who lent their expertise to the settlement movement. By 1910, Hull House was the epitome of settlement work.

But Catholics remained ambivalent toward Addams. The *New World* voiced official opinion:

> But really, is Hull House the chief agency for diffusing culture and teaching civilization in Chicago? We do not so believe. When we reflect upon the tremendous number of German Catholic churches and schools, Irish Catholic churches and schools, and Catholic churches and schools for Poles, Bohemians, Italians, Austrians and even Syrians, we feel obligated to enter a protest for the sake of truth. . . . The Catholic Church . . . is building a civilization here after which Hull House does not appreciate. It is a fact visible to God that the Catholic Church in Chicago is doing more to create a snow-white dawn among all races surging into this great, restless, terrible city than fifty Hull Houses could do.[81]

The majority of Catholics, fearing Addams's Protestant upbringing, were unable to see the good she had done.

Catholicism responded to the settlement movement with houses of its own. There were 250 Catholic settlements in the United States by 1915—one of these was Madonna Center, at 712 South Loomis Street.[82] Madonna Center grew out of the pioneering efforts of Father Paul Ponziglione, S.J., who began English-language classes for newly arrived Italians at Holy Catholic laity from Sacred Heart Academy. He continued his work by establishing Holy Guardian Angel Mission in 1897. Mary Agnes Amberg, daughter of William A. Amberg, recalled that the founding of the mission was an act of providence: "We did not choose those whom we wished to serve. They were already there, a class of immigrants who needed us badly, and we undertook to serve them in whatever way we were able."[83] Like Addams and others who went before them—whether Catholic or Protestant—the founders of this Catholic settlement were educated, well-to-do women. Seeking a way to serve mankind, they found an outlet for their energies in the settlement movement.

The Catholic settlement was a miniature parish, for it directly encouraged the Americanization of its flock. Mrs. William A. Amberg, the mother of Mary Agnes, obtained the use of Dante Public School for evening classes in English, reading, and writing, as well as basic courses in government.[84] By 1904, the Board of Education granted the mission exclusive use of the school for summer vacation courses. The teachers, both Protestant and Catholic alike, had one goal in mind, "the Americanization of their pupils."[85] Guardian Angel soon took on the appearance of a Hull House, with classes in dressmaking, millinery, and drawing; youth clubs and parties, and a modest library offering English-language books. As Mary Berger observed in 1909: "Here patiently, perseveringly and against desperate odds . . . these children of a sunny south land have been molded with a view of making them ideal citizens—ideal Americans because ideal Catholics."[86]

But Guardian Angel had to change with the times. The archdiocese informed the parish that it would have to move the mission to another location since the parish needed the building for other purposes. St. Francis of Assisi School, at 1226 West Newberry Street, soon became available, with eight classrooms. Mary Agnes Amberg and Catherine Jordan, who moved into the building in 1911, transformed the mission into a modern settlement. Guardian Angel Social Center, as it came to be called, offered a variety of activities for the Americanization of its residents. Reading, billiards, sewing, and club meetings took up five classrooms; dancing and entertainment occupied the auditorium on the third floor; debating and social clubs helped young people meet one another; and dressmaking classes prepared young women for their future roles as homemakers and wives. Harriet Vitum, head resident of Northwestern University Settlement, expressed the sentiment of many when she called the mission "a centre from which radiates all manner of good, especially to our vast foreign population, the potential American citizens of our great cities."[87]

As war fever engulfed America, the mission faced another crisis in 1915. Archbishop Mundelein informed Misses Amberg and Jordan that they would have to move again, since the parish needed the building for regular school. By mid-August, they reopened the center at 927-931 Polk Street, a predominantly Italian, Greek, and Mexican neighborhood. By 1918, the settlement was again in operation, with a number of activities for young and old alike—social clubs and athletic groups, home economics classes, and a variety of activities for neighborhood youth. When Andrea Lespina, an aide to Al Capone and Anthony D'Andrea, was shot to death in front of his home at 718 Loomis Street in 1922, the settlement found a bizarre opportunity to expand. Mrs. Lespina approached Misses Amberg and Plamondon on the possibility of selling her house to the settlement: "I will sell it to you, Miss Mary, cheap. For a song. I have lost my husband. I care for nothing now. Nothing, anymore."[88] They bought the house and renamed it Madonna Center, with its main offices in a two-story structure directly north of the main building, at 712 South Loomis Street. Misses Amberg, Plamondon, and Jordan, who moved into their new home in 1922, remained there for the rest of their active lives.

Madonna Center continued to function as a focus of ethnicity at its new location. It encouraged native customs and folklore through dances, *feste*, and art. Encouraging the young to appreciate their traditions, Madonna Center soon found that "the old country took on a new importance, and parents gained in stature before their children." Miss Amberg noted that "we never discussed Italian origins without paralleling our talk with a discussion of the effect of Italian culture upon America." But Italian culture was inexorably tied to Catholicism, and it was Catholicism that united all these activities and made the Catholic settlement an entity unto itself. As Miss Amberg recalled: "I should like to reemphasize here the religious feeling we try to infuse into all our activities at Madonna Center. We strive to make this both explicit and implicit in all we do . . . ours is the singing strength of Catholicism."[89]

Americanization efforts at Madonna Center began at the lowest level. It offered prenatal classes for young mothers-to-be; it provided kindergarten classes for the older children; and doctors from Elizabeth McCormick Memorial Fund examined the young for free. The center encouraged sound nutrition and healthy eating habits.

The settlement also affected older children. It organized two Boy Scout troops, which Henry Littleton and Robert Ward, grandnephews of Mary Agnes Amberg, financed. As they themselves said, "The scouts learned to live and get along with other boys, to begin, finish, and hold onto the privilege of a camp task. They learned the practical as well as the spiritual value of being good instead of being bad. They were being trained to be Americans."[90] Marie Plamondon organized a Girl Scout troop in 1921, at a time when there were only five troops in all Chicago—Madonna Center, St. Clement's, St. Vincent's,

St. Sebastian's, and St. Xavier College. The center also provided athletic facilities for basketball, baseball, and football. Girls from Providence High School, Sienna High School, and the Academy of the Sacred Heart helped with storytelling, choral singing, and other academic programs. All these activities directly fostered a sense of Americanization at Madonna Center.

The Catholic settlement continued to Americanize the Italian through the 1920s. Mrs. Anthony Serritella recalled that Madonna Center was a meeting place for young men and women: "We were just kids then. We used to go on Saturdays or after school. They danced and we played games—arts and crafts, we'd sew. They had a lot of nice things. It was the only place you could go for diversion."[91] The center also provided trips to the Field Museum, the Art Institute, and the Museum of Science and Industry. Plays with patriotic themes also encouraged Americanization. And as the children grew into adults, the settlement provided legal help, homes for abandoned children, and advice to unwed mothers. It tried to moderate the expensive weddings and funerals that most Italians could not afford. Its library provided hundreds of English-language volumes, and its printing press sent out various bulletins in Italian and English through the 1920s and 1930s.

During the Great Depression, assisting in the general effort toward relief, the settlement supplemented the regular government agencies. It kept food, clothing, medicine, fuel, and soap in reserve for the needy of the area. A nutrition clinic helped housewives conserve food and rations. Misses Amberg and Plamondon continued to guide the settlement through the ensuing decades. Awarded the National Red Cross for her service to the Italian people during World War I, Amberg and Plamondon both received citations for distinguished service from the alumnae association of Sacred Heart Academy in Lake Forest in 1950. Their lives enriched their Italian brothers and sisters for more than forty years. And their institution provided a place where Italian culture and Americanization could proceed at the same pace.

The history of Madonna Center parallels the ethnic parish itself. It was an invaluable institution that met the needs of Chicago's Italian Americans for a half a century. It provided a focus for all the national and ethnic feelings Italians had in them. But it also followed them through their new life in America. It educated thousands of new Americans through English classes, vocational courses, and basic hygiene. It provided a place for socializing and interethnic contact. Indeed, it helped the vast majority succeed in a new and strange land.

Chicago's Italians, unhindered by the cultural shock of World War I, effectively continued traditions through fifty years of war, prosperity, and depression. While German Americans quickly merged into the general population after 1918, Italian Americans kept their identity as Italians well past World War II. And it was the ethnic parish that provided the focus for their dual culture and loyalty. Father Luigi Giambastiani consistently maintained the need for Italian parishes like St. Philip Benizi. In 1945, he wrote Samuel Cardinal Stritch of Chicago: "Today it is too late to envision the possibility of a fusion of the Italian element with the general make-up of St. Vincent Parish . . . they are a group of their own, a complete ethnic unit, an Italian community entitled to a social standing of their own, to a religious atmosphere in keeping with their Christian way of living." He noted that "some evolution and assimilation will take place. . . but this, in order to be beneficial, will have to be by degrees and only individually as forced amalgamation and absorption of the whole group would bespeak, in my humbled opinion, a certain lack of respect to their *ethnic* identity." In handwritten notes on Stritch's negative reply, Giambastiani stressed that the Italian people still retained *"ethnic feeling"* after losing their native language. While closing these parishes might be "the easiest way out . . . is it the best for the soul? . . . Since the Church takes care of its souls, the raison d'etre of a parish is how these souls can be best served."[92] And for Father Luigi, it was the national parish that best served the Italian people. St. Philip's and other Chicago Italian parishes were largely successful in carrying on the native traditions of these proud people. Local societies and *feste*, parish priests and sermons, as well as parochial schools and settlement houses joined forces to provide a way station for Italian culture. For the majority, it was the only way station that acknowledged their ethnic needs.

But the national parish also Americanized its parishioners. Anthony Serritella, Jr., a Chicago lawyer and articulate spokesman for the third-generation Italian, noted that the "Catholic Church was *the* socializer for the Italian people." He called the ethnic parish "the invisible church—they brought the people together, in the process educated them. That's how the church would find out about their problems. If there were individual problems they would go out and help the individual. If they were social problems they would get involved in social organizations. I think maybe what the church did for them was let the people do something for the church and in the process of doing that solved a lot of their problems." Serritella felt that Americanization went on through the almost invisible structure that brought people together and opened their horizons beyond themselves and their local village. But it was the parish that was the focus of everything, since it was the one concrete organization with which the immigrant could identify. As Serritella asked, "What poor dirt farmer had a sophisticated organization to join? Or what dirt farmer had the opportunity to help a sophisticated organization? It's almost like the invisible hand of the church pushing these people into American life."[93] I maintain that the parish did exactly that. Local societies, schools, archdiocesan programs, and settlement houses all combined to ease the adjustment to American life. That they were largely successful is a tribute to the unique nature of the ethnic parish.

FIVE

The Decline and Perseverance of Ethnicity: 1930 and Beyond

Chicago remained an immigrant city through the 1920s. The city was still either two-thirds foreign-born or the children of foreign-born in 1929. Charles Merriam estimated that approximately 1,000,000 Chicagoans were Catholic, 429,265 Protestant, and 400,000 Jewish.[1] The Irish, Polish, and Italian segments were largely Catholic, while the Germans and Bohemians were equally divided between the two denominations; Scandinavians, native-born, and blacks remained largely Protestant.

German America declined during the 1920s, as "the interest of prosperous, middle-class city dwellers of German ancestry in German affairs largely disappeared."[2] H. L. Mencken, editor of the *American Mercury*, scorned America's Germans for abdicating cultural and political leadership during the postwar decade.[3] But despite immediate losses, Chicago's Germans continued to support "the German oak tree." One hundred thousand gathered at Municipal Pier to celebrate German Day in 1923. And three thousand gathered in Humboldt Park to support Chicago's *Deutschtum* in 1925. Sullivan and Adler's Schiller Building, which seated 1,300, housed Chicago's German Theater until it was razed in 1961. The Victoria Theater, at Sheffield and Belmont, supported productions through the late twenties and thirties. And as movies became popular, the Kino opened its doors on North Avenue near Halsted; it presented German films exclusively from 1931 to the early 1960s.[4]

But Chicago's Germans did not remain static. As they entered the American mainstream, they moved north and northwest of their original settlements. Census data reveal that Germans remained the leading foreign group in eighteen of Chicago's seventy-five communities in 1930. They were the second largest minority in thirteen of the remaining fifty-seven communities."[5] German foreign-born numbered 111,366 citywide, or 3.3 percent of Chicago's total population (3,376,848). Lincoln Park, with 11,318 foreign-born, was the largest German community, while Lakeview, with 9,383 was the second largest. Germans were also dominant in North Center, with 6,932 foreign-born (53.2 percent of the area's total foreign-born community): Uptown, 4,081 (16.4 percent); Irving Park, 4,184 (26.3 percent); Logan Square, 5,650 (16.7 percent); Portage Park, 3,422 (22.5 percent); Humboldt Park, 3,098 (12.2 percent); and West Town, 3,276 (4.6 percent). Although the North Side claimed the largest proportion of Germans, the South Side also had its share, led by West Englewood, with 2,902 foreign-born (19.8 percent), Englewood with 2,721 (14.0 percent), and New City with 2,070 German foreign-born (8.1 percent).

Some Germans moved out of the city to suburbia.[6] By 1930, Germans were the dominant foreign group in twelve suburbs with more than twenty-five thousand population. Those with the highest percentage were Aurora, with 6,885 foreign-born (or 14.8 percent of the total foreign-born population), Highland Park (10.9 percent), Joliet (9.4 percent), and Hammond, Indiana (10.7 percent). Berwyn followed with 4,515 German foreign-born, and Elgin, with 4,244 foreign-born. In general, Germans moved sporadically throughout the suburbs, never concentrating in one area. Their dispersion tended to further the process of Americanization and lessen the ties of ethnicity.

Between 1931 and 1940, 114,065 Germans immigrated to the United States. During the same ten-year period, 35,536 Germans returned to Germany. In fact, between 1932 and 1935, 14,182 Germans immigrated to the United States, while 17,696 emigrated.[7] Few were attracted to the rantings of Fritz Kuhn and his Nazi cohorts. Indeed, "the pro-German element in the United States during those years preceding World War II were a lunatic fringe, hardly to be compared in numbers . . . with the Kaiser's adherents of 1914-1917." Statistics indicate that only 1 percent of America's German population was militantly Nazi in 1938, while 70 percent were completely indifferent to Hitler's Third Reich.[8]

Chicago's Germans suffered through the Depression as much as any other group. Some who could not survive returned to Germany during the 1930s. Other Germans stayed in Chicago but lost their Germanity along the way. Otto Hilbert was one of these Germans. Born in the *Schwarzwald* in Bavaria, Hilbert immigrated to America in 1923. After living in Cleveland and

Chicago, he returned to New York to work on a South American steamer. He soon married an Austrian girl, and moved back to Chicago in 1927. Starting out as a baker's apprentice, he bought his own bakery at Sixty-ninth and Normal by the end of the decade. Riding the trolleys east and west as far as they would go, Hilbert sold his fresh-baked goods to all the riders traveling to and fro. Since he lived on the South Side, Mr. Hilbert had no opportunity to join German clubs or societies, although he did have his children baptized at St. Martin's Church during the late thirties and forties. He remembered a German hour on the radio during the 1920s, a group of German Hungarians who lived in Chicago in the 1930s, and the Goldblatt brothers who opened a chain of department stores in the early 1920s. While his brother read German newspapers, Hilbert himself abandoned them for English papers. He moved to Logansport, Indiana, in 1944, "a big German town . . . German newspapers, German schools, German churches . . .[but] not anymore, nothing."[9]

While the experiences of Mr. Hilbert demonstrate how one German became American, the experiences of other Germans show how Chicago's *Deutschtum* lived on at the parochial level. Indeed, it was the German parish that effectively continued this tradition through the Great Depression and beyond. In 1937, Cardinal Mundelein listed eight parishes as distinctly German: St. Michael, St. Alphonsus, St, Augustine, St. Benedict, St. Martin, St. Theresa, St. Mathias, and St. Philomena.[10] Mrs. Henry Hahn, who lived on the Northwest Side of Chicago for fifty years, recalled that parishioners at St. Alphonsus Parish were still arguing about the use of German in church services as late as 1935. She noted that "in our home it never made a difference if one was Catholic or non-Catholic." Indeed, her father, who had come to the United States from Bavaria in the early 1900s, became a Lutheran when there was no Catholic church to attend in his native village. He returned to Catholicism after working at the Alexian Brothers Hospital in Chicago.[11] The archdiocesan archives note that a 9:30 A.M. Mass was still celebrated at St. Alphonsus and the priests themselves were still involved in German affairs as late as 1970.

Other parishes also furthered German ethnicity during these decades. St. Michael's, Chicago's third German parish, continued to conduct evening services *auf Deutsch* in honor of St. Joseph through the 1930s. St. Paul's conducted stations of the cross in German, as well as special devotions to St. Benedict during the same decade. St. George's Parish celebrated its golden jubilee in 1934 with a German musical program.[12] And St. Benedict's Parish, which hosted the German delegation to the 1926 Eucharistic Congress, participated in the German exhibition at the 1933 Century of Progress Exposition. St. Benedict's continued to show an interest in things German through the 1940s, as it helped "distressed Germans" in the postwar era and was commended by Samuel Cardinal Strit as one of Chicago's leading German parishes. Finally, St. Gregory's Parish, on the Far North Side, asked: "Our parishioners? Who are they? Was this a German Parish? Were the Irish to continue to St. Ita's?" While the pastor despised nationalism, it ran rampant among the parishioners as late as 1937.[13]

As the United States prepared for another world conflict, Americans of all ethnic backgrounds joined forces against Hitler and the Nazi threat. But the hysterical hatred of everything German did not manifest itself as it had during World War I. There was even an increase in German language classes, as refugees flocked to America to escape the coming war. German pamphlets poured out of Washington, as the Army Specialized Training Program maintained German as one of its principal languages.[14] Indeed, America's *Deutschtum* continued to exist as it had before World War I in rural America. Walter Stahlke of Skokie recalled that his parents carried on Germanic traditions when he was growing up in rural Minnesota. "My parents had eleven children, and they taught us all German, which sort of demonstrates the pride they had in their cultural heritage—even though they had no acquaintances in Germany, never went there, and never corresponded, with anybody there. Yet they sort of cling to this German language and many of the foods they ate and things they did came out of this German heritage."[15] His wife Lorna had a much different experience, even though she grew up on a farm a few miles away:

> I was kind of ashamed of being German until we came to Chicago and met educated German people. The Germans in Minnesota were mostly farmers. They'd come to the movies, and you'd smell the cow manure on their shoes. When I grew up I never told anyone I was German. I didn't learn to speak it. That was World War II then. In Minnesota, we wouldn't have dreamt of joining a German organization. But when we came here [Chicago], our daughter found that her friends were going to Hebrew school, or Greek school, or whatever. If you didn't have an ethnic group, you were kind of out of it.[16]

Chicago was fairly open-minded about its German population during the war, although there were still many vestiges of anti-Germanism remaining. Joseph and Paula Cottmann, who came to Chicago in 1927 and 1929 respectively, operated a bakery and deli during the Great Depression. When hard times forced them to close in 1938, they found that many Americans had become anti-German. The Cottmanns would have been eligible for citizenship in normal years, but the State Department declared that no Germans could be naturalized for two years. Although praising Chicago as one of the few cities that allowed its German dailies to publish during the war, they also remembered that it was dangerous to speak German on city buses or sidewalks for fear of reprisals. As Joseph Cottmann noted: "We all get investigated. All our mail was opened, and some who had a little bit more mouth than they should suddenly would be gone, taken to a concentration camp somewhere. . . . But nobody bothered us, and we had no kick coming. We were free here. Every time I go to Germany and they ask my about it, I say, 'What do you think if there had been Americans over here then?' They say, 'We'd have put them in jail.' "[17]

Theresa Krutz, who supplied many valuable insights regarding Chicago's German community, recalled similar feelings. "My father had the Schwaben Stube Restaurant [3500 North Lincoln] and they did not suffer—they were never boycotted. It was neighborhood restaurant. I think one year they didn't have the Schwaben picnic and that there were problems in the schools—anyone who had a German name was automatically equated with a Nazi." As for the war itself, "there was feeling on both sides for and against it. The prevailing notion was there was nothing to do but condemn Hitler and that was what we were being taught. You couldn't imagine anyone getting into that kind of situation." When the war was over, the Krutzes immediately began relief activities to the Fatherland, and "our back porch was an assembly line for packages—my sister just went to Germany—and friends and relatives of my father greeted us as family and a lot are far better off financially than we are right now. But they still remember when they didn't have any clothes or food."[18]

As the twentieth century turned fifty, German Americans drifted into the American middle class. Between 1951 and 1960, only 477,765 Germans came to America; between 1961 and 1973, only 214,767.[19] Some Germans turned to local groups to nourish their Germanity. Mrs. Krutz gave a vivid account of the present state of the Schwabenverein:

> The Untersutzungsverein is dwindling rapidly. What you had to do to belong to that was pay $2 a month. When you die you get $150 to $200. And you put that in a couple of times over! We belong to that too. You pay your $24 a

year—every time someone died you gotta send in two more dollars . . . the *Sterbegeld*. There are a number of my cousins and one of my brothers and we belong—we keep putting money into this thing. About two years ago my cousin Rudi's son became 18 years old and Rudi's father—my uncle George—is very active. So what did they do but propose Jack for membership. Well it had been so long since anybody joined that they couldn't find a membership application! They finally had to Xerox one that wasn't in real good shape. There is just no more support. It's not practical, its no kind of insurance. But on the other hand it did keep this brotherhood alive.[20]

Other Germans established new societies. The German-American National Congress (Deutsch Amerikanischer National Kongress), with headquarters at 4240 North Western Avenue, was established in 1958 to promote German-American friendship, preserve *die deutsche Sprache*, and promote German culture among third- and fourth-generation German Americans.[21]

Germans continued to move further from Chicago into the far suburbs through the fifties and sixties. By 1960, only seventeen of Chicago's seventy-five communities were predominantly German.[22] The Near North Side decreased from 9.6 percent German in 1930 (7,657) to 2.7 percent in 1960 (2,026). Rogers Park decreased from 10.3 percent (5,944) to 5.0 percent (2,860); Jefferson Park from 19.7 percent (4,018) to 9.4 percent (2,587); and Austin from 10.9 percent (14,344), to 4.6 percent (5,787) during the same thirty-year period. Eastern and southern Europeans gradually replaced many Germans in Chicago's communities. For example, Russians, who moved into Rogers Park after World War II, numbered 6,756 by 1960 (11.6 percent of the total population). Italians, who forced out many Germans in Austin, numbered 13,384 first- and second-generation immigrants by 1960 (10.6 percent). Many Germans settled in such suburbs as Buffalo Grove, Elgin, Elmhurst, and Maywood. German stock constituted the dominant element in thirteen suburbs over 25,000. Arlington Heights numbered 1,627 foreign stock in 1960 (or 5.8 percent of the total population); Highland Park had 1,204 foreign stock (4.7 percent); Desplaines, with 2,633 (7.5 percent); and Park Ridge, 2,230 (7 percent). Statistics also indicate that Germans spread themselves throughout Chicagoland, with pockets as small as 670 in East Chicago to a large settlement of 4,548 in Elgin.

But despite decades of Americanization, German Americans still remained the second largest ethnic group in Chicago. Nineteen-seventy census data indicate that there were 49,990 foreign-born Germans in Chicago, with foreign stock numbering 235,665. The greatest concentration was the area bounded by Fullerton, the Kennedy and Edens expressways, and Bryn Mawr Avenue. Within this areas, the heart of Chicago's *Deutschtum* lay in the square formed by Belmont, Western, Irving Park, and Ashland, with concentrations west of the Kennedy Expressway and a few pockets in Hyde Park, South Shore, Gage Park, and the area just north of Marquette Park to Midway Airport. Mrs. Krutz recalled that "until a few years ago in the stores up and down Lincoln Avenue there were signs, 'Deutsch wird hier gesprochen' ['German is spoken here']. Germans were all over. It seems to me that the people on the block were German." Chicago's Germans also carried on a variety of activities: 38,490 trips to Germany; over one hundred *Vereine*, including athletic, gymnastic, and ski clubs; 1,000 soccer club members; and some 2,500 *Gesangvereine*. German businesses comprised more than a third of the firms in the Oak Mill Shopping Mall, at 7900 North Milwaukee Avenue, while three hundred German Americans studied German in Glenview and Palatine.[23]

Two defeats in this century's wars did not foster a sense of pride among German Americans. The Hollywood caricatures of the 1940s and 1950s depicted the German as obstinate and stupid. Yet, despite these reversals, Germans today are redefining their natural roots. More are willing to talk about their Germanity than remain quiet. The majority maintain that the Germans who marched in World War II were not marching for *der Fuhrer* alone, but for the Fatherland and all that it stood for. Most feel that the ordinary German did not know that concentration camps existed, while the American government did secret things on its own. Lorna Stahlke of Skokie stated it this way: "I'm proud of all the good things my German heritage has given me. The Germans who come to America are ready in every way to contribute to our culture, and they bring us a lot of things. You don't find better carpenters, bricklayers, metalworkers, than ones from Germany. They take pride in their work, and our country needs that more than ever before." Both she and her husband agree that "these ridiculous neo-Nazis are just starting the whole thing over again," while the typical German is a "gentle, sharing person who works hard for the good of all and in the process himself."[24]

While German Americans struggled to survive during the thirties, Italian Americans intensified their national identity. The Sons of Italy boasted twenty-five thousand adult members in Boston alone, with five thousand junior members by 1935. The Benito Mussolini Club attracted thousands of members, who saw in *Il Duce* a symbol of Italian pride and nationalism, a pride they did not have when they came to America. As Charles Trout observed, "instead of becoming more assimilated, much of Boston's Italian community manifested greater tendencies toward separatism."[25]

Chicago's Italian communities also survived the ravages of the Depression. By 1930, their numbers had increased to 73,950 foreign-born. The growth of Chicago's Italian community is mirrored in the growth of its seventy-five community areas.[26] The Near West Side remained the largest Italian community, with 17,161 foreign-born (or 44.8 percent of the area's total foreign-born population). The community included the Nineteenth Ward, as well as parts of the Eighteenth and Twentieth wards. West Town was the second largest Italian community, with 8,290 foreign-born (11.5 percent of the area's total foreign-born), which included the Seventeenth Ward of the city. The Near North Side still numbered 5,876 foreign-born (28 percent), a good majority of whom belonged to St. Philip Benizi Parish at Oak and Cambridge. East Garfield Park, just west of the Near West Side, numbered 3,773 Italians, while Armour Square on the South Side numbered 3,000 foreign-born. Other leading Italian communities included: Austin (2,449), Belmont (2,316), Lincoln Park (2,294), Humboldt Park (2,224), and West Pullman (2,220). By 1940, the Near West Side was still the largest Italian community, with 11,849 foreign-born (40.9 percent of the area's total foreign-born population), while Humboldt Park jumped from ninth to third, with 5,062 foreign-born (24.6 percent). Italians were obviously moving west of their original settlements. East Garfield Park increased its Italian settlement to 4,649 (35.0 percent), while Austin's community numbered 2,487 in 1940 (11.7 percent). The Near North Side lost the most by World War II, as the community decreased from 5,876 in 1930 to 2,397 in 1940. The communities of Belmont (2,275), Armour Square (2,139), and West Pullman (1,822) remained relatively stable during this period, while the community of North Lawndale directly west of West Town increased from 797 foreign-born in 1930 to 1,747 in 1940. The 1930s was a decade of change and transition for Chicago's Italians, as thousands moved out of their old neighborhoods into newer ones.

But it was the ethnic church that contributed most to the continuation of Italian culture and tradition in Chicago. The ethnic parish actively supported and nourished *Italianita* through the first four decades of the century. Father Luigi Giambastiani of St. Philip Benizi Parish actively supported Italian causes through the 1930s and 1940s, welcoming foreign dignitaries in his school and church. He made St. Philip's one of Chicago's leading Italian parishes. But even after the parish declined, hundreds came back to be married or buried at old St. Philip's. Father George Charbonneau, O.S.M., of St. Dominic's Parish, noted that a large number of parishioners returned to the Near North Side for these important liturgical events, even though they had moved miles away to Elmwood Park, Broadview, Park Ridge, River Forest, and other western and northern suburbs.[27] Indeed, the history of St. Philip Benizi Parish was a continuous unfolding of Italian ethnicity and tradition. And it was the Catholic parish which provided the institutions and resources to do precisely that.

But other ethnic parishes did as much. St. Mary of Mt. Carmel Parish fostered its annual *feste* in honor of San Rocco and Our Blessed Lady through the late 1960s. St. Anthony of Padua Parish, which welcomed Italian officials through the 1930s, became a "thriving Italian center for *religion* as well as for *patriotism*." Santa Maria Incoronata Parish hosted 6,000 Italian Americans for its annual procession in 1944. And Our Lady of Pompeii Parish, which still survives on the Near West Side, hosted the annual Columbus Day celebration for Chicago's Italian community throughout the 1970s.[28] Mr. and Mrs. Anthony Serritella, as well as their son James, testified to the enduring Italianness of Our Lady of Pompeii. Finally, St. Callistus Parish, at 2167 West Bowler Street (and the only Italian parish established by Cardinal Mundelein), nourished Italian ethnicity through the thirties and forties as well. It established a Department of Italian in its higher grades in 1937, celebrated a ten-day carnival, and fostered the traditional Sicilian table in honor of St. Joseph throughout the 1950s.[29] Chicago's Italian parishes fostered Italian ethnicity through the second half of the century. They were true way stations of Italian culture.

Chicago's Italians also moved to the suburbs as they improved their economic lot.[30] Berwyn and Cicero already numbered 1,025 and 3,632 foreign stock respectively in 1930. By 1960, Berwyn's Italian population had increased to 2,493, while Cicero's grew to 4,499. Highland Park numbered 1,439 Italians by 1960, while Joliet and Gary maintained a relatively stable Italian population, with 3,016 and 2,488 respectively. Oak Park increased its Italian stock to 2,227, while Skokie rose to 1,025 the same year. Illinois was the sixth largest Italian state in 1960, with 72,139 foreign-born and 249,873 claiming Italian parentage. Only New York, New Jersey, Pennsylvania, California, and Connecticut surpassed Illinois in sheer numbers of Italian Americans.

But as Italians moved to the far suburbs, they did not bring their ethnic church with them. It is significant that no new national parish was established after the original settlements were abandoned. While most returned to their ethnic churches for marriages and funerals, they did not bring these traditions to newer parishes in the suburbs. Recent studies indicate that Italian Catholics largely abandoned their old world attitudes in favor of an American-style church. But this church was largely Irish-orientated, with Irish priests and nuns imparting a Jansenistic and conservative viewpoint. Indeed, "although some unique social identity persists, the Italian cultural expression of Catholicism has undergone strong Irish influence and their value system has become very much that of the American Middle Class."[31] A survey of three generations of Italian Americans indicates that these assumptions are true. Mass attendance was always high on the Irish religious scale—over 95.7 percent attended Sunday Mass. While the first-generation Italian was not as faithful, the second and succeeding generations gradually approached the Irish ideal, with 83 percent attending Sunday Mass by the second generation. Church contributions were also a significant Irish-American thermometer of religiosity, a function that Irish priests originally berated the Italians for not doing. But Italian participation in this aspect of American church life also increased, as more and more contributed to the support of the church. Indeed, like the Germans who came before them, Chicago's Italians slowly drifted into the American mainstream.[32] But like the Germans of today, they are also rediscovering the roots from which they came.

The ethnic parish was a central factor among Chicago's immigrants during the first half of the twentieth century. It was a focus of all their ethnic feelings and needs. The national parish served as a true way station of ethnicity and Americanization through decades of war, prosperity, and change. Indeed, the Catholic parish was a necessary stop for the immigrant between the main stations of his ethnic heritage (where he was coming from) and the wider American culture (where he was going to). As the nineteenth-century railroad station provided necessary physical nourishment, the Catholic parish provided both physical and spiritual necessities. During the late nineteenth and early twentieth centuries, the German and Italian parish fostered ethnicity through traditional liturgies, parish celebrations, and numerous societies. As the century progressed, men like Charles Rempe and Luigi Giambastiani continued to foster ethnicity through a vast network of parish schools, church bulletins, and an active involvement in Chicago's political and economic life. At the same time, church leaders like Quigley and Mundelein established archdiocesan and nationwide organizations to further the adjustment of Chicago's immigrants. Indeed, Chicago's ethnic parishes faithfully served its immigrant flock for more than fifty years. Its thirty-three German and eleven Italian parishes were a vital force in the history of Chicago itself. Chicago has always been a city of immigrants. And the Catholic parish was a vital force in that development.

Notes

CHAPTER ONE

1. *Historic City: The Settlement of Chicago* (Chicago: Department of Development and Planning, 1976), p. 2. An excellent bibliography on the early history of Illinois is found in Theodore C. Pease, *The Story of Illinois*, rev. ed. (Chicago: University of Chicago Press, 1965), pp. 301-14. See in particular the following works: Clarence W. Alvord, *The Illinois Country, 1673-1818*, The Centennial History of Illinois, vol. 1 (Chicago: A. C. McClurg & Co., 1918-1920); Sister Mary Borgias Palm, *The Jesuit Missions of the Illinois Country, 1673-1763* (Cleveland: Sisters of Notre Dame, 1933); and Milo M. Quaife, *Checagou, 1673-1835* (Chicago: University of Chicago Press, 1933).
2. The Miami Indians, who occupied the Chicago area shortly after 1650, left the region around 1800 for the area between the Ohio, Wabash, Maumee, and Great and Little Miami Rivers in Indiana. The Potawatomi Indians (which included the Chippewa and Ottawa tribes) moved into the Chicago area shortly after the Miami headed east; they remained there until 1835, when a treaty with the United States government forced them to give up all lands east of the Mississippi; they subsequently left for a five-million-acre reservation in Kansas.
3. Marquette, a French Jesuit, steadfastly resisted the dreams of empire concocted by numerous officials during the French period of Illinois history (1673-1763). An example of such dreams was Robert Cavellier, Sieur de la Salle, who came to Illinois in 1666. His plan was to establish a series of posts to the mouth of the Great Lakes, linking the fur trade of Fort Frontenac on Lake Ontario to New Orleans. These dreams were repeatedly destroyed by Indian resistance to French rule (Pease, *Illinois*, pp. 5-10).
4. England acquired title to the French territory east of the Mississippi River in 1763. As Pease notes: "France had failed in the Illinois because she had not materials for building a strong colony. England had failed because by her regulations she defied great human forces" (ibid., p. 33).
5. See Robert L. Schuyler, *The Transition in Illinois from British to American Government* (New York: Columbia University Press, 1909).
6. The history of Illinois during the early part of the eighteenth century is very limited. Life was rough, and there were only a handful of French and American frontiersman in the territory. Inadequate census data indicate that there were

some 2,500 inhabitants in Illinois in 1800; by 1806 the figure rose to 4,300; and by 1812, 12,282 (Pease, *Illinois*, p. 70).
7. *Historic City*, p. 7. Chicago's first elections were held in 1826, with thirty five voters participating.
8. Statistical data for the city of Chicago are summarized in *The People of Chicago: Who We Are and Who We Have Been* (Chicago: Department of Development and Planning, 1976), pp. 9-10.
9. Bessie L. Pierce, *A History of Chicago*, 3 vols. (New York: Knopf, 1937-57), 1: 185; for an account of Chicago before 1848, see pp. 43-122, 172-221.

As can be seen from this quote, earlier immigrants were not always friendly to newer ones; Chicago's first mayor, William E. Odgen, called them "poor and vicious foreigners" (ibid., p. 186).
10. See ibid., vol. 2. For related studies, see Arthur C. Cole, *The Era of the Civil War, 1848-1870: The Centennial History of Illinois* (Chicago: A. C. McClurg & Co., 1918-1920), vol. 3. and Paul W. Gates, *The Illinois Central Railroad and Its Colonization Work* (Cambridge: Harvard University Press, 1934).
11. While the pioneers of Illinois moved west at the turn of the century, newcomers from New England, Germany, Sweden, and French Canada invaded Illinois's boundaries. The expansion of the Illinois Central Railroad was largely responsible for this growth, as 814,891 emigrants settled in eastern and suburban Illinois in 1860 (Pease, *Illinois*, p. 137).
12. Other ethnic groups in 1860 included: French (883), Swedes (816) and blacks (955) (*People of Chicago*, p. 11). See also Pierce, *History of Chicago*, 2: 9-13.
13. The history of Chicago's public works is admirable: first waterworks (1842), first sewers (1856), first paid fire department (1858), and first police department (1855) (*Historic City*, p. 27).
14. Ibid., p. 42.
15. See Pierce, *History of Chicago*, vol. 3.
16. Pease, *Illinois*, pp. 186-87.
17. Silvano M. Tomasi and Madeline H. Engel, eds., *The Italian Experience in the United States* (Staten Island: Center for Migration Studies, 1970), p. 163.
18. The panic of 1873 began a general depression that culminated in an ethnic march on City Hall in December of that year. But times were difficult, as 528 strikes marred the city peace between 1887 and 1894 (*Historic City*, p. 45).
19. Ibid., p. 60. The city itself tripled in area by 1889, when 125 square miles were added to the city proper on July 15 and scores of suburbs joined the protection that Chicago offered.
20. Not everyone agreed with this assessment of Chicago's potential. Rudyard Kipling exclaimed in 1900 that, "Having seen it, I urgently despair never to see it again. It is inhabited by savages" (Harold M. Mayer and Richard C. Wade, *Chicago: Growth of a Metropolis* [Chicago: University of Chicago Press, 1969], p. 272); and Lincoln Steffens stated a few years earlier that Chicago was "first in violence, deepest in dirt; loud, lawless, unlovely, ill-smelling, irreverent, new . . . the 'tough' among cities" (Lincoln Steffens, *The Shame of the Cities*, quoted

in Graham Taylor, *Pioneering on Social Frontiers* [Chicago: University of Chicago Press, 1926; reprint ed., New York: Arno Press, 1976], p. 35). But the vast majority would probably have agreed with Julian Street, a novelist, when he stated: "Chicago is stupifying. It knows no rules. . . . It stands apart from all the cities of the world, isolated by its own individuality, an Olympian freak, a fable, an allegory, an incomprehensible phenomenon, a prodigious paradox in which youth and maturity, brute strength and soaring spirit are harmoniously confused" (Stephen Longstreet, *Chicago 1860-1919* [New York: David McKay Co., 1973], p. 460).

21. Mayer and Wade, *Chicago*, p. 252.
22. In 1912, "even where the city administration does not recognize a black 'ghetto' . . . the real estate agents who register and commercialize what they suppose to be universal race prejudice are able to enforce one in practice" (Edith Abbot, *The Tenements of Chicago, 1908-1935* [Chicago: University of Chicago Press, 1936]; quoted in Mayer and Wade, *Chicago* p. 252). Census data indicate the growing importance of blacks for Chicago's future: 44,103 (1910); 109,458 (1920); 233,903 (1930); and 277,731 (1940) (*People in Chicago*, pp. 29-39).
23. Abbot, *Tenements of Chicago*.
24. Longstreet, *Chicago*, pp. 369-479.
25. Taylor, *Social Frontiers*, p. 188.
26. Many authors cite 1917 as a turning point in Chicago's history. "In a sense the story of Illinois and Chicago as a distinct social and economic entity may be said to end with the first World War. The organization of the United States for victory in 1917-1918 necessitated vast extensions of federal agencies in regions hitherto left to the state, to the municipality or to individual enterprise" (Pease, *Illinois*, p. 226).
27. Mayer and Wade, *Chicago*, pp. 290, 346.
28. Ibid., p. 348.
29. Steel mill and railroad agents moved South to seek black help in their respective industries. But old hatreds remained strong; riots broke out in the summer of 1919, leaving a half dozen dead and scores injured. "These old epidemics of hatred broke out anew between native and foreign-born, black and white, Jew and Gentile, Catholic and Protestant. But their virulence proved to be pathological" (Taylor, *Social Frontiers*, p. 239).
30. Mayer and Wade, *Chicago*, p. 316.
31. Some areas did not develop as fast as others. For example, a tract of land just west and south of Seventy-ninth and Western was laid out with sidewalks and utilities during the 1920s, but remained "dead" until after World War II (ibid., p. 327).
32. Berwyn increased from 4,000 residents in 1920 to 47,000 in 1930; Riverside was transformed from a quiet village to a twentieth-century suburb during the same period; Evanston doubled its population, from 32,000 to 63,000 in 1930; Wilmette, Winnetka, Glencoe, and Highland Park also shared in the general building boom of the 1920s (ibid., p. 342).

33. Charles E. Merriam, *Chicago, A More Intimate View of Urban Politics* (New York: Macmillan Co., 1929), p. 151. Merriam felt that the transition from foreign to American loyalty was difficult to determine; it could happen when a foreign-born married a native, when he learned English in preference to his own native tongue, or when he returned to Europe and discovered that he was a stranger to his own native land. Merriam noticed that with the rise of new nationalism in Germany, Italy, and Russia, "there is a strong sentiment of adherence not only to the mores of the fatherland, but also to the national political unity itself. This is not only true in the case of the new Germany, the new Italy, the new Czechoslovakia, but to some extent the new Soviet Russia" (p. 140).
34. The seventy-five community areas, which were first delineated by the Social Science Research Committee of the University of Chicago in 1930, were based on the pioneering work of the Local Community Research Committee, with cooperation of the U. S. Census Bureau. The following data are taken from Louis Wirth and Eleanor H. Bernert, eds., *Local Community Fact Book of Chicago* (Chicago: University of Chicago Press, 1949).
35. Merriam, *Urban Politics*, pp. 137-38.
36. For ethnics and politics, see John M. Allswang, *A House for All peoples: Ethnic Politics in Chicago 1890-1936* (Lexington, Kentucky: University of Kentucky Press, 1971).
37. Primary sources for the early history of Catholicism in Chicago include Gilbert J. Garraghan, *The Catholic Church in Chicago, 1673-1871* (Chicago: Loyola University Press, 1921), and John Gilmary Shea, *A History of the Catholic Church in the United States*, 4 vols. (New York: Merscham, 1886-92), vol. 4.
38. April 11, 1815, St. Louis University Archives, St. Louis, Missouri, quoted in Garraghan, *Catholic Church Chicago*, p. 28.
39. *Annales de la Propagation de la Foi*, 3:342, quoted in Garraghan, *Catholic Church Chicago*, p. 39.
40. Alfred T. Andreas, *History of Chicago*, 3 vols (Chicago: A. T. Andreas, 1884-86), 1:289, quoted in Garraghan, *Catholic Church Chicago*, p. 45.
41. The legal history of the diocese of Illinois (and Chicago) was complicated during the early history of the United States. The area that encompassed Chicago was first under the jurisdiction of Quebec (1675-1784); it then came under the Prefecture Apostolic of the United States until 1789, when the diocese of Baltimore was created as the first American see. When Bardstown, Kentucky, was formed as the westernmost diocese in the United States in 1808, Illinois and Chicago were transferred to its jurisdiction. Chicago came under the jurisdiction of the bishop of St. Louis in 1833, and the bishop of Vincennes, Indiana, in 1834. It remained under Indiana's jurisdiction until September 2, 1844 (ibid., p. 28).
42. September 2, 1844, ibid., p. 108.
43. St. Peter's moved to Clark and Polk streets in 1853, and to 110 West Madison Street in 1910.

44. Garraghan, *Catholic Church Chicago*, p. 136. Other significant events of Quarter's episcopate included the chartering of the University of St. Mary of the Lake in 1844 and the establishment of St. Xavier's Academy for women by the Sisters of Mercy in 1846 (St. Xavier's College at 103rd Street and Pulaski Avenue remains the oldest such institution in Chicago).
45. December 13, 1849; see Garraghan, *Catholic Church Chicago*, pp. 137-66, for a summary of Van de Velde's ministry.
46. Ibid., pp. 109, 173.
47. Ibid., pp. 169, 173.
48. It is interesting that among the ecclesiastical personages mentioned, there is little evidence of anti-Protestantism. Indeed, both Catholics and Protestants tended to help each other at this early frontier stage of Catholicism's development. This is clearly seen in a letter of Bishop Brute (Vincennes, Ind.) to the *Catholic Telegraph* of Cincinnati: "Of this place the growth has been surprising, even in the West, a wonder amidst its wonders. . . . Here the Catholics have a neat little church. Americans, Irish, French and Germans meet at a common altar. . . . They already have their choir supported by some of the musicians of the garrison. Many of the officers and a number of the most respectable Protestants attend. The Bishop on his arrival in the diocese had been invited to fix his residence among them" (May 7, 1835, quoted in Garraghan, *Catholic Church Chicago*, p. 79).
49. Ibid., p. 90.
50. *People of Chicago*, pp. 13-15.
51. James J. McGovern, *Souvenir of the Silver Jubilee in the Episcopacy of His Grace the Most Rev. Patrick Augustine Feehan* (Chicago: Privately printed, 1891), pp. 196-201.
52. Ibid., pp. 202-6. Protestants and Jews reciprocated by allowing Catholic congregations that had perished in the fire to do the same. See Mary Agnes Amberg, *Madonna Center* (Chicago: Loyola University Press, 1976), p. 22.
53. Italians established schismatic parishes in Hackensack, New Jersey, and Chicago (St. Anthony of Padua Parish, 1899). For a complete discussion of schismatic churches within Catholicism see Richard Linkh, *American Catholicism and European Immigrants, 1900-1924* (Staten Island, New York: Center for Migration Studies, 1975), pp. 100ff.
54. For a complete discussion of German Americans, see Colman J. Barry, *The Catholic Church and German-Americans* (Milwaukee: Bruce, 1952); Philip Gleason, *Conservative Reformers* (South Bend, Ind.: University of Notre Dame Press); and T. T. McAvoy, *The Great Crisis in American Catholic History, 1895-1900* (Chicago: Regenery Press, 1957). The general theme of these controversies was the place of Catholicism in American culture. While German Americans played a prominent role in many of these discussions, there were other more widely spread controversies: the theories of Henry George, the legitimacy of the Knights of Labor, the founding of the Catholic University of America, and the place of parochial schools in American society.
55. January 1, 1908, quoted in Linkh, *American Catholicism*, p. 29.

56. July 29, 1981, Barry, *German-Americans*, p. 154. President Benjamin Harrison replied to Gibbons in the following letter: "Foreign and unauthorized interference with American affairs cannot be viewed with indifference. I was very much pleased with the opinion that you expressed publicly in the matter . . . this is no longer a missionary country like others which need missionaries from abroad. It has an authorized hierarchy and well-established congregations. Of all men, the Bishops of the Church should be in full harmony with the political institutions and sentiments of the country" (pp. 156-67).
57. See McGovern, *Souvenir Feehan*, pp. 190-230; and Walsh, *Catholic Church Chicago*, pp. 1-6; also W. J. Madaj, "The First Archbishop of Chicago," *New World*, August 16, 1974, pp. 7-9.
58. Leo XIII declared that ethnic parishes could exist only for the *first*-generation immigrant; but Feehan, seeing their necessity, simply recognized their existence and allowed them to continue.
59. McGovern, *Souvenir Feehan*, pp. 288-89.
60. Ibid., pp. 281-82.
61. Charles H. Schanabruch, "The Catholic Church's Role in the Americanization of Chicago's Immigrants: 1833-1928" (Ph.D. dissertation, University of Chicago, 1975), pp. 190-230; and John P. Walsh, "The Catholic Church in Chicago and the Problems of an Urban Society, 1893-1915" (Ph.D. dissertation, University of Chicago, 1948), pp. 1-6; Ibid., pp. 324-25.
62. Ibid., p. 331.
63. Ibid., pp. 344-45.
64. Its predecessor was the *Catholic Home*, a weekly newspaper owned by Dr. McGovern, and edited by Judge John Hyde. Feehan bought the newspaper and transformed it into the *New World* on September 10, 1892.
65. Madaj, "First Archbishop," p. 9.
66. Feehan was also an astute Americanizer, who did not pass up the World's Columbian Exposition in 1893 to show off Catholicism to the world. Hosting a Catholic Congress at the exposition from September 4-9, he brought up such topics as labor problems, workingmen's organizations, blacks, poverty, immigration, public and private charities, as well as education (ibid., p. 8).
67. *New World*, September 10, 1892, p. 5.
68. Catholic statistics taken from Gerald Shaughnessy, *Has the Immigrant Kept the Faith?* (New York: Macmillan Co., 1925), quoted in Marvin R. Schafer, "The Catholic Church in Chicago, its Growth and Administration" (Ph.D. dissertation, University of Chicago, 1929), p. 56.
69. François Houtart and Jean Remy, *Milieu Urbain et Communauté Chrétienne* (Tours: Mame, 1968), pp. 143, 181.
70. *People of Chicago*, p. 33.
71. Houtart, *Milieu Urbain*, pp. 181, 143. Statistics for 1950 indicate that German parishes still averaged 2,098 parishioners per parish, while Italian ones averaged 4,579 (p. 181).
72. For the life of Archbishop Quigley, see Walsh, "Catholic Church Chicago," pp. 280-320; W. J. Madaj, "The Second Archbishop of Chicago," *New World*,

August 23, 1974, pp. 7-10; Schanabruch, "Catholic Church Chicago," pp. 300-25; and various issues of the *New World*, 1903-15.
73. *New World*, March 14, 1903, p. 6.
74. Ibid., p. 14; *New World*, November 26, 1904, p. 3.
75. Ibid., July 16, 1904, p. 4.
76. Ibid., February 22, 1908, p. 4.
77. Ibid., September 17, 1915, p. 10.
78. P. J. Muldoon, *Immigration to and Immigrants in the United States* (Chicago: J. S. Hyland and Co., 1913), p. 134, quoted in Linkh, *American Catholicism*, p. 37.
79. Edmund Dunne, *The Church and the Immigrant, in Catholic Builders of the Nation*, ed. C. E. McGuire (Boston: Continental Press, 1923), 2:6-7. The vast majority of Catholic thinkers favored this pluralistic approach. They particularly disliked the view of the Anglo-American majority, who felt that the eastern and southern European immigrant was inferior to the earlier northern immigrants. "America's crucible . . . Germans and Frenchmen, Irishmen and Englishmen, Jew and Russian—into the crucible with you all. God is making the American" (Israel Zangwill, *The Melting Pot* [New York: Jewish Publication Society of America, 1909], p. 37). Catholicism accepted the uniqueness of each immigrant group and refused to deny their individual differences. Through ethnic parishes and schools, Catholicism effectively met these immigrants' needs.
80. Joseph J. Parot, "The American Faith and the Persistence of Chicago Polonia, 1870-1920" (Ph.D. dissertation, Northern Illinois University, 1971), p. 301.
81. *New World*, September 16, 1915, p. 5.
82. *Official Catholic Directory*, 1910-1920. Quigley's 1913 Report to Rome included the following statistics on Chicago's Catholics: English—274,686; Polish—174,642; German—75,951; Italian—56,200; Bohemian—32,700; Lithuanian—24,600; Slovak—9,224; Croatian—8,000; and Hungarian—1,600. W. J. Madaj, "The First Cardinal of the Archdiocese of Chicago," *New World*, August 30, 1974, p. 7.
83. Madaj, "Mundelein," p. 7.
84. *New World*, April 16, 1915, p. 11.
85. Parot "Chicago Polonia," p. 301. The archdiocese was further reduced by the erection of the Rockford diocese in 1908, with the Right Reverend P. J. Muldoon, then vicar-general of the archdiocese, first bishop. Diocesan priests increased from 417 to 496 during the same span of time, while religious increased from 149 to 294; only 25 parishes remained without a resident priest. Quigley, who was also solicitous for the Poles of the archdiocese, allowed them to establish St. Hedwig's Industrial School for Girls in 1910, an institution that later became St. Hedwig's Orphanage. Quigley also consecrated the Reverend Paul P. Rhode as the first Polish American auxiliary bishop in 1909.
86. While Quigley remained a progressive on immigrant matters, he was a traditional bishop on others. He denounced Social Democracy as a "recent importation from Continental Europe," marked by "unbelief, hostility to religion and hatred of the Catholic Church" ("Social Democracy: Bishop Quigley

strongly condemns it," *Northwestern Chronicle*, March 8, 1902, quoted in Aaron I. Abell, *American Catholicism and Social Action* [South Bend, Indiana: University of Notre Dame Press, 1963], p. 150); he also condemned pragmatism as a "barbaric nudity," whose offshoots were strikes, tyranny, and absolutism (Schanabruch, "Catholic Church Chicago," p. 360); finally, he remained aloof from the woman suffrage controversy, and said, "We do not so much object to votes for women as to the methods which women are employing to reach the ballot" (*New World*, April 6, 1912, p. 4).

87. *New World*, September 23, 1915, pp. 1ff. A select group of fifteen pallbearers included six Americans, five Irishmen, three Germans, and one Pole; and the Laymen's Committee that arranged the funeral included twenty-seven Germans out of a total one hundred committeemen.

88. For the life of Cardinal Mundelein, see Paul R. Martin, *The First Cardinal of the West* (Chicago: New World Publishing Co., 1934); George W. Mundelein, *Letters of a Bishop to His Flock* (New York: Benziger Brothers, 1927); George W. Mundelein, *Two Crowded Years* (Chicago: Extension Press, 1919); Schanabruch, "Catholic Church Chicago," pp. 400-30; and various issues of *New World*, 1916-1939; W. J. Madaj, "First Cardinal of the Archdiocese of Chicago," *New World*, August 30, 1974, pp. 7-9.

89. The laity formally greeted Mundelein at LaPorte, Indiana, where Richard Gannon welcomed the new archbishop as "representatives and descendants from almost every country and clime" (*New World*, February 11, 1916, p. 6). The welcome in Chicago was even more tumultuous, as five hundred autos formed a mile-long procession down Michigan Avenue. Mundelein himself noted "how good God has been to the Church in Chicago; how it has become one of the choice spots of His vineyard. . . . What fools we would be to let sordid ambition, to let a lack of unity, to let a spirit of neglect and indifference blight the wonderful harvest that is preparing before our eyes" (Martin, *First Cardinal*, pp. 54-56). For a complete account of Mundelein's installation, see *New World*, February 11, 1916.

90. Madaj, "First Cardinal," p. 8.
91. Mundelein, *Two Crowded Years*, pp. 54-55; 164-65.
92. Martin, *First Cardinal*, pp. 71-96.
93. The society was founded by Blessed John Vercelli, O.P., in 1274, to combat the insults and blasphemies of the Albigensians and Moors. The society, which was approved by Pius IV in 1564, quickly spread through the Western world (*New World*, September 27, 1979). The first Chicago union was established in 1914, under the directorship of Msgr. Edward J. Kelley.
94. "His Eminence Addresses the Holy Name," *New World*, January 10, 1936, p. 1. Mundelein's attitude toward the society was clear: "The trouble with us in the past has been that we were too often allied or drawn into an alliance on the wrong side. Selfish employers of labor have flattered the church by calling it the great conservative force, and then called upon it to act as a police force while they paid but a pittance of wage to those who worked for them. . . . Our place

is beside the poor, behind the working man. They are our people, they build our churches, they occupy our pews, their children crown our schools, our priests came from their sons" (*National Catholic Welfare Conference Bulletin*, October 2, 1939, p. 3).
95. "Holy Name Big Brothers Take Care of 2,507 Boys in Past 12 Months," *New World*, March 11, 1921. Big Brothers counseled the boys and found them jobs. Mundelein stated: "Let us start a probationary system of our own, a Big Brother movement that is really worthwhile" (*National Catholic Welfare Conference Bulletin*, October 2, 1939, p. 5).
96. Samuel Cardinal Stritch continued Mundelein's policy that the Holy Name "be the core of Catholic Action in his lay apostolate" (*New World*, May 2, 1943, p. 4).
97. See Patrick Mallon, "The Society of St. Vincent de Paul," *Messenger of the Sacred Heart* 67, no. 9 (September 1929): 11-15; and Walsh, "Catholic Church Chicago," pp. 63-94.
98. Ibid.
99. Mundelein, *Crowded Years*, p. 203.
100. Address to Annual Meeting of St. Vincent de Paul Society, Palmer House, December 12, 1937 (*New World*, December 17, 1937, p. 5). Chicago conferences numbered 212 in 1937, with 2,594 members; they visited 64,689 families and spent $526,765.59 for depression relief.
101. Elmer Von Feldt, "Knights of Columbus," *New World*, May 28, 1976, p. 6.
102. The society was established to counteract the influence of early unions that were quasi-religious and anti-Catholic. The knights gained national attention during the Mexican Campaign of General John J. Pershing, when the society established nineteen Catholic centers from Brownsville to El Paso, Texas. The knights were allotted $25 million for charitable activities during World War I.
103. *New World*, June 26, 1931, p 4. Ethnic parishes also joined the Knights of Columbus, as they contributed thousands to general relief.
104. Edward J. Geiger, sports editor of the *Chicago Herald American*, noted that "In Bishop Sheil we have a champion, a man with a heart bigger than Chicago itself, a man with a kindly understanding, a man who does charitable work willingly and cheerfully, a man who guides hundreds of boys away from the path of corruption and turns their course into the road that leads to honesty and splendid manhood" (December 11, 1936).
105. Ibid., July 12, 1940.
106. Italians also established a CYO Community Center at Vernon Park on the North Side as a recreational and occupational center for young Italian immigrants. The center, which offered sporting facilities, arts and crafts, shopwork, weaving, dancing, sewing, radio engineering, and story hours, served over 5,000 boys and girls a week. See also John Gibson, "Another Kind of Night Life in Chicago Revealed," *New World*, September 22, 1938; and December 16, 1978.
107. Over 3,000 scouts participated in the 1932 Scout Retreat at Mayslake, Illinois; The *New World* noted that "1,200 gallons of milk and other foodstuffs were

consumed" (September 1, 1932). See also "A 'New Deal' for Scouting is inaugurated by the CYO," *New World*, September 14, 1933. The CYO wanted a troop in every parish and a Sea Scout Patrol in every troop two years old; it also offered four-year scholarships to active Eagle Scouts who passed a competitive exam.
108. "A Million People Greet Cardinal," *New World*, May 16, 1924, pp. 1-2.
109. Mundelein, *Crowded Years*, p. 146.
110. Ibid., p. 308.
111. Ibid., pp. 157-58. Mundelein's patriotism is clearly stated: "This is the kind of patriotism that we preach and that we practice. It does not consist of much waving of the flag . . . but in the present and the future, even as in the past, when our country needs us, we will be there to do our share and even more" (p. 150).
112. *New World*, May 18, 1937, p. 1; June 29, 1937, p. 1.
113. *Catholic Herald*, St. Louis, Missouri, October 6, 1939.
114. Cited in Schanabruch, "Catholic Church Chicago," p. 478.
115. Mundelein to Most Rev. P. Fumasoni-Biondi, apostolic delegate, Washington, D.C., March 7, 1927; quoted in James W. Sanders, *The Education of an Urban Minority: Catholics in Chicago, 1833-1965* (New York: Oxford University Press, 1977), p. 52.
116. February 6, 1925, quoted in ibid., p. 53.
117. "Brooklyn German Societies Bid Farewell to Most Rev. G. W. Mundelein, D.D.," *New World*, January 28, 1916, p. 1.
118. *New World*, May 12, 1933.
119. While Mundelein did bargain with his recalcitrant Europeans, he did not attempt to bridge the color line that swept across Chicago like a giant web. In a 1917 address to the black Catholics of St. Monica's Church, he said: "Because of the circumstances that exist in this city I am convinced that our colored Catholics will feel themselves very much more comfortable, far less inconvenienced and never at all embarrassed if, in a church that is credited to them, they have their own sodalities and societies, their own church and choir, in which they alone will constitute the membership. . . . It would be puerile for us to ignore the fact that a distinction as to color enters very often into the daily happenings of our city. I am not going to argue as to the reasons for or against this line of distinction which causes so much bitterness, nor will I say anything as to the justice or injustice of it. It is sufficient to say that it does exist and that I am convinced that I am quite powerless to change it" (Mundelein, *Crowded Years*, pp. 59-60).
120. Madaj, "First Cardinal," p. 8.
121. Schanabruch, "Catholic Church Chicago," p. 433.
122. Mundelein was both a national and international figure. He was a friend of Franklin Roosevelt, James A. Farley, Fiorello La Guardia, and Al Smith. Congress, which honored him for his patriotic services in 1939, noted that his contributions toward general relief "constitute an epic that merits the attention and study of every American" (*New World*, November 10, 1939, p. 1). United

States senator Scott Lucas (Ill.) called Mundelein "a true symbol of the American way of life" (*New World*, October 13, 1939, p. 1). But Mundelein also represented the entire Catholic Church in America. He presided at the Eighth National Eucharistic Congress in New Orleans in 1938; he was the first American cardinal to officiate at a Vatican beatification ceremoney (for Mother Francis X. Cabrini); he attended the papal election of 1939, which elevated Cardinal Eugenio Pacelli to the Papacy as Pius XII; and he became an international celebrity for denouncing Hitler.

CHAPTER TWO

1. *People in Chicago*, pp. 9, 24-26, 30-39. Foreign stock includes only the foreign-born and their children. The third and subsequent generations are counted as native-born; statistically, the heritage is lost in the census after the second generation.
2. See Michael F. Funchion, "Chicago's Irish Nationalities, 1881-1890," (Ph.D. dissertation, Loyola University of Chicago, 1963); Ruth M. Piper, "The Irish of Chicago, 1848 to 1871" (master's thesis, University of Chicago, 1936); Joseph J. Thompson, "The Irish in Chicago," *Illinois Catholic Historical Review* 2 (April 1920): 458-73; and Ellen Skerrett, "Irish Catholic Parish: Schools, Politics, Parades," *New World*, February 6, 1976, p. 15: "St. Anne's, St. Cecilia's—Distinctly Irish," *New World*, March 19, 1976, p. 15; "Irish Twins: Holy Angels, St. Elizabeth," *New World*, May 7, 1976, p. 27.
3. Thomas N. Brown, *Irish-American Nationalism, 1870-1890* (Philadelphia: J. B. Lippincott, 1966), pp. 34-35.
4. Skerrett maintains that the Irish clung to their parishes long after they left their original ghettos, for the parish provided a "sense of belonging," a place where friends, mates, and other Irishmen met and kept friendships (Skerrett, "Irish Catholic Parish," p. 15).
5. Lake Township grew from 3,360 inhabitants in 1870, to 18,780 in 1880; Hyde Park also grew accordingly. Feehan established the following South Side parishes: Visitation (843 West Garfield Boulevard), St. Gabriel's (4522 South Wallace Street), St. Cecilia (4515 South Wells Street), St. Elizabeth (4049 South Wabash), Holy Angels (607 East Oakwood), and Corpus Christi (4920 South King Drive).
6. Houtart, *Milieu Urbain*, pp. 208-9.
7. Sanders, *Education Urban Minority*, p. 113.
8. Skerrett, "Irish Catholic Parish," p. 15. Bridgeport alone numbered nearly 5,000 voters.
9. Richard O'Connor, *The German-Americans* (Boston: Little, Brown and Co., 1968), p. 376.
10. Joseph Lopreato, *The Italian-Americans* (New York: Random House, 1970), p. 36.

11. Germans played a prominent role in American history even before 1800. They established Germantown, Pennsylvania, as their first important settlement in America, in 1683; by the outbreak of the American Revolution, more than 225,000 Germans had settled the frontier from New York to Georgia, as far west as the Allegheny Mountains. Indeed, they were the first to enter Kentucky and Tennessee. See Albert Faust, *The German Element in the United States*, 2 vols. (New York: Houghton Mifflin, 1909), 1:1-285; Robert H. Billigmeier, *Americans from Germany* (Belmont, California: Wadsworth Publishing Co., 1974), pp. 7-20.
12. August 7, 1932, quoted in Rudolf Hofmeister, *Germans of Chicago* (Champaign: University of Illinois Press, 1976), p. 23.
13. Germans began the westward trek from the East as early as 1802, when David Ziegler, a former general under George Rogers Clark, became the first mayor of Cincinnati, Ohio. Many immigrants, following roads through Maryland and West Virginia, founded such towns as Canton, Massillon, Alliance, and Steubenville, Ohio; others, following a northern route, founded such Ohio cities as Berlin, Hanover, Strassburg, Dresden, Frankfort, Potsdam, Freiburg, and Saxon. By the 1820s, Germans were pushing west into Illinois and Missouri. Billigmeier, *Americans from Germany*, pp. 47-48.
14. Ex-mayor Long John Wentworth, addressing the German Old Settlers' picnic in Wright's Grove, on September 6, 1876, claimed that there were at least fifty Germans in Chicago by 1839. See Townsend, *Germans of Chicago*, pp. 24-25.
15. Chicago's brewery business grew rapidly, as eight brewers opened their doors by 1854; by 1870, the total value of Chicago's brewery business was $4,523,945. Pierce, *History of Chicago*, 1:89.
16. Faust, *German Element*, 1:585.
17. Townsend, *Germans of Chicago*, pp. 26-27.
18. See Townsend, *Germans of Chicago*, pp. 28-39. The German Forty-eighters, never a majority among the immigrants, opposed the entire established order, both religious and lay. Although they were first attracted to the Democratic Party, they later switched allegiance to the Republican since it had taken a decided antislavery position in the pre-Civil War decades.
19. Vivien M. Palmer, gen. ed., "History of Communities," 6 vols. (Chicago: Chicago Historical Society, 1928), vol. 6: "Documentary History of Lower North Side," Document 14. (Mimeographed.)
20. Emil Dietzsch, *Chicago's deutsche Männer* (Chicago: Max Stern & Co., 1885), p. 30.
21. On the early history of German Catholicism in America, see Lambert Schrott, *Pioneer German Catholics in the American Colonies, 1734-1784* (New York: U.S. Catholic Historical Society, 1933). Early statistics indicate that there were 952 German Catholics in all of Pennsylvania in 1757. German Catholics were the first to evolve a "national parish," as well as the first to be involved in a trustee controversy. A 1796 dispute led to an early schism, which was healed in 1802. A group of Austrians established the Leopoldine Foundation in 1829 as an immigrant-aid society for Germans and Austrians abroad.

22. Joseph Salzbacher, *Meine Reise nach Nord-Amerika in Jahre 1842* (Vienna, 1845), quoted in Emmet H. Rothan, *The German Catholic Emigrant in the United States, 1830-1860* (Washington: Catholic University of America Press, 1946), p. 14. Other Catholic cities included St. Louis (7,000 German Catholics), Pittsburgh (8,000), New Orleans (8,000), and Louisville (4,600).
23. Gleason, *Conservative Reformers*, pp. 19-23. Archbishop Hughes noted that "the German Catholics are exceedingly prone to divisions and strife among themselves, and with their pastors"; and a German priest exclaimed, "Oh, the disunity among the Germans!" (Jay Dolan, "Urban Catholicism: New York City 1815-1865" [Ph.D. dissertation, University of Chicago, 1970], p. 212). For a lively account of the New York Church at midcentury, see Jay Dolan, *The Immigrant Church: New York's Irish and German Catholics, 1815-1865* (Baltimore: Johns Hopkins University Press, 1975).
24. Gleason, *Conservative Reformers*, p. 9. Dolan maintains that the parish was more central for Germans than it was for the Irish, since among the German Catholics, more so than among the Irish, the local parish was the center around which much of their community activities revolved" ("Urban Catholicism," p. 215).
25. Dolan observes that the German parish was not a response to rural or urban conditions, but "the result of an intensely religious nationalism which measured faith in terms of language . . . once the religious nationalism of the German Catholics began to decline, then the ethnic parish began to dissolve" ("Urban Catholicism," p. 194).
26. *People of Chicago*, p. 11.
27. Approximately five hundred senior officers in the Union Army were German-born; these included General Carl Schurz, General Adolph von Steinwehr, General William Rosencrans, and General Herman Haupt. There were few German Confederate soldiers, as most Germans lived in the northern cities and countryside. Hofmeister, *Germans of Chicago*, p. 89.
28. Ibid. On Germans' reactions to Lincoln, see Townsend, *Germans of Chicago*, pp. 47-53; and Billigmeier, *Americans from Germany*, pp. 88-90.
29. Palmer, "History of Communities," 3: Documents 9-11. The first Turner Hall was located where the old Sherman Hotel stood (Dearborn and Randolph). The Lederkranz, the forerunner of the Germania Club, put on operas at the McVickers Theatre.
30. *People of Chicago*, p. 13.
31. Hofmeister, *Germans of Chicago*, p. 58.
32. Pierce, *History of Chicago*, 1:589.
33. Some 250,630 came in 1882 alone. Barry, *German-Americans*, p. 6. A significant number of Slavic Germans arrived in the United States after 1873. Joining a previous group who had settled in Sandusky, Ohio, in 1847, these Black Sea Germans settled in the Midwest, particularly the Dakota Territory. The history of these Eastern European Germans is complex, as it follows their settlement in Russia during the eighteenth and nineteenth centuries and their gradual immigration to the United States for a new life. See George Aberle,

From the Steppes to the Prairies (Bismarck, North Dakota: n.p., 1963); and George Rath, *Die Russlanddeutschen in den Vereinigten Staaten von Nord-Amerika* (Bismarck, North Dakota: Heimatbuch der Deutschen aus Russland, 1963). Barry (p. 6) estimates that 30 percent of the Germans who came to the United States between 1865 and 1900 were Roman Catholic; the majority lived in the triangle formed by Cincinnati, St. Louis, and Milwaukee. German Catholics were generally more conservative than their Protestant co-nationals; Catholics supported Stephen Douglas in 1860, George McClellan in 1864, and Horace Greeley in 1872; they did not follow Carl Schurz into the liberal Republican movement. Howard B. Furer, ed., *The Germans in America* (Dobbs Ferry, N.Y.: Oceana Publications, 1973), p. 53.

34. Wayne Moquin and Charles Van Doren, eds., *A Documentary History of the Italian Americans* (New York: Praeger, 1974), pp. 37-38. The most significant migration prior to 1880 was to South America, particularly Brazil and Argentina. But transportation costs and economic opportunities lured the majority to the United States after 1880. Nelli, *Italians in Chicago*, pp. 3-4.
35. The first Italian immigrants came from northern Italy, particularly Piedmont and Liguria. While some went to California and started profitable vineyards, others, from the poorer regions of Venetia, Latium, and the Marches, settled in the East and Midwest. But the situation changed dramatically in the 1880s, when Italian migration shifted southward, to the region known as the Mezzogiorno. Of 5,058,776 Italians who migrated to the United States between 1876 and 1930, 80 percent were from the Mezzogiorno. Sicily led the statistics, with 1,205,788 immigrants (29.9 percent of the total immigration); Campania (Naples) followed close behind, with 1,105,802 immigrants (27.4 percent). Lopreato, *Italian-Americans*, p. 35.
36. Humbert Nelli, *Italians in Chicago, 1880-1930* (New York: Oxford University Press, 1970), pp. 23-25.
37. Ibid.
38. Ibid., pp. 25-28. There were 4,091 Italians in Chicago in 1884.
39. Virgil P. Puzzo, "The Italians in Chicago, 1890-1930" (master's thesis, University of Chicago, 1937), pp. 29-32.
40. Barry, *German-Americans*, p. 57.
41. Tomasi and Engel, *Italian Experience*, pp. 196-97. Tomasi and Engel also list preconceived religious ideas, ethnic antipathies, and Protestant proselytizing as part of the "Italian problem."
42. New York's St. Patrick's Cathedral accommodated hundreds of Italians from 1882 on, when the parish celebrated an Italian Mass in the church basement; between 1882 and 1890, over 1,000 marriages and 5,000 baptisms were performed there. Ibid., pp. 173-93.
43. The Scalabrinian Pietro Bandini established the San Raffaele Society in New York for the care of immigrant women and children; by 1890, it had cared for more than 20,000 Italians who arrived on Ellis Island. Luciano J. Iorizzo and Salvatore Mondello, *The Italian-Americans* (New York: Twayne, 1971), pp. 180-81.

44. The Precious Blood Fathers, another Italian Order, established Our Lady of Mt. Carmel Parish in West Englewood in 1892.
45. Tomasi and Engel, *Italian Experience*, p. 192. Some writers disagree with this assessment. For example, Andrew F. Rolle, in *The American Italians* (Belmont, California: Wadsworth Publishing Co., 1972), p. 105 argues that the church taught Italians "how to be Americans by running away from our cultural heritage, our accents, our languages, our food."
46. Taylor, *Social Frontiers*, pp. 195-98.
47. Joseph Lopreato, *Italian-Americans*, (p. 89).
48. Taylor, *Social Frontiers*, p. 196.
49. Palmer, "History of Communities," 3: Documents 25, 16.
50. The western section of North Center was called Hamlin Park, bounded by the Northwestern Railroad, Addison Avenue, and the Chicago River (north branch). One resident recalled that "German was spoken on the street up to the time of the war. Since then, the Germans have given up their daily use of the language and the whole atmosphere of the district has become different" (ibid., Document 7).
51. Ibid., Document 8. Riverview Amusement Park grew out of this early German shooting society; two Germans bought the property and opened Riverview on July 2, 1904.
52. Ibid., Document 5. An eighty-year-old pioneer recalled in 1928 that when the area first began to develop, Germans would help one another raise their homes ($300 in lumber would do it). "It was just like a picnic, for everyone was interested in the building and helped the newcomers to settle. . . . Other summers the woods west of Western would be filled with picnic parties on Saturdays and Sundays and I and my helpers were kept busy selling beer" (Document 6).
53. Ibid., 4: Document 8.
54. It was a tough area at the beginning of the century, as this early ditty recalls: "De furder y'go, de tougher it gets—I live at Toity-toid an de tracks, De last house on de corner, An dere's blood on de door." Irish gangs fought German gangs, while the former fought black gangs to the east (ibid., Document 6).
55. Ibid., 5: Document 5. Some Germans moved south of Grand Boulevard to Greater Grand Crossing. A 1924 survey noted that "any attempt to divide the groups into neighborhoods on the basis of nationality seems futile, since racial ties are fast losing their effectiveness in maintaining the solidarity of the national group."
56. Ibid., 6: Documents 4-5.
57. Ibid. Although German-speaking, Austrians always considered themselves a distinct nationality separate from Germans. There was also a large number of German-speaking people in present-day Hungary, and many times native-born Americans confused them with Hungarians. A North Side resident recalled: "German-Hungarians came to this North Side directly from Hungary. They are Schwabian-Hungarians who speak the German language and often call

themselves Germans. . . . The real Hungarians came about fifteen years ago" (ibid., 3: Document 19).
58. Ibid., 6: Document 4.
59. Schanabruch, "Catholic Church Chicago," pp. 87-88. The best estimates for German Catholic immigration during this period come from Shaughnessy, *Has the Immigrant Kept the Faith?*, as quoted in Gleason, *Conservative Reformers*, p. 47. Between 1881 and 1890, over 400,000 German Catholics immigrated to America; between 1891 and 1900, 105,000 immigrated.
60. Barry, *German-Americans*, pp. 9-12.
61. Ibid.
62. Dolan, "Urban Catholicism," pp. 237-40.
63. Hofmeister, *Germans of Chicago*, pp. 209-13.
64. *New World*, October 3, 1903, p. 26; March 14, 1930, p. 26.
65. Schanabruch, "Catholic Church Chicago," p. 93; Sanders, *Education Urban Minority*, pp. 108-11.
66. Hofmeister, *Germans of Chicago*, pp. 170-75.
67. *People of Chicago*, p. 27.
68. O'Connor, *German Americans*, p. 366.
69. Barry, *German-Americans*, p.8.
70. O'Connor, *German Americans*, p. 375.
71. Shaughnessy, *Has the Immigrant Kept the Faith?*, p. 30.
72. Gleason, *Conservative Reformers*, pp. 14, 15, 49. German Catholics began to publish their own newspapers in 1837, to such an extent that there were over sixty-four weekly or daily newspapers by 1900. But between 1900 and 1914, fourteen publications ceased operations, and only three more began publication between 1900 and 1937.
73. Nelli, *Italians in Chicago*, p. 29.
74. The densest area of population was at Polk, Desplaines, Taylor, and Jefferson streets; by 1913, land values had risen to $300 per square foot, as manufacturing and business concerns moved into the area. Ibid., p. 31.
75. Ibid., pp. 13-21.
76. Palmer, "History of Communities," 4: Document 5.
77. Ibid.
78. The director of the South Parks System noted that, "With the exception of the Italian and Chinese communities, the district is scarcely more than a geographical area, possessing but little organized community life and depending almost entirely upon other communities for commercial and business centers. The Italians have preserved their old world traditions to a marked degree and thus have a well-organized social life" (ibid., 4: Document 1).
79. Archives of the archdiocese of Chicago, hereafter cited as AAC. Typewritten paper in St. Francis de Paula file.
80. Palmer, "History of Communities," 5: Document 1.
81. Ibid., 6: Document 8; 13.
82. Nelli, *Italians in Chicago*, pp. 73-86.
83. Ibid., pp. 94-97.

84. Moquin and Van Doren, *Italian Americans*, p. 307.
85. Nelli, *Italians in Chicago*, p. 72. While some Italians did take advantage of adult education courses at the YMCA, settlement houses, and the public schools, the overall effort on behalf of education paled to insignificance next to the German effort. Germans established parochial schools even before they built their churches, and had always been in the forefront of educational innovation, from the time of Friedrich Frobel, who introduced the first kindergarten in 1855. Leading Germans directly influenced the establishment of the public school system in Chicago.
86. Merriam, *Urban America*, p. 142.
87. Quoted in Moquin and Van Doren, *Italian Americans*, p. 360.
88. Nelli, *Italians in Chicago*, p. 98.
89. Both Germans and Italians adhered to the Republican Party through the early part of the twentieth century. But both groups failed to select a dynamic leader who could rise to the political fame of a Fiorella La Guardia in New York City. When an Italian delegate to the Democratic nominating commission appealed for an Italian alderman, an Irishman exclaimed: "Well, ye got the Pope, ain't ye? Wot'n'll more d'ye want?" (Merriam, *Urban America*, p. 138).
90. Nelli, *Italians in Chicago*, p. 104.
91. Ibid., pp. 112, 106, 127. *Cosmopolitan* magazine reinforced this view when it said, "There is no central organization. There are no blood-sealed oaths. There is no international association. The Black Hand is the generic name of innumerable small groups of criminals operating under its flag to blackmail and murder" (June 1909, p. 31).
92. Nelli, *Italians in Chicago*, p. 115. Graham Taylor was an eyewitness to one of these vendettas, when he saw two Italians run after a third, shoot him, and leave him for dead in the street. When Taylor tried to assist, the wounded man said that he would take care of himself and his attackers.
93. On post-World War I criminality, see ibid., pp. 130-54, and Moquin, *Italian Americans*, pp. 105-50.
94. See Andrew Jacke Townsend, "The Germans of Chicago," pp. 178-230, for a detailed description of the development of Chicago's German newspapers.
95. Hofmeister, *Germans of Chicago*, p. 166.
96. See Humbert S. Nelli, "Role of the 'Colonial' Press in the Italian-American Community of Chicago, 1886-1921" (Ph.D. dissertation, University of Chicago, 1965), pp. 26-80.
97. Ibid., p. 65. Durante also founded *Il Corriere dell' Italia* in 1888, which emphasized provincial over national news.
98. Ibid., pp. 38-41. Nelli maintains that "the press was probably the most powerful institution in influencing the daily lives of the immigrants . . . the newspapers reached a larger audience than other agencies, and did so more quickly than the benevolent societies and the Church" (p. 26).
99. Chicago's Italian newspapers generally branded Catholicism "a pagan cult, a fetish materialism of a pagan origin" (*La Fiaccola*, April 12, 1917, cited in Nelli, "Colonial Press," p. 90). Even conservatives like Durante condemned the papacy

as a rival for Italian influence, and there was a constant feud between them and the Catholic press.

100. Hofmeister, in *Germans of Chicago*, p. 114, relates that an old saying in Chicago was, "Put three Germans together and in five minutes you'll have four clubs."
101. Townsend, "Germans of Chicago," pp. 90-120.
102. The Chicago Symphony, which began as the Theodor Thomas Orchestra in 1890, changed its name to its present title in 1913. Since a large number of its members were Germans, there was some attempt during World War I to disband it. Although this never happened, four members were expelled and the conductor forced to resign for allegedly showing German sympathies. Hofmeister, *Germans of Chicago*, pp. 77-80.
103. "Der Gegenseitiger Unterstützungs-Verein von Chicago," *Deutsch-Amerikanische Geschichtsblätter* 31 (1931): 137-56.
104. The club welcomed distinguished Germans from abroad, such as Baron von Hollegen, ambassador to the United States from Germany, in 1902; Richard Strauss, the composer, in 1904; Albert Einstein in 1920; the Dresden Cross Chorus in 1930; and Dr. Konrad Adenauer, chancellor of postwar Germany, 1952. Hofmeister, *Germans of Chicago*, p. 100.
105. The Chicago archdiocesean archives note that the union was still active in 1926, with Nicholas Q. Kluetsch, of St. Augustine's parish, president; Fred A. Gilson of St. Benedict's, secretary; and Bishop Henry J. Althoff, of Belleville, Illinois, protector. AAC 12 1926 E 856.
106. *New World*, March 23, 1917, p. 1.
107. Ibid., November 21, 1919, p. 3.
108. While there were some counterparts for these societies in Italy, the Italian-American variety seems to have arisen on American soil, as a response to economic and social needs. Nelli, *Italians in Chicago*, pp. 170-72.
109. Ibid., p. 180.
110. Puzzo, "Italians in Chicago," pp. 65-68.
111. Moquin and Van Doren, *Italian Americans*, p. 330.
112. Nelli, "Colonial Press," p. 92.
113. LaVern Rippley, in *Of German Ways* (Minneapolis: Dillon Press, 1970), p. 69, notes that "nationalism vs. regionalism—these seeming contradictions are still the main sweeping generalizations that can be made about Germany." The Main River divided Germany into the stern, Protestant, cosmopolitan North and the fun-loving, Catholic, rural South. Bavaria was strongly patriotic to its own culture and history throughout the eighteenth century, while Hannover linked itself to King George's England. Small states like Mecklenberg, Hessen-Darmstadt, and Württemberg maintained fairy-tale-like governments at public expense. Austria always had a history of its own, although its Catholic background linked it to the fortunes of southern Germany.
114. Dolan, "Urban Catholicism," p. 192.
115. Hermann Hagedorn, *The Hyphenated Family: An American Saga* (New York: Macmillan Co., 1960), p. 27.

116. Dean W. Kohlhoff, *Missouri Synod Lutherans and the Image of Germany, 1914-1945* (Chicago: University of Chicago Press, 1973), p. 8. An extensive bibliography indicates a continued sense of being Saxon among twentieth-century German Americans. See John Foisel, *Saxons through Seventeen Centuries* (Cleveland: Central Alliance of Transylvania Saxons of the United States, 1965); Carl E. Schneider, *The German Church on the American Frontier* (St. Louis: Eden Publishing House, 1939); and various articles in the *Deutsch-Amerikanische Geschichtsblätter*, 1900-1910.
117. Palmer, "History of Communities," 3: Document 5.
118. John Bright, *Hizzoner Big Bill Thompson* (New York: Jonathan Cape and Harrison Smith, 1930), p. 104.
119. Interview with Mrs. Henry Hahn, Chicago, Illinois, May 30, 1978.
120. Interview with Theresa Krutz, Chicago, Illinois, August 20, 1978.
121. "Schwaben-Verein Chicago," *Deutsch-Amerikanische Geschichtsblätter*, 31(1931): 127-36. The earliest Chicago meetings were held at Klases Hall, at 70 North Clark Street. The society soon established the everpresent *Sängerbund* and embarked on a series of projects that culminated in the erection of Schiller Monument in Lincoln Park on May 15, 1886. The society eventually raised funds for similar statues in Humboldt Park (to Fritz Reuter) and Berlin (to Otto von Bismarck).
122. Another significant provincial group were German Hungarians, Germans who were Hungarian nationals but spoke *Deutsch* nevertheless. Otto Hilbert, whom I interviewed on October 25, 1977, noted that there were many *Donau-Deutsche* in Chicago during the thirties and forties. A monthly *Nachrichten der Donauschwaben* appeared in 1955 to disseminate news about these German Hungarians.
123. Lopreato, *Italian-Americans*, pp. 102-04; 135.
124. Ibid.
125. Marie Hallets, *Rosa: The Life of an Italian Immigrant* (Minneapolis: University of Minnesota Press, 1970), p. 209.
126. Palmer, "History of Communities," 3: Document 28. A parishioner from St. Philip Benizi noted that "there is as much difference between a Sicilian and a man from Tuscani as there is between an Irishman and an Englishman" (ibid., Document 27).
127. Serritella interview. Mr. Serritella also recalled that there was a sense that some parishes, like St. Michael's, were exclusively northern Italian, while others, like Our Lady of Pompeii, were southern. There "were enclaves where all the people from a certain town would stay. People from Tuscany at Twenty-fourth and Western, People from this town near Chinatown."
128. For a general survey of German Americans and World War I, see O'Connor, *German-Americans*, pp. 348-413; Hagedorn, *Hyphenated Family*; and for Chicago, Townsend, *Germans of Chicago*, pp. 113-77.
129. William E. Leuchtenburg, *The Perils of Prosperity, 1914-1932* (Chicago: University of Chicago Press, 1958), pp. 44-45.

130. Hofmeister, *Germans of Chicago*, p. 66,
131. William Stuart described this fanaticism in *The Twenty Incredible Years* (Chicago: n.p., 1935), p. 69: "Hunting the Hun became a pastime. The propaganda of hate was on. Chicago was doing her part as a great American city which never failed in a national crisis . . . there was a demand that a page in the school histories that praised the Kaiser be torn out. . . . Every day there was a report that this or that prominent German had been sent to a federal prison—false reports but serving a purpose."
132. See Roland G. Usher, *Pan-Germanism* (Boston: Houghton Mifflin Co., 1913), and Mildred S. Wertheimer, *The Pan-German League, 1890-1914* (New York: By the author, 1924).
133. The Ancient Order of Hibernians and the German National Alliance, who lobbied together to persuade Congress to avoid international alliances in 1907, celebrated St. Patrick's Day together in 1915.
134. Longstreet, *Chicago*, p. 456.
135. *New World*, January 8, 1915, p. 3; February 2, 1915, p. 2; April 16, 1915, p. 3.
136. Hofmeister, *Germans of Chicago*, pp. 63-64; Townsend, *Germans of Chicago*, pp. 113-15.
137. Ibid., pp. 128-29; 132-35; 137-40.
138. Numerous events led up to this declaration. The 1916 presidential election was a bitter campaign, as Germans turned to the Democratic candidate Charles Evans Hughes. They bitterly denounced Theodore Roosevelt as a "blatant swashbuckler," as well as "the ruinous policy of the president. He will not see Germany's side of the controversy. He forgets the millions of German-Americans among his citizens and the serious internal problems he is awakening" (ibid., pp. 145-48).
139. O'Connor, *German-Americans*, pp. 405-06.
140. Townsend, *Germans of Chicago*, pp. 166-69.
141. Philip Gleason, "Frederick P. Kenkel," *New World*, September 3, 1976, p. 6.
142. April 7, 1917, and June 10, 1917, cited in Nelli, "Colonial Press," pp. 180-81.
143. Ibid.
144. Niles Carpenter, *Immigrants and Their Children 1920* (Washington, D.C.: Government Printing Office, 1927), p. 119; Edward P. Hutchinson, *Immigrants and Their Children 1850-1950* (New York: John Wiley and Sons, 1956), p. 49.
145. Theodore Huebener, *The Germans in America* (New York: Chilton Co., 1962), p. 153.
146. Hofmeister, *Germans of Chicago*, pp. 79; 245-50. The first exclusively German theater in Chicago was the Kino, on North Avenue at Halsted; it showed German films intermittently between 1931 and 1960. By 1976, only the Mozart Theater, at 4614 North Lincoln Avenue, showed German films.
147. *People of Chicago*, pp. 30-39; Evelyn M. Kitagawa and Karl E. Tauber, eds., *Local Community Fact Book* (Chicago: University of Chicago Press, 1963).
148. Kitagawa and Tauber, *Community Fact Book*.

149. Palmer, "History of Communities," 3: Document 28.
150. Nelli, *Italians in Chicago*, pp. 189-91.
151. Moquin and Van Doren, *Italian Americans*, pp. 152; 361; 368-69.
152. Billingmeier, *Americans from Germany*, pp. 146-48. Julis Gobel, a writer for the German-American Historical Society of Illinois, noted that, "The real German malady is *Teilnahmlosigkeit* [public inactivity]."
153. O'Connor, *German-Americans*, pp. 431-42.
154. Hofmeister, *Germans of Chicago*, pp. 113-14.
155. "Schwaben-Verein Chicago," p. 136.
156. Krutz interview.
157. "German Delegates Meet the Cardinal," *New World*, October 8, 1920, p. 1.
158. Mary Filser Lohr, "Der Nationale Katholische Frauenbund," in Georg Timpe, *Katholishes Deutschtum in den Vereingten Staaten von Amerika* (Freiburg im Breisgau: Herder, 1937), pp. 64-67.
159. Schanabruch, "Catholic Church Chicago," p. 539.
160. Interview with Hugo Stobba.

CHAPTER THREE

1. *Centennial, All Saints-St. Anthony of Padua Parishes, 1875-1975* (Chicago: Privately printed, 1975), p. 18. German festivities were still evident at St. Anthony's in 1930, when parishioners hosted a farewell dinner for Monsignor John Dettmer. Fifty boys met the Monsignor at the rectory, where they sang a *Sonntagslied* and several German folk songs; over five hundred people attended the affair, many dressed in native German costumes (*New World*, March 14, 1930, p. 3).
2. Thompson, *Archdiocese of Chicago*, p. 453.
3. *Golden Jubilee, St. Augustine's Parish, 1886-1936* (Chicago: Privately printed, 1936), p. 304. The district lay outside the city of Chicago at this time, extending from Thirty-ninth Street to Eighty-seventh Street on the north and south, and from State Street to No Man's Land on the east and west. Known as the Town of Lake, it was annexed to the city in 1886.
4. Ibid., pp. 35-36, 43.
5. Thompson, *Archdiocese of Chicago*, pp. 497-99, 500-01, 407-09.
6. Ibid., pp. 491-93.
7. *St. Martin Parish, Diamond Jubilee, 1886-1961* (Chicago: Privately printed, 1961), p. 18.
8. *Golden Anniversary, St. Martin's Parish, 1886-1936* (Chicago: Privately printed, 1936), p. 21. Otto Hilbert, of Logansport, Indiana, testified to the enduring German character of St. Martin's, when he had his children baptized there even though he lived several miles south of the parish. Interview with Otto Hilbert, Chicago, Illinois, October 25, 1977.

9. Thompson, *Archdiocese of Chicago*, pp. 241-43. The souvenir program of 1926, *Old St. Joseph's* (Chicago: Privately printed, 1926) indicates that the parish declined from a high of 258 baptisms in 1886, to a low of 39 in 1926.
10. *Centennial, St. Michael Church, 1852-1952* (Chicago: Privately printed, 1952), pp. 16, 24. Statistics indicate that St. Michael's steadily grew, from 302 baptisms and 300 schoolchildren in 1860, to 387 baptisms and 1,791 school children in 1902. *Gedenkblätter zum goldenen Jubiläum der St. Michaels Gemeinde* (Chicago: Privately printed, 1902), p. 115.
11. Palmer, "History of Communities," 3: Document 11,
12. Thompson, *Archdiocese of Chicago*, p. 491.
13. Palmer, "History of Communities," 3: Document 1, 26.
14. Kitigawa and Tauber, *Community Fact Book*.
15. Thompson, *Archdiocese of Chicago*, pp. 542-43, 621-23.
16. Kitigawa and Tauber, *Community Fact Book*.
17. See F. L. Kalvelage, *The Annals of St. Boniface Parish, 1862-1926* (Chicago: Privately printed, 1926) and *Centennial, St. Boniface Church, 1864-1964* (Chicago: Privately printed, 1964).
18. Nicholas Dreher, a Rhinelander, started the first school west of the Chicago River the same year the mission was established. Known as The Little White School House, it continued the long-established German tradition of building schools before churches.
19. *St. Boniface Church*. Albrecht continued another tradition by establishing a mutual-aid society, the St. Bonifacius Unterstätzungs-Verein, his first year.
20. Kalvelage, *Annals St. Boniface*, pp. 31-56.
21. Ibid., p. 32. Venn also encountered the wrath of some die-hard Germans, who accused him of making the parish Irish, since he occasionally preached in English for the sons of his immigrants.
22. *New World*, April 22, 1936, p. 6.
23. The *Pfarrbote der St. Bonifacius Germeinde* provided valuable information on St. Boniface Parish through the 1930s; the only existing copies are located at St. Boniface Rectory, Chicago. Other information on Fr. Evers's pastorate is found in Kalvelage, *Annals St. Boniface*, pp. 57-108; and *St. Boniface Parish*.
24. *Pfarrbote*, June 5, 1904.
25. Ibid., September 1902, p. 13; June 1907.
26. Ibid., January 1907.
27. Kalvelage, *Annals St. Boniface*, p. 83.
28. Ibid., pp., 101-20.
29. *St. Boniface Church*.
30. Kalvelage, *Annals St. Boniface*, p. 103.
31. Mundelein to C. A. Rempe, August 25, 1917, AAC 4 1917 20.
32. *St. Boniface Church*.
33. *St. Aloysius Parish Diamond Jubilee, the Seventy-Five Years of St. Aloysius Parish, 1884-1959* (Chicago: Privately printed, 1959); Schanabruch, "Catholic Church Chicago," pp. 290-95.

34. Rev. A. J. Thiele to Archbishop Mundelein, May 1, 1918, AAC 5 1918 M 342.
35. Although Thompson, in *Archdiocese of Chicago* (p. 641), considers the parish German and English, there is no indication other than this reference that Germanity survived at St. William's. *St. Williams Fiftieth Anniversary 1916-1966* (Chicago: Privately printed, 1961) does not even mention a German presence in its brief history of the parish.
36. Thompson, *Archdiocese of Chicago*, p. 535; AAC St. Philomena Files; interview with St. Philomena secretary, Chicago, Illinois, May 6, 1976.
37. Thompson, *Archdiocese of Chicago*, pp. 429-31.
38. Ibid., pp. 523-24. Although St. Henry's was usually classified as a German parish, it was formally known as the Church of the Luxemburgers. As a contemporary noted, "The Ridge St. Henry's was a kind of clearing house for the natives of Luxembourg. Emigrating into this country the Luxemburger's first protracted stopover was usually the Ridge. From here if he did not remain he went to . . . wherever a settlement of his countrymen was to be found" (Palmer, "History of Communities," 3: Document 18).
39. *The St. Gregory Story, 1904-1954* (Chicago: Privately printed, 1954), pp. 2, 36; *Album mit Illustrationen zur zehnten Jahresfeier der Gründung der St. Gregorius Gemeinde, 1904-1914* (Chicago: Privately printed, 1914), p. 10.
40. *Historic City*, p. 66. See also *Golden Jubilee Celebration, St. Benedict Parish, 1902-1952* (Chicago: Privately printed, 1952); "St. Benedict Parish Plans Seventy-Fifth Jubilee Celebration," *New World*, July 8, 1977, p. 1; and Thompson, *Archdiocese of Chicago*, pp. 588-89.
41. Archbishop Mundelein to Rev. Joseph Zimmerman, January 19, 1917, AAC 4 1917 2 3.
42. German parishioners to Archbishop Mundelein; AAC 5 1919 M 34.
43. Archbishop Mundelein to C. A. Rempe, November 16, 1916, AAC 3 1916 R 25.
44. M. E. Huhnke and Catherine Baer to Msgr. Hoban, April 30, 1917, AAC 4 1917 H 95.
45. Schanabruch, "Catholic Church Chicago," pp. 291-92.
46. St. Benedict's was still predominantly German during World War I, as "nerves frayed and tempers flared" during the four-year conflict. Most parishioners remained loyal to Germany and Austria, since the majority still had relatives in those countries. *St. Benedict's Golden Jubilee*, pp. 21-22.
47. Ibid., p. 30; *New World*, March 28, 1947, p. 1.
48. Mrs. Henry Hahn, interview. *St. Michael's Diamentes Jubileum 1852-1927* (Chicago: Privately printed, 1927) notes that "though the World War caused a great change of attitude toward the use of the German language in the country, St. Michael's still maintains its title of a German parish . . . it has been . . . consistently true to its early tradition." Devotions continued to be conducted in German throughout the 1930s; and even as late as 1966 St. Michael's celebrated its 100th anniversary with a Meister Brau Westphalian horse team provided by the Peter Hand Brewery (*New World*, November 13, 1966, p. 1).

49. Theresa Krutz, interview.
50. *St. Augustine Golden Jubilee*, pp. 117-18; 215.
51. Angel Guardian Orphanage, a German institution from its foundation, was established by the Board of Administration of St. Boniface Cemetery on ten acres of land in Rosehill. The pastors of St. Henry Parish serviced the orphanage from 1865 to 1882, after which the archbishop of Chicago appointed priests to minister to its needs. Palmer, "History of Communities," 3: Document 19.
52. St. Boniface *Pfarrbote*, July 1907, p. 21; June 1907, p. 11. St. Boniface noted that "we have given in to the assimilation process, but we have lost much and won nothing . . . it therefore follows that we should stop this process more than speed it up" (*Pfarrbote*, July 1907, p. 21).
53. Pastoral letters of C. A. Rempe, 1919-1926, St. Boniface Rectory, Chicago, Illinois.
54. St. Augustine's *Pfarrbote* announced a "Deutsche Retreat in Mayslake" as late as December 1926.
55. Thompson, *Archidocese of Chicago*, p. 361. The *New World* noted on April 22, 1936, p. 6, that "St. Boniface has been a favorite shrine of old settlers of Chicago." It pointed to the famous skull of St. Ann, whose relics came to St. Boniface from Fueren's miraculous shrine in Germany. St. Augustine's celebrated an annual *Herbstfest* (fall festival), the objective of which was "to bring former parishioners back to the parish to awaken in them past times and joys" (*Pfarrbote*, October 1926, p. 22).
56. *St. Benedict Golden Jubilee*, p. 30; *New World*, January 31, 1930, p. 31; *Gedenkblatter*, p. 5.
57. *St. Augustine Golden Jubilee*, p. 230. St. Clement's celebrated its own feast day with a "carol for St. Clement"; although newspaper articles do not delineate the feast, it would seem that it was Germanic in origin. See "North Side Parish Plans Big Festival," *New World*, October 10, 1919, p. 3; "St. Clement's Day North Side Church in Unique Historic Celebration, *New World*, November 21, 1919, p. 3.
58. St. Boniface *Pfarrbote*, June 1902, p. 11.
59. Ibid., August 1902. Some of this rivalry was productive: "It is hoped that there will be a return of the old-time rivalry for the offices because rivalry means growth and growth means a greater number of Catholic young men enrolled" (*New World*, January 16, 1904, p. 26). St. Augustine's listed 16 *Sodalitäten und Vereine* in 1911, including the St.-Aloysius-Junglings-Sodalität, the Marianische Jungfrauen Sodalität, and the Third Order of St. Francis. The latter began in 1886, introduced an English branch in 1920, but kept its German branch through 1940 (*St. Augustine Golden Jubilee*, pp. 270-72).
60. Theresa Krutz, interview.
61. Der *Pfarrbote*, "Fronleichnam," June 1920, p. 3; Rippley, *Of German Ways*, pp. 126-27.
62. Theresa Krutz, interview.

63. *Der Pfarrbote*, February 1920, p. 36; *St. Augustine Golden Jubilee*, pp. 275-79.
64. *St. Augustine Golden Jubilee*, pp, 285-86; 205-10.
65. Ibid., pp. 22, 219-20.
66. *Der Pfarrbote*, March 1922, p. 32.
67. *St. Aloysius Parish*, pp. 96-109.
68. St. Augustine's established a City Improvement Club in 1901 to instruct parishioners on social and political questions (*St. Augustine Golden Jubilee*, p. 105). Father Rempe of St. Boniface put political pressure on a local politician: "I could tell our alderman, unless you do this or that, there are going to be eight hundred solid votes against you at the next election . . . every man and woman should be a registered voter" (Fr. Rempe Letters, 1920).
69. Rippley, *Of German Ways*, pp. 157-60; Billigmeier, *Americans from Germany*, pp. 84-130.
70. See Sanders, *Education Urban Minority*, pp. 55-60.
71. Ibid., p. 61.
72. *Der Pfarrbote*, September 1911, p. 9.
73. Mrs. Henry Hahn, interview.
74. Theresa Krutz, interview. It is interesting that German Lutheran schools had the same objective as Catholic parochial schools; namely, the retention of German as a viable language and culture. Lutheran schools devoted up to ten hours to German reading and up to five hours to German speaking and song, while relegating English to a mere seven hours a week. Chicago's Missouri Lutheran schools reached their peak in 1927-1928, when the synod operated forty-five such schools in the Chicago area alone. Although this number dropped to forty-three schools in 1930, there were still 5,823 students enrolled in Chicago's Missouri Lutheran schools. Dean Wayne Kohlhoff, "Missouri Synod Lutherans and the Image of Germany, 1914-1945" (Ph.D. dissertation, University of Chicago, 1973), pp. 118-61.
75. *St. Aloysius Parish*, p. 36; *St. Martin Parish*, pp. 28-32. "There is no question but that this higher source of education made St. Boniface School very attractive and brought about . . . the healthful growth of the parish" (Kalvelage, *Annals of St. Boniface*, p. 149). St. Benedict's commercial program was designed to make stenographers of young women by the age of sixteen; when the government refused to accredit it, Monsignor Fasnacht decided to supplant its courses with a regular four-year high school, a dream that did not reach realization until 1950 (*St. Benedict Golden Jubilee*, p. 40).
76. *St. Michael's Church*, p. 50. St. Aloysius began a three-year high school program in 1903, which continued until 1932; its sister school was Josephinum High School, at 1501 North Oakley Boulevard. Opening in 1890 with 75 girls, Josephinum grew to a four-year high school by 1909, with a two-year commercial course on the side; its enrollment increased to 600 by 1959. *St. Aloysius Parish*, p. 40.
77. *St. Augustine Golden Jubilee*, p. 255.
78. "Kolping Societies Celebrate 100th Anniversary in Nation," *New World*, August 21, 1970, p. 1.

79. Hans Dexl, "Die Kolpingsvereine in den Vereinigsten," in George Timpe; *Katholishes Deutschtum*, pp. 156-61.
80. Ibid., p. 158. The Kolping Society also sponsored three newspapers during its century-long development: *St. Joseph Post* (Dayton, Ohio), 1896-98; *Arbeiterfreund*, 1919-21; and *Kolping Banner*, 1929-81.
81. Fr. Matthias E. Fischer, Chicago Kolping House, private publication, 1962. The Society's headquarters then moved to 5826 North Elston Avenue, where it continues to function as one of Chicago's few remaining German societies. See also, "Kolping House nears 90-Year Milestone," *New World*, November 9, 1962, p. 3; "Kolping House Hoping for Second Chance," August 21, 1970, p. 4; and "Says Kolping Group Fires, Inspires Youth of Germany," August 24, 1941, p. 2.
82. Fr. Hermann Weber to Mundelein, March 19, 1923; AAC 7 1923 W 7; 1926 W 7.
83. "Kolping House Marks Seventy-fifth Year—Here at Convention This Week," *New World*, August 29, 1947, p. 1.
84. St. Philomena Files, AAC 5 1918 R 26.
85. *St. Augustine Golden Jubilee*, p. 309; *Der Pfarrbote*, March 1921, p. 25.
86. *St. Michael Diamond Jubilee*, p. 24. At St. Benedict's, "nerves frayed and tempers flared" during the war (*St. Benedict Golden Jubilee*, pp. 21-22); and at St. Glare's in Woodlawn, "some of their number tried to uphold the German element and this of course caused friction" (Palmer, "History of Communities," 3: Document 3a).
87. *New World*, October 8, 1920, p. 1.
88. See *Achtundzwanzigste internationaler eucharistischer Kongress zu Chicago, Ill., U.S.A.* (Techny, Ill.: Mission Press, 1926); *XXVIII International Eucharistic Congress* (Chicago: Privately printed, 1926); *New World*, June 18, 1926, pp. 8-30.

CHAPTER FOUR

1. Thompson, *Archdiocese*, pp. 481-83.
2. Ibid., p. 555; *St. Mary of Mt. Carmel Church, 1892-1976* (Chicago: Privately printed, 1976); and Palmer, "History of Communities," vol. 6: "History of West Englewood Community," Documents 7-7a.
3. Thompson, *Archdiocese*, pp. 578-79.
4. "Maria Incoronata Parish: Chicago Melting Pot," *New World*, February 17, 1915, p. 1.
5. Thompson, *Archdiocese*, pp. 579-80.
6. *New World*, September 2, 1938.
7. Fr. Vincent J. Giese, "A Little Bit of Italy," *Chicago Catholic*, June 23, 1978, pp. 10-11.
8. *New World*, March 15, 1944, p. 12.

9. St. Philip Benizi is the focal point of my study of Chicago's Italian parishes. Its records and archives were made available through the kind assistance of Fr. Conrad Borntrager, O.S.M., Our Lady of Sorrows Basilica, 3121 West Jackson Boulevard; St. Philip's records are now kept at Assumption Parish, 323 West Illinois Street.
10. St. Philip's institutional history is recorded in *The Silver Book, by the Servite Fathers, for the Twenty-Fifth Anniversary of St. Philip Benizi Church* (Chicago: Privately printed, 1929); and *Golden Jubilee Celebration* (Chicago: Privately printed, 1954).
11. *The Golden Jubilee St. Philip Benizi Parish*, noted that when the church was finally ready for worship, "you could see that they loved the Church; they felt that St. Philip was not only the House of God, but also their Church, like the Church of their home town, under whose shadow they were born and raised way back in Sicily" (p. 12).
12. Palmer, "History of Communities," vol. 3: "History of Lower North Side," Document 61.
13. Father Luigi stated: "It will neutralize, for the time being, their proselytizing efforts and give a chance to hear Mass on Sunday to hundreds of Italians who would not come to St. Philip at present on account of the distance" (L. Giambastiani to Msgr. Hoban, January 25, 1921 AAC 6 1921 H 220).
14. Palmer, "History of Communities," 3: Document 27a, Document 13.
15. The 1900 census listed 30,150 blacks in Chicago, out of a total population of 1,698,575. By 1920, the number of blacks had increased to 109,458, and by 1930 to 233,903. Hill, *People of Chicago*, pp. 24-36.
16. Fr. Liugi Giambastiani to Chicago Housing Authority, September 30, 1942, Archives of St. Philip Benizi parish (hereafter ASPB), II, VI, 59.
17. Palmer, "History of Communities," 3: Document 27.
18. Holy Rosary served the needs of a Venetian colony, whose parishioners had moved west from Santa Maria Addolorata, and "the history of Holy Rosary Parish is very much the history of the Italian people of the West Side of Chicago" (Thompson, *Archdiocese*, p. 612).
19. Ibid., p. 645.
20. Father Anthony Cogo introduced the teaching of Italian in the parochial grammar school in 1937. Italian *feste* attracted parishioners through the 1950s. But by 1976, the parish was only 15 percent Italian, with 85 percent Spanish. *New World*, September 11, 1936, p. 10; March 25, 1955, p. 8.
21. *New World*, September 18, 1936, p. 3.
22. AAC, in files under St. Francis de Paula Parish.
23. Fr. Angelo Barsi to Fr. Luigi Giambastiani, January 1925, ASPB, II, VI, 51.
24. ASPB, October 2, 1935, II, VI, 41; September 20, 1935, II, 41; August 15, 1936, II, 41.
25. Serritella interview.
26. The parish continued to trouble Mundelein through the 1920s. The archbishop consistently denied funeral services to many San Rocco parishioners "because

of the known lawlessness of their lives" (Cardinal Mundelein to M.R. Fumasoni Biondi, September 29, 1926 AAC 12 1926 F225).
27. *Il Calendario Italiano* (hereafter *ICI*), October 1923, p. 21.
28. The bulletin notes: "The Church of St. Philip is and ought to be considered the Italian Church on the North Side. This means that the Italians ought to go to Mass and all the functions at St. Philip's, and not other churches, just as the Irish go to St. Dominic's, and the Germans to St. Joseph's or St. Michael's. For this reason the priests of St. Dominic are Irish, while those of St. Joseph's or St. Michael's are German; and while concord and harmony is a beautiful and holy thing, it is also just that each one to be with his own kind. It is true that some *idealists* dream of an American millenium when all races will be fused into one new American race—but in the meantime it is good that each one think of his own, while looking towards the future, but always with one's feet on the ground in the present. And the needs of the present demand that the Italians go to the Italian Church . . . Italians be united to your churches . . . give your offerings to the Italian churches who need it . . . the Irish, Polish, and Germans work for their own churches, do the same yourself . . . the Italian church ought to be not only a symbol of glory for you, but a symbol of union, of faith, and of race" ("San Filippe e La Vostra Chiesa," *ICI*, June 1922, pp. 8-9).
29. Ibid., p. 9.
30. "Ai Nostri Amici Lontani," *ICI*, May 1925, pp. 8-10.
31. St. Philip Benizi baptismal records, now kept at St. Dominic Parish, 257 West Locust Avenue, Chicago, Illinois.
32. Serritella interview.
33. Palmer, History of Communities, 3: Document 27.
34. *ICI*, September 1926, p. 12.
35. ASPB, I, II, 6; II, V, 29.
36. *ICI*, September 1922, p. 6; September 18, 1938, p. 2.
37. ASPB, II, VIII, 70.
38. *ICI*, September 1923, p. 9. The parish souvenir of 1954 notes that "these festivals had the good effect of keeping the masses of immigrants faithful to their traditions and the devotions to the Home Saints, which couldn't but strengthen their ties and affiliation to Mother Church" (ibid.).
39. Ibid., December 1925, p. 6; September 1937, pp. 4-5.
40. Serritella interview.
41. ASPB, June 14, 1939, II, 41.
42. Ibid.
43. "Alla Gioventù Italo-Americana che sente la vocazione al Sacerdozio," *ICI*, September 1937.
44. ASPB, II, V, 29.
45. Ibid., II, 50.
46. *ICI*, April 1924, p. 13. *ICI* also noted that Mussolini himself strongly supported a Catholic Italy: "I protect Catholicism and because I desire to collaborate with it. . . . Italy would be annihilated if it did not have its religion and the morality that it teaches" (December 1923, p. 15).

47. ASPB, II, 105.
48. *ICI*, October 1926, pp. 9-10; December 1924, pp. 11-12; October 1925, p. 6.
49. Taylor, *Social Frontiers*, p. 194.
50. *ICI*, April 1924, p. 13. Graham Taylor expressed these sentiments when he said: "Only Italy fully interprets the Italian in America. Its everywhere present art account for the love of beauty prevailing more among Italians than in any other race" (Taylor, *Social Frontiers*, p. 195).
51. Ibid., December 1926, pp. 14-16. "We may reasonably hope to make these children grow up to be good Catholic men and women, an honor to the church, their parents, and their country" (June 1922, p. 20).
52. *The Silver Book*, n.p. The Parish archives noted that St. Julian's Day Nursery sought "the best development of the children in their *physical, mental*, and *spiritual* life; to foster cooperation between the Sisters and the mothers . . . to promote acquaintances among its members" (II, X, 96).
53. The nursery was granted an Illinois charter as a nonprofit organization in 1938. Its objectives were defined as follows: "The furtherance of *social, physical*, and *educational* development and activity with a view toward improving the mind, body, and *social welfare* of the parents and the children in the community known as St. Philip Benizi Parish . . . to render such aid and assistance and conduct social activities and to conduct and operate a kindergarten" (ASPB II, X, 99).
54. *ICI* put it this way:

"As the threat to the spiritual life of our young girls and to their morals *transcends nationality*, so should this effort to safeguard them from perils be made in every parish without reference to its nationality. Italian and Pole and Slovak and Croatian and Lithuanian and German and Irish—what the racial stock—our children go out to the same dangers, meet the same enemies and must be protected and safeguarded by a common effort.

"Can we make that effort for them in any better fashion than by offering them for their imitation the Virtues of Our Lady, by promising her very vividly to them for their patterns and so securing them from danger with the traditional safeguards of their sex." ("Increasing Dangers of the Age Call for Strong Sodalities," *ICI*, November 1929, p. 27.)
55. ASPB, II, V, 29.
56. Serritella interview.
57. Palmer, *History of Communities*, 6: Document 7.
58. *ICI*, January 1923, p. 20.
59. Ibid., October 31, 1926.
60. *ICI* characterized the society as American and Catholic: "The spirit of the Holy Name members is the spirit of the true Catholic . . . membership in the Holy Name Society is the great apostleship of the Catholic layman, that has rallied to the support of our Church in recent years, the strength and vigor of our Catholic citizenship. In a country like ours, where public sentiment means influence and power, we can hardly estimate the tremendous moral force of our

large and growing organizations. . . . The Holy Name Society of the *city, state*, and *nation* should be the vanguard of the Catholic faith" (November, 1923, p. 20).
61. May 1924, pp. 16-17.
62. "The CYO at St. Philip's," March 1932, p. 20.
63. The organization also sponsored the Lewis Holy Name School of Aeronautics, which taught young men the art of flying. The Knights of Columbus, a nationwide Catholic organization, also furthered Americanization by sponsoring sporting clubs, movies and dances, and other activities that brought the young people of Chicago together. The knights acted on the parish level by recruiting members from existing ethnic societies.
64. ASPB, II, VI, 53.
65. *ICI*, January 1925, p. 10; May 1924, p. 19; June 1926, p. 17. *ICI* contrasted the efforts of Italians with other nationalities in these words: "It is fortunate that next to the Italian colonies there are other groups of true Catholics like the Irish, Polish, and Germans, who practice their religion and understand their duties" (October 1924, pp. 10-11).
66. The ethnic parish also emphasized the merits of confession and Holy Communion (*ICI*, May 1923, pp. 14-15); the need for good Catholic marriages (*ICI*, June 1922, p. 18); and the central role of the pastor as supreme ruler within the parish (*ICI*, June 1922, p. 20). It united with other Catholic parishes against the immodest dress of the day (*ICI*, March 1923, p. 18) and the lack of morality in movies (May 1924, p. 10), and like other Catholic parishes, it encouraged Catholic literature and pictures in the home (*ICI*, March 1924, p. 10; January 1924, pp. 22-23).
67. Fr. L. Giambastiani to Fr. Hoban, July 30, 1918; AAC 4 1918 H 190.
68. *ICI*, April 1924.
69. *New World*, September 10, 1915, p. 3; January 8, 1910, p. 2.
70. Sanders, *Education Urban Minority*, p. 71.
71. *ICI*, September 1925, pp. 8-9,
72. *ICI*, September 1925, p. 9.
73. *New World*, November 8, 1929, p. 3. Our Lady of Pompeii also taught its children their native language through the 1930s. Sisters from Mother Cabrini Hospital conducted weekly classes in Italian through 1950. Serritella interview.
74. Serritella interview.
75. *ICI*, October 1925, p. 18.
76. *ICI*, June 1922, p. 19; September 1924, pp. 10-11; February 1924, p. 18.
77. Ibid., June 1922, pp. 14-15.
78. "What is more important: work or school? Look at the frenetic activity which produces a skyscraper in a few weeks or months. Look at the different workers, from the manual laborer, who is constantly dirty, to the architect, who makes his plans in a well-lit office and gives orders which no one dares to refuse. And when the building is finished, makes 100 times more than the ordinary laborer.

What would you want to be: the worker or the architect? The former represents work, the latter school" ("Scuola o Lavor," *ICI*, June 1922, pp. 10-11).
79. Jane Addams, *Twenty Years at Hull House* (New York: Macmillan, 1910), p. 97.
80. Allen F. Davis, *Spearheads for Reform* (New York: Oxford University Press, 1967), p. 89.
81. *New World*, February 23, 1913, p. 1.
82. See Amberg, *Madonna Center*.
83. Ibid., p. 30.
84. The process of securing this school was largely brought about through the efforts of Charles A. Plamondon, father of Marie Plamondon, who was a co-worker at Guardian Angel. Mr. Plamondon was vice-president of the Board of Education, and he requested public school textbooks for night classes in English. William A. Bogan, principal of Washington Elementary School, secured teachers and books for reading, writing, and government.
85. Amberg, *Madonna Center*, p. 65.
86. Mary Berger, "Catholic Settlement Workers," *Extension* 4 (June 1909): 27.
87. "Bishop McGavick extols work at Italian Center," *New World*, October 22, 1915, p. 1. Leading Catholic Chicagoans came together at the Auditorium Theater in October to discuss the future of Chicago's Catholic settlements. Besides Bishop McGavick and Miss Vitum, participants included the Rev. Frederick Siedenberg, S.J., of Loyola University; Judge Edward E. Brown, former justice of the Appellate Court; Leonara Z. Meder, head of all social service agencies in Cook County; and Professor W. H. Cahill, dean of engineering, Loyola University. A fundraising drive connected with the meeting netted $6,000.
88. Amberg, *Madonna Center*, p. 120.
89. Ibid., p. 79.
90. Ibid., pp. 143-44.
91. Serritella interview.
92. ASPB, II, VI, 41. Stritch's views are contained in a letter to Giambastiani: "It is a fact that national groups are passing phenomena in our cities. In time these groups no longer use their own vernacular and they become part of the general population in every way, retaining however their Catholic faith. We should not make the mistake of building chapels not urgently needed which will in time become problems" (Stritch to Giambastiani, November 17, 1945; ASPB, II, 41).
93. Serritella, interview.

CHAPTER FIVE

1. Merriam, *Rise of Urban America*, p. 148.
2. Billigmeier, *Americans from Germany*, p. 146.

3. H. L. Mencken, "Die Deutschamerikaner," *Die Neue Rundschau* 40 (November 1928): 486-95.
4. Hofmeister, *Germans of Chicago*, p. 79; 245-50.
5. Wirth and Bernert, *Local Community Fact Book*. In 1930, 67.4 percent of Chicago's population was either foreign-born or children of foreign-born; in other words, 2,174,430 Chicagoans were foreign-stock Americans. Poles were the leading nationality, with 149,622 foreign-born residents (or 17.8 percent of the total foreign-born population). Germans were the second largest nationality, with 111,366 foreign-born (13.2 percent); followed by Russians with 78,462 (9.3 percent); Swedes with 75,178 (8.9 percent); and Italians with 73,960 (8.8 percent).
6. Kitagawa and Tauber, *Local Community Fact Book*, pp. 305-8.
7. Hofmeister, *Germans of Chicago*, pp. 14, 47. The end of the Weimar Republic in 1933 marked the beginning of another immigration of Germans to America. This migration, although many times smaller than the nineteenth century ones, was an intellectual immigration, which brought such men as Albert Einstein, Paul Tillich, and Bertolt Brecht to America. See Donald Fleming and Bernard Bailyn, *The Intellectual Migration, Europe and America, 1930-1960* (Cambridge: Harvard University Press, 1969).
8. O'Connor, *German-Americans*, p. 437; Furer, *Germans in America*, p. 78.
9. Hilbert interview.
10. Letter of Cardinal Mundelein to the German parishes of Chicago, August 23, 1937.
11. Mrs. Henry Hahn interview.
12. *New World*, January 12, 1934, p. 10; March 14, 1930, p. 8; April 27, 1934, p. 4.
13. *St. Benedict Golden Jubilee*, p. 34; *St. Gregory Story*, pp. 51-52.
14. Huebener, *Germans in America*, p. 156,
15. Jack Hurst, "Ja, Chicago Still Has Lots of German Soul," *Chicago Tribune Magazine*, October 30, 1977, sec. 9, pp. 23-52.
16. Ibid, p. 49.
17. Ibid.
18. Theresa Krutz interview.
19. Hofmeister, *Germans of Chicago*, p. 14.
20. Theresa Krutz interview.
21. Hurst, "Ja, Chicago," p. 49.
22. 1960 census statistics only indicate the number of foreign-stock Germans (foreign-born plus their children) in proportion to the total population. See Kitagawa and Tauber, *Local Community Fact Book*, pp. 305-8; Hofmeister, *Germans of Chicago*, p. 51.
23. Hurst, "Ja, Chicago," pp. 49-50; Theresa Krutz interview.
24. Hurst, "Ja, Chicago," p. 50.
25. Charles Trout, *Boston, the Great Depression, and the New Deal* (New York: Oxford University Press, 1977), p. 258. For a complete discussion of Boston's

Italian community, see Herbert Gans, *The Urban Villagers* (New York: Free Press, 1962).
26. Wirth and Bernert, *Local Community Fact Book*. While Chicago's O'Hare International Airport constitutes its seventy-sixth community area, there are a thousand residents within its boundaries.
27. Interviev with Fr. George Charbonneau, O.S.M., Chicago, Illinois, October 18, 1977.
28. Interview, Fr. Joseph Gentili; *New World*, September 18, 1936, p. 3; October 16, 1970, p. 1; James Serritella interview.
29. *New World*, May 30, 1919, p. 1; September 6, 1935, p. 1; September 11, 1936, p. 1; March 25, 1955, p. 2.
30. Kitagawa and Tauber, *Local Community Fact Book*, pp. 305-8.
31. Tomasi and Engel, *Italian Experience in United States*, p. 190.
32. Nicholas J. Russo, "Three Generations of Italians in New York City," in ibid., pp. 195-209.

Bibliography

Books

Abbot, Edith. *Historical Aspects of Immigration.* Chicago: University of Chicago Press, 1926.
_____. *Immigration.* Chicago: University of Chicago Press, 1924.
_____. *The Tenements of Chicago, 1908-1935.* Chicago: University of Chicago Press, 1936.
Abbot, Edith, and Sophonisba P. Breckenridge, *Truancy and Non-Attendance in the Chicago Schools.* Chicago: University of Chicago Press, 1917.
Abell, Aaron I. *American Catholicism and Social Action.* South Bend, Ind.: University of Notre Dame Press, 1963.
Aberle, George P. *From the Steppes to the Prairies.* Bismarck, N.D.: n.p., 1963.
Achtundzwanzigste internationaler eucharistischer Kongress zu Chicago, Illinois. Techny Press, Ill.: Mission Press, 1926.
Addams, Jane. *Twenty Years at Hull House.* New York: Macmillan Co., 1910; New York: Signet, 1960.
Allswang, John M. *A House for All Peoples: Ethnic Politics in Chicago 1890-1936.* Lexington, Ky.: University of Kentucky Press, 1971.
Amberg, Mary Agnes. *Madonna Center.* Chicago: Loyola University Press, 1976.
Andreas, Alfred T. *History of Chicago.* 3 vols. Chicago: A.T. Andreas, 1884-86.
Annalen der Glaubensverbreitung. Munich: Ludwig-Missionsverein, 1848-1918.
Barnard, Harry. *Eagle Forgotten: The Life of John Peter Altgeld.* New York: Bobbs-Merrill Co., 1938.
Barry, Colman J., Father. *The Catholic Church and German-Americans.* Milwaukee: Bruce Publishing Co., 1953.

Benson, William S., James J. Walsh, and Edward J. Hanna, *Catholic Builders of the Nation*. 4 vols. Boston: Continental Press Inc., 1925.

Berichte der Leopoldinen-Stiftung im Kaisterthume Österreich. Vienna: n.p., n.d.

Billigmeier, Robert H. *Americans from Germany*. Belmont, Calif.: Wadsworth Publishing Co., 1974.

Billington, Ray Allen. *The Protestant Crusade, 1800-1860*. New York: Macmillan Co., 1938.

Bittinger, Lucy. *German Religious Life in Colonial Times*. Philadelphia: J. B. Lippincott Co., 1906.

_____. *The Germans in Colonial Times*. Philadelphia: J. B. Lippincott Co., 1901.

Blied, Benjamin J. *Austrian Aid to American Catholics 1830-1860*. Milwaukee: By the author, 1944.

_____. *Three Archbishops of Milwaukee*. Milwaukee: By the author, 1940.

Bright, John. *Hizzoner Big Bill Thompson*. New York: Jonathan Cape and Harrison Smith, 1930.

Brophy, Mary Liguori, Sister. *The Social Thought of the German Roman Catholic Central Verein*. Washington: Catholic University of America Press, 1941.

Brown, Thomas N. *Irish-American Nationalism, 1870-1890*. Philadelphia: J. B. Lippincott Co., 1966.

Browne, Henry J. *The Catholic Church and the Knights of Labor*. Washington: Catholic University of America Press, 1949.

Burgess, Ernest W., and Charles Newcomb, eds. *Census Data of the City of Chicago, 1920*. Chicago: University of Chicago Press, 1931.

_____. *Census Data of the City of Chicago, 1930*. Chicago: University of Chicago Press, 1933.

Burgler, F. C. *Geschichte der katholische Kirche, Chicagos*. Chicago: Wilhelm Kuhlmann, 1889.

Burns, James. *The Growth and Development of the Catholic School System in the United States*. New York: Benziger Brothers, 1912.

Butt, Ernest. *Chicago Then and Now*. Chicago: Aurora, Finct & McCullough, 1933.

Callahan, Daniel. *The Mind of the Catholic Layman*. New York: Charles Scribner's Sons, 1963.

Campbell, Edney Fay, Fanny R. Smith, and Clarence F. Jones. *Our City—Chicago*. New York: Charles Scribner's Sons, 1930.

The Catholic Church in the United States. 3 vols. New York: Catholic Editing Co., 1912.
Catholic Guide of Chicago Archdiocese. Chicago: Catholic Service Co., 1938.
Chada, Joseph. *Czech American Catholics, 1850-1920.* Lisle, Ill.: Center for Slav Culture, 1964.
Child, Clifton James. *The German-Americans in Politics, 1914-1917.* Madison, Wisc.: University of Wisconsin Press, 1939.
Ciesluk, Joseph E. *National Parishes in the United States.* Washington, D.C.: Catholic University of America Press, 1944.
Cipriani, Lisi. *Italians in Chicago.* Chicago: n.p., 1933.
Cogley, John. *Catholic America.* New York: Dial Press, 1973; New York: Image Books, 1974.
Community Area Data Book, 1970. Chicago: Chicago Association of Commerce and Industry, 1970.
Condit, Carl W. *The Chicago School of Architecture: A History of Commercial and Public Building in the Chicago Area, 1875-1925.* Chicago: University of Chicago Press, 1964.
Connelly, James F. *The Visit of Archbishop Caetano Bedini to the United States of America.* Rome: Libreria Editrice dell' Università Gregoriana, 1960.
Connelly, Nicholas P. *The Canonical Erection of Parishes.* Washington, D.C.: Catholic University Press, 1938.
Cordasco, Francesco. *Italians in the United States.* New York: Oriole Editions, 1972.
_____. *Studies in Italian-American Social History.* Totowa, N.J.: Rowman and Littlefield, 1975.
Cronau, Rudolf. *German Achievements in America.* New York: n.p., 1916.
Cross, Robert D. *The Emergence of Liberal Catholicism in America.* Cambridge: Harvard University Press, 1958.
Davis-Dubois, Rachel, and Emma Schweppe, *The Germans in American Life.* New York: Thomas Nelson and Sons, 1936.
DeCourcy, Henry. *The Catholic Church in the United States.* New York: Edward Dunigan and Brother, 1857.
Desmond, Emmett. *Fabulous Chicago.* New York: Random House, 1935.
Diamond, Sander A. *The Nazi Movement in the United States, 1924-1941.* Ithaca, N.Y.: Cornell University Press, 1974.
Di Donato, Pietro. *Christ in Concrete.* New York: Bobbs-Merrill, 1939.
Dietzsch, Emil. *Chicago deutsche Manner.* Chicago: Max Stern and Co., 1885.

Dignan, Patrick J. *A History of the Legal Incorporation of Church Property in the United States.* n.p., 1933.

Dolan, Jay. *The Immigrant Church: New York's Irish and German Catholics, 1815-1865.* Baltimore: Johns Hopkins University Press, 1975.

Douglas, Paul. *The Story of German Methodism.* New York: The Methodist Book Concern, 1939.

Eisenach, George J. *A History of the German Congregational Churches in the United States.* Yankton, S.D.: The Pioneer Press, 1938.

Ellis, John Tracy. *American Catholicism.* 2d ed. Chicago: University of Chicago Press, 1969.

_____. *Documents of American Catholic History.* Milwaukee: Bruce Publishing Co., 1956.

_____. *A Guide to American Catholic History.* Milwaukee: Bruce Publishing Co., 1959.

_____. *John Lancaster Spalding, First Bishop of Peoria, American Educator.* Milwaukee: Bruce Publishing Co., 1961.

_____. *The Life and Times of Cardinal Gibbons, Archbishop of Baltimore, 1834-1921.* 2 vols. Milwaukee: Bruce Publishing Co., 1952.

_____. *Perspectives in American Catholicism.* Baltimore: Helicon Press, 1963.

Faust, Albert B. *The German Element in the United States.* 2 vols. New York: Houghton Mifflin, 1909.

Fecher, Vincent J. *A Study of the Movement for German National Parishes in Philadelphia and Baltimore, 1787-1802.* Rome: Apud Aedes Universitatis Gregorianae, 1955.

Felici, Icilio. *Father to the Immigrants: The Life of John Baptist Scalabrini.* New York: P. J. Kennedy & Sons, 1955.

Foerster, Robert F. *The Italian Emigration of Our Times.* Cambridge: Harvard University Press, 1919.

Foisel, John. *Saxons through Seventeen Centuries.* Cleveland; Central Alliance of Transylvania Saxons of the United States, 1965.

Forster, Walter. *Zion on the Mississippi.* St. Louis: Concordia Publishing House, 1953.

Fox, Paul. *Poles in America.* New York: George H. Dorn Co., 1952.

_____. *The Polish National Catholic Church.* Scranton, Pa.: School of Christian Living, 1956.

Furer, Howard B., ed. *The Germans in America.* Dobbs Ferry, N.Y.: Oceana Publications, 1973.

Gabriel, Brother Angelus, F.S.C. *The Christian Brothers in the United States 1848-1948*. New York: Declan S. McMullen So., 1948.

Gallery, Mary Onahan. *Life of William J. Onahan*. Chicago: Loyola University Press, 1929.

Gallo, Patrick J. *Ethnic Alienation: The Italian-Americans*. Rutherford, N.J.: Fairleigh Dickinson University Press, 1974.

Gans, Herbert J. *The Urban Villagers*. New York: Free Press, 1962.

Garraghan, Gilbert J. *The Catholic Church in Chicago, 1673-1871*. Chicago: Loyola University Press, 1921.

Gillard, John T., S.J. *The Catholic Church and the American-Negro*. Baltimore: St. Joseph Society Press, 1929.

Ginger, Ray. *Altgeld's America: The Lincoln Ideal Versus Changing Realities*. Chicago: Quadrangle Books, 1965.

Glazer, Nathan, and Daniel P. Moynihan. *Beyond the Melting Pot*. Cambridge: Massachusetts Institute of Technology Press, 1963.

Gleason, Philip. *Catholicism in America*. New York: Harper and Row, 1970.

_____. *The Conservative Reformers*. South Bend, Ind.: University of Notre Dame Press, 1968.

Gordon, Milton M. *Assimilation in American Life: The Role of Race, Religion and National Origins*. New York: Oxford University Press, 1964.

Gosnell, Harold F., and Charles E. Merriam, *Machine Politics: Chicago Model*. Chicago: n.p., 1937.

Gottfried, Alex. *Boss Cermak of Chicago*. Seattle, Wash.: n.p., 1962.

Greeley, Andrew M. *The Catholic Experience*. Garden City, N.Y.: Doubleday & Co., 1967; Image Books, 1969.

_____. *That Most Distressful Nation: The Taming of the American Irish*. Chicago: Quadrangle Books, 1972.

_____. *Why Can't They be Like Us?* New York: Institute of Human Relations Press, 1969.

Grente, Georges. *Le beau voyage des cardinaux français aux Etats-Unis et au Canada*. Paris: Librairie Plon, 1927.

Grossman, Ronald P. *The Italians in America*. Minneapolis: Lerner Publications, 1966.

Guilday, Peter. *A History of the Councils of Baltimore, 1791-1884*. New York: Macmillan Co., 1932.

_____. *The Life and Times of John England*. 2 vols. New York: The America Press, 1927.

Guilday, Peter. *The National Pastorals of the American Hierarchy, 1792-1919.* Washington, D.C.: National Catholic Welfare Conference, 1923.
Habig, Marion A., O.F.M. *The Franciscans at St. Augustine's and in Chicagoland.* Chicago: Franciscan Herald Press, 1961.
Hagedorn, Hermann. *The Hyphenated Family.* New York: Macmillan Co., 1960.
_____. *Where do You Stand?* New York: Macmillan Co., 1918.
Handlin, Oscar. *Al Smith and His America.* Boston: Little, Brown and Co., 1958.
_____. *Boston's Immigrants, 1790-1865: A Study in Acculturation.* Cambridge: Harvard University Press, 1941.
_____. *Immigration as a Factor in American History.* New York: Doubleday and Co., 1959.
_____. *Race and Nationality in American Life.* New York: Doubleday and Co., 1957.
_____. *The Uprooted.* 2d ed. Boston: Atlantic-Little, Brown, 1971.
Hannemann, Max. *Das Deutschtum in den Vereingten-Staaten.* Gotha: J. Perthes, 1936.
Hanson, Marcus L. *The Immigrant in American History.* Cambridge: Harvard University Press, 1948.
Harrison, Carter, II. *Growing Up with Chicago.* Chicago: n.p., 1944.
_____. *Stormy Years.* Indianapolis: n.p., 1935.
Hauser, Philip M., and Evelyn M. Kitagawa, eds. *Local Community Fact Book of Chicago, 1950.* Chicago: University of Chicago Press, 1953.
Hawgood, John A. *The Tragedy of German America.* New York: G. P. Putnam's Sons, 1940.
Hays, Samuel P. *The Response to Industrialism, 1885-1914.* Chicago: University of Chicago Press, 1968.
Higham, John. *Strangers in the Land.* New York: Atheneum, 1971.
Historic City. Chicago: Department of Development and Planning, 1976.
Hofmeister, Rudolf, *The Germans of Chicago.* Champaign, Ill.: University of Illinois Press, 1976.
Houtart, François. *Aspects sociologiques de Catholicisme Americain.* Paris: Les Editions Ouvrieres Economie et Humanisme, 1957.
Hoyt, Homer. *One Hundred Years of Land Values in Chicago.* Chicago: University of Chicago Press, 1933.
Huber, Raphael. *Our Bishops Speak.* Milwaukee: Bruce Publishing Co., 1951.

Huebener, Theodore. *The Germans in America*. New York: Chilton Co., 1962.

Hyland, J.S., ed. *Progress of the Catholic Church in America and the Great Columbian Catholic Congress of 1893*. Chicago: n.p., 1897.

Iorizzo, Luciano J., and Salvatore Mondello. *The Italian-Americans*. New York: Twayne Publications, 1971.

Iverson, Noel. *Germania, U.S.A., Social Change in New Ulm, Minnesota*. Minneapolis; University of Minnesota, 1966.

Iwicki, John. *The First One Hundred Years: A Study of the Apostolate of the Congregation of the Resurrection in the United States, 1866-1966*. Rome: Gregorian University Press, 1966.

Jones, Maldwyn A. *American Immigration*. Chicago: University of Chicago Press, 1960.

Kenneally, Finbar, Fr., ed. *United States Documents in the Propaganda Fidei Archives*. 2 vols. Washington, D.C.: Academy of American Franciscan History, 1966-68.

Kinsman, Frederick J. *Americanism and Catholicism*. New York: Longmans, Green and Co., 1924.

Kirkfleet, Cornelius J. *The Life of Patrick Augustine Feehan*. Chicago: Matre and Co., 1922.

Kitagawa, Evelyn M., and Karl E. Tauber, eds. *Local Community Fact Book: Chicago Metropolitan Area, 1960*. Chicago: University of Chicago Press, 1963.

Köstering, J. F. *Auswanderung der sachsischen Lutheraner im Jahre 1838*. St. Louis: n.p., 1866.

Lait, Jack, and Mortimer Lee. *Chicago Confidential*. New York: Crown Publishers, 1950.

The Lakeside Annual Directory of the City of Chicago. Chicago: Williams, Donnelley and Co., 1874-1917.

Leckie, Robert. *American and Catholic*. Garden City, N.Y.: Doubleday and Co., 1970.

Leuchtenburg, William E. *The Perils of Prosperity, 1914-1932*. Chicago: University of Chicago Press, 1958.

Linkh, Richard. *American Catholicism and European Immigrants, 1900-1924*. Staten Island, New York: Center for Migration Studies, 1975.

Longstreet, Stephen. *Chicago 1860-1919*. New York: David McKay Co., 1973.

Lopreato, Joseph. *The Italian-Americans*. New York: Random House, 1970.

Luebke, F. C. *Immigrants and Politics: The Germans of Nebraska, 1880-1900.* Lincoln: University of Nebraska Press, 1969.

McAvoy, Thomas T., C.S.C. *The Great Crisis in American Catholic History, 1895-1900.* Chicago: Henry Regnery Co., 1957.

_____. *A History of the Catholic Church in the United States.* South Bend, Ind.: University of Notre Dame Press, 1969.

_____. *Roman Catholicism and the American Way of Life.* South Bend, Ind.: University of Notre Dame Press, 1960.

McGirr, John E. *The Life of the Rt. Rev. Wm. Quarter, D.D., First Bishop of Chicago.* Des Plaines, Ill.: St. Mary's Training School Press, 1920.

Martin, Paul R. *The First Cardinal of the West.* Chicago: New World Publishing Co., 1934.

Marty, Myron A. *Lutherans and Roman Catholicism: The Changing Conflict, 1917-1963.* South Bend, Ind.: University of Notre Dame Press, 1968.

Mayer, Harold M., and Richard C. Wade. *Chicago: Growth of a Metropolis.* Chicago: University of Chicago Press, 1969.

Merriam, Charles E. *Chicago, A More Intimate View of Urban Politics.* New York: Macmillan Co., 1929.

Merwick, Donna. *Boston Priests, 1848-1910.* Cambridge: Harvard University Press, 1973.

Mondello, Salvatore. *The Italian Immigrant in Urban America, 1880-1920.* N.p., n.d.

Montay, Mary Innocenta, Sister. *The History of Catholic Secondary Education in the Archdiocese of Chicago.* Washington, D.C.: Catholic University of America Press, 1953.

Montgomery, Louise. *The American Working Girl in the Stockyards Districts.* Chicago: University of Chicago Press, 1913.

Moquin, Wayne, and Charles Van Doren, eds. *A Documentary History of the Italian Americans.* New York: Praeger Publishers, 1974.

Moses, John, and Joseph Kirland. *History of Chicago.* 2 vols. Chicago: Munsell & Co., 1895.

Mundelein, George W. *Letters of a Bishop to His Flock.* New York: Benziger Bros., 1927.

_____. *Two Crowded Years.* Chicago: Extension Press, 1919.

Murphy, John. *Catholic Attitude Toward the Immigrant and the Negro, 1825-1925.* Washington, D.C.: Catholic University of America Press, 1939.

Musmanno, Michael A. *The Story of the Italians in America.* New York: Doubleday & Co., 1965.

Nelli, Humbert. *Italians in Chicago, 1880-1930: A Study in Ethnic Mobility.* New York: Oxford University Press, 1970.
Newcomb, Charles, and Richard O. Lang, eds. *Data of the City of Chicago, 1934.* Chicago: University of Chicago Press, 1934.
Novak, Michael. *The Rise of the Unmeltable Ethnics.* New York: Macmillan Co., 1972.
The Official Catholic Directory. Milwaukee: M. H. Wiltzius Co., 1903-1910; New York: P. J. Kennedy & Sons, 1920-1940.
Palmieri, Aurelio. *Il grave Problema religioso italiano negli Stati Uniti.* Florence: n.p., 1921.
Panunzio, Constantine M. *The Soul of an Immigrant.* New York: Macmillan Co., 1921.
Pasley, Fred D. *Al Capone.* New York: n.p., 1930.
Pease, Theodore C. *The Story of Illinois.* Rev. ed. Chicago: University of Chicago Press, 1965.
Pierce, Bessie L. *As Others See Chicago: Impressions of Visitors, 1673-1933.* Chicago: University of Chicago Press, 1933.
——. *A History of Chicago.* 3 vols. New York: A. A. Knopf, 1937-57.
Polk's Chicago Directory. Chicago: n.p., 1923; 1928-29.
Riley, Thomas J. *The Higher Life of Chicago.* Chicago: University of Chicago Press, 1905.
Rippley, LaVern. *Of German Ways.* Minneapolis: Dillon Press, 1970.
Roemer, Theodore, O.F.M. *The Leopoldine Foundation and the Church in the United States, 1829-1839.* New York: United States Historical Society, 1933.
——. *The Ludwig-Missionsverein and the Catholic Church in the United States, 1839-1918.* Washington, D.C,: Catholic University of America Press, 1933.
Rolle, Andrew F. *The American Italians.* Belmont, Calif.: Wadsworth Publishing Co., 1972.
——. *The Immigrant Unpraised.* Norman: University of Oklahoma Press, 1968.
Sanders, James W. *The Education of an Urban Minority: Catholics in Chicago, 1833-1965.* New York: Oxford University Press, 1977.
Schiavo, Giovanni E. *Four Centuries of Italian-American History.* New York; Vigo Press, 1952.
——. *Italian-American History.* 2 vols. New York: Vigo Press, 1947-49.

_____. *The Italians of Chicago: A Study in Americanization.* Chicago: Italian American Publishing Co., 1928.

Schneider, Carl E. *The German Church on the American Frontier.* St. Louis: Eden Publishing Co., 1939.

Schnuker, George. *Die Ostfriesen in Amerika.* Cleveland: Central Publishing House, 1917.

Schrott, Lambert. *Pioneer German Catholics in the American Colonies, 1734-1784.* New York: United States Catholic Historical Society, 1933.

Shannon, James P. *Catholic Colonization on the Western Frontier.* New Haven: Yale University Press, 1957.

Shaughnessy, Gerald. *Has the Immigrant Kept the Faith?* New York: Macmillan Co., 1925.

Shea, John Gilmary. *A History of the Catholic Church in the United States.* 4 vols. New York: Merscham Co., 1886-92.

Spith, Arthur L. *The Deutschtum of Nazi Germany and the United States.* The Hague, Netherlands: Martinus Nyhoff, 1965.

Spaulding, E. Wilder. *The Quiet Invaders: The Story of the Austrian Impact upon America.* Vienna: Osterreichischer Bundesverlag, 1968.

Stead, William T. *If Christ Came to Chicago.* Chicago: Laird and Lee, 1894.

Sweeney, Francis D. *The Life of John Lancaster Spalding: The First Bishop of Peoria, 1840-1916.* New York: Herder & Herder, 1965.

Taylor, Graham. *Pioneering on Social Frontiers.* Chicago: University of Chicago Press, 1926; reprint ed., New York: Arno Press, 1976.

Thompson, Joseph. *The Archdiocese of Chicago, Antecedents and Development.* Des Plaines, Ill.: St. Mary's Training School Press, 1920.

_____. *A History of the Knights of Columbus in Illinois.* Chicago: Universal Press, 1921.

Timpe, Georg. *Katholishes Deutschtum in den Vereinigten Staaten von Amerika.* Freiburg im Breisgau: Herder, 1937.

Tomasi, Lydio F. *The Italian-American Family.* New York: Center for Migration Studies, 1972.

Tomasi, Silvano M., and Madeline H. Engel, eds. *The Italian Experience in the United States.* Staten Island, N.Y.: Center for Migration Studies, 1970.

Trisco, Robert F. *The Holy See and the Nascent Church in the Middle Western United States, 1826-1850.* Rome: Gregorian University Press, 1962.

Trout, Charles. *Boston, the Great Depression, and the New Deal.* New York: Oxford University Press, 1977.

Usher, Roland G. *Pan-Germanism.* Boston: Houghton Mifflin Co., 1913.

Verga, Giovanni. *Little Novels of Sicily*. New York: n.p., 1883; New York: Grove Press, 1953.
Walburg, Anton. *The Question of Nationality*. Cincinnati: Herder, 1889.
Walker, Mack. *Germany and the Emigration 1816-1885*. Cambridge: Harvard University Press, 1964.
Ward, David. *Cities and Immigrants*. New York: Oxford University Press, 1971.
Wendt, Lloyd and Herman Kogan. *Bosses in Lusty Chicago*. Bloomington, Ind.: Indiana University Press, 1943.
Wilk, Gerard. *Americans from Germany*. New York: German Information Center, 1976.
Wirth, Louis, and Eleanor H. Bernert, eds. *Local Community Fact Book of Chicago*. Chicago: University of Chicago Press, 1949.
Wirth, Louis, and Margaret Furez, eds. *Local Community Fact Book, 1938*. Chicago: Chicago Recreation Commission, 1938.
Wittke, Carl F. *German-Americans and the World War*. Columbus, Ohio: The Ohio State Archeological & Historical Society, 1936.
_____. *The German-Language Press in America*. Louisville, Ky.: University of Kentucky Press, 1957.
_____. *Refugees of Revolution: The German Forty-eighters in America*. Philadelphia: University of Pennsylvania Press, 1952.
_____. *We Who Built America: The Saga of the Immigrant*. New York: Prentice-Hall, 1945.
Wust, Klaus. *The Virginia Germans*. Charlottsville, Va.: University of Virginia Press, 1969.
Zglenicki, Leon, ed. *The Poles of Chicago, 1837-1937*. Chicago: Polish Pageant Inc., 1937.
Zorbaugh, Harvey W. *The Gold Coast and the Slums*. Chicago: University of Chicago Press, 1929.

Articles

Abramson, Harold J. "Ethnic Diversity within Catholicism: A Comparative Analysis of Contemporary and Historical Religion." *Journal of Social History* 4 (Summer 1971): 359-88.
Agnew, W. H. "Pastoral Care of Italian Children." *American Ecclesiastical Review* 28 (March 1913): 257-67.

Bandini, Albert R. "Concerning the Italian Problem." *American Ecclesiastical Review* 62 (March 1920): 278-85.

Barry, Colman, J. "German Catholic Immigrants." *New World*, January 2, 1976, p. 6.

Berger, Mary. "Catholic Settlement Workers." *Extension* 4 (June 1909): 27.

Boyer, Brian. "Chicago's Italians." *Chicago Sun-Times*, July 14, 1968, sec. 9, p. 6.

Browne, Henry J. "The 'Italian Problem' in the Catholic Church of the United States, 1880-1900." *United States Catholic Historical Society* 35 (1946): 46-72.

Castiglioni, A. "Numero, provenience e distribuzione degli italiani residenti in Chicago." *Bolletino dell'Emigrazione* (1915): n.p.

Cressey, Paul F. "Population Succession in Chicago: 1898-1930." *American Journal of Sociology* 44 (July 1938): 56-69.

Cross, Robert D. "The Changing Image of the City Among American Catholics." *Catholic Historical Review* 48 (April 1962): 33-52.

Cushing, Richard J. "Italian Immigrants." *Catholic Mind*, October 1954, 604-09.

Dolan, Jay. "Immigrants in the City: New York's Irish and German Catholics." *Church History* 41 (September 1972): 354-68.

Dore, Grazia. "Some Social and Historical Aspects of Italian Emigration to America." *Journal of Social History* 2 (Winter 1968): 95-115.

Dunne, Edmund M. "Memoirs of 'Zi Pre.' " *Ecclesiastical Review* 49 (1913): 192-203.

Epstein, Francis J. "History in the 'Annuals' of the Leopoldine Association." *Illinois Catholic Historical Review* 1 (October 1919): 225-33.

Esslinger, D. R. "American German and Irish Attitudes toward Neutrality, 1914-1917: A Study of Catholic Minorities." *Catholic Historical Review* 53 (July 1967): 194.

Femminella, Francis S. "The Impact of Italian Migration and American Catholicism." *American Catholic Sociological Review* 22 (Fall 1961): 233-41.

Franchi, F. J. "The Italian Catholics." *America*, March 21, 1931, p. 584.

Gallery, John I. "The Chicago Catholic Institute and Chicago Lyceum." *Illinois Catholic Historical Review* 2 (January 1920): 303-22.

Garraghan, Gilbert J. "Early Christianity in Illinois." *Illinois Catholic Historical Review* 1 (July 1918): 8-28.

Giacosa, Giuseppe. "Chicago e la sua colonia." *Nuova Antologia* 124 (March 1, 1893): 15-33.
Giese, Vincent J., Fr. "A Little Bit of Italy." *Chicago Catholic*, June 23, 1978, pp. 10-11.
Gleason, Philip. "Frederick P. Kenkel." *New World*, September 3, 1976, p. 6.
―――. "Immigration and American Catholic Intellectual Life." *Review of Politics* 26 (April 1964): 33-44.
"Greeks and Italians in the Neighborhood of Hull House." *American Journal of Sociology* 21 (November 1915): 285-315.
Greeley, Andrew M. "Impact of Italian Migration and American Catholicism." *American Catholic Sociological Review* 22 (Winter 1961): 333.
Herriot, F. I. "The German of Chicago and Stephen A. Douglas." *Deutschamerikanische Geschichtsblatter* 12 (1912): n.p.
Holwick, F. G. "Reverend Gasper Henry Ostlangenburg." *Illinois Catholic Historical Review* 3 (July 1920): 43-52.
Hurst, Jack. "Ja, Chicago Still Has Lots of German Soul." *Chicago Tribune*, October 30, 1977, sec. 9, pp. 23-52.
Lagnese, J. G. "Italian Catholic." *America* 44 (February 21, 1931): 475-76.
Larkin, Helen M. "Catholic Education in Illinois." *Illinois Catholic Historical Review* 4 (April 1922): 339-54.
Lee, Berthon T. "Apostolate to Italo-Americans." *Catholic Mind* 51 (April 1953): 211-19.
McAvoy, T. T. "The Catholic Minority after the Americanist Controversy, 1899-1917: A Survey." *Review of Politics* 11 (January 1959): 53-82.
McMahon, Charles A. "Bishop Muldoon's War and Reconstruction Service." *Illinois Catholic Historical Review* 10 (April 1929): 295-300.
McManamin, Francis G. "Peter J. Muldoon: First Bishop of Rockford, 1862-1927." *Illinois Catholic Historical Review* 48 (October 1962): 365-78.
Madaj, W. J. "The First Archbishop of Chicago." *New World*, August 16, 1974, pp. 7-9.
―――. "The First Cardinal of the Archdiocese of Chicago." *New World*, August 30, 1974, pp. 7-9.
―――. "The Second Archbishop of Chicago." *New World*, August 23, 1974, pp. 7-10.
Mastrovalerio, Alessandro. "Remarks upon the Italian Colony in Chicago." In *Hull House Maps and Papers*. New York: T. Y. Crowell & Co., 1895.
Murphy, A. J. "Father Siedenburg, S.J." *Catholic Charities Review* 23 (March 1939): 85-86.

Nicolay, C. L. "Berlin, A German Settlement in Waterloo County, Ontario, Canada." *German-American Annals*, n.s. 1 (January-February 1907): 105-21.

Nolan, J. Allen. "Right Reverend Peter James Muldoon, D.D. First Bishop of Rockford, 1683-1927." *Illinois Catholic Historical Review* 10 (April 1928): 291-94.

Norton, Grace P. "Chicago Housing Conditions. VII. Two Italian Districts." *American Journal of Sociology* 18 (1913): 509-42.

Onahan, William J. "Catholic Progress in Chicago—Personal Recollections of Catholic Progress and Activities in Chicago during Sixty-four Years." *Illinois Catholic Historical Review* 1 (October 1918): 176-83.

Prindiville, Kate G. "Italy in Chicago." *Catholic World* 77 (July 1903): 452-61.

Ridpath, John C. "The Mixed Population of Chicago." *Chautaugan* 12 (January 1891): 483-93.

Riordan, D. J. "The University of St. Mary of the Lake." *Illinois Catholic Historical Review* 2 (October 1919): 135-60.

Rothenstiener, John. "Interesting Facts Concerning Chicago's First Four Bishops." *Illinois Catholic Historical Review* 9 (October 1926): 151-61.

Russo, Nicholas J. "Three Generations of Italians in New York City: Their Religious Acculturation." In Tomasi and Engel, *The Italian Experience in the United States*, pp. 195-209.

Skerrett, Ellen. "Irish Catholic Parish: Schools, Politics, Parades." *New World*, February 6, 1976, p. 15.

Spiro, M. E. "The Acculturation of American Ethnic Groups." *American Anthropology* 107 (1955): 1240-52.

Thompson, Joseph J. "The Illinois Missions." *Illinois Catholic Historical Review* 1 (July 1818): 38-63.

_____. "The Irish in Chicago." *Illinois Catholic Historical Review* 2 (April 1920): 458-73.

_____. "Momentous Moment in the American Church." *Illinois Catholic Historical Review* 7 (July 1924): 3-94.

Tolino, John V. "Solving the Italian Problem." *Ecclesiastical Review* 99 (September 1938): 248-56.

_____. "The Future of the Italian-American Problem." *Ecclesiastical Review* 101 (September 1939): 221-32.

Tolino, John V. "The Church in America and the Italian Problem." *Ecclesiastical Review* 101 (January 1939) 22-32.

———. "Priest in the Italian Problem." *Ecclesiastical Review* 109 (November 1943): 321-30.
Tomasi, Silvano M. "Italian-American Catholic." *New World*, January 23, 1976, p. 7.
———. "The Ethnic Church and the Integration of Italian Immigrants in the United States." In Tomasi and Engel, *The Italian Experience in the United States*, pp. 163-93.
Trepte, Helmut. "Deutschtum in Ohio." *Deutsch-amerikanische-Geschichtsblätter* 32 (1932): 161-405.
"The Untold Story of Catholic Chicago." *Chicago Daily News*, December 1966, p. 12.
Vecoli, Rudolph J. "Contadini in Chicago: A Critique of the Uprooted." *Journal of American History* 51 (December 1964): 404-17.
———. "Prelates and Peasants: Italian Immigrants and the Catholic Church." *Journal of Social History* 2 (Spring 1969): n.p.
Wolkovich, William, Fr. "Lithuanians in America." *New World*, January 16, 1976, p. 6.
Wunsch, Paul I. "The Italian Catholic." *America*, March 21, 1931, p. 584.

Parish Histories

Album mit Illustrationen zur zehten Jahresfeier der Gründung der St. Gregorius Gemeinde, 1904-1914. Chicago: Privately printed, 1914.
Brons, Joseph, and Harry Gerardin. *Old St. Joseph*. Chicago: Privately printed, 1926.
Centennial, All Saints-St. Anthony of Padua Parishes, 1873-1973, 1875-1975. Chicago: Privately printed, 1975.
Centennial, St. Boniface Church, 1864-1964. Chicago: Privately printed, 1964.
Centennial, St. Michael Church, 1852-1952. Chicago: Privately printed, 1952.
Gedenkblätter zum goldenen Jubiläum der St. Michaels Gemeinde, 1852-1902. Chicago: Privately printed, 1902.
Geschichte der St. Aloysius-Gemeinde. Chicago: Privately printed, 1909.
Golden Anniversary, St. Martin's Parish, 1886-1936. Chicago: Privately printed, 1936.
Golden Jubilee Celebration, St. Benedict Parish, 1902-1952. Chicago: Privately printed, 1952.

Golden Jubilee Celebration, St. Philip Benizi Church, 1904-1954. Chicago: Privately printed, 1954.
Golden Jubilee, St. Augustine's Parish, 1886-(1881)-1936. Chicago: Privately printed, 1936.
Golden Jubilee, St. Francis Xavier Parish, 1888-1938. Chicago: Privately printed, 1938.
Golden Jubilee, St. Mary of Mount Carmel Parish, 1892, 1942. Chicago: Privately printed, 1942.
A Historical Sketch of St. Clement's Church, Chicago, 1905-1930. Chicago: Privately printed, 1930.
Illustrative Souvenir of the Archdiocese of Chicago. Chicago: R. H. Fleming Publishing Co., 1916.
Kalvelage, F.L., Fr. *The Annals of St. Boniface Parish, 1862-1926.* Chicago: Privately printed, 1926.
Kelley, Francis C. *Archbishop Quigley, a Tribute.* Chicago: Privately printed, 1915.
McGovern, James J. *Souvenir of the Silver Jubilee in the Episcopacy of His Grace the Most Rev. Patrick Augustine Feehan, Archbishop of Chicago, 1865-1890.* Chicago: Privately printed, 1891.
Notre Dame de Chicago, 1887-1937. Chicago: Privately printed, 1937.
One Hundred Years, the History of the Church of the Holy Name. Chicago: Privately printed, 1949.
St. Aloysius Parish Diamond Jubilee, the Seventy-five Years of St. Aloysius Parish, 1884-1959. Chicago: Privately printed, 1959.
The St. Gregory Story, 1904-1954. Chicago: Privately printed, 1954.
St. Martin Parish, Diamond Jubilee, 1886-1961. Chicago: Privately printed, 1961.
St. Maurice Parish, Diamond Jubilee, 1890-1965. Chicago: Privately printed, 1964.
St. Michael's Diamentes Jubileum, 1852-1927. Chicago: Privately printed, 1927.
St. Philomena Church, Seventy-fifth Anniversary, 1894-1969. Chicago: Privately printed, 1969.
St. William's Fiftieth Anniversary, 1916-1966. Chicago: Privately printed, 1966.
Seventy-fifth Anniversary, St. Maria Incoronata Church, 1897-1972. Chicago: Privately printed, 1972.
The Silver Book, by the Servite Fathers, for the Twenty-fifth Anniversary of St. Philip Benizi Church. Chicago: Privately printed, 1929.

Unpublished Materials

Abramson, Harold J. "The Ethnic Factor in American Catholicism: An Analysis of Inter-ethnic Marriage and Religious Involvement." Ph.D. dissertation, University of Chicago, 1969.

Briggs, John W. "Church Building in America: Divergent and Convergent Interests of Priests and Lay People in Italian-American Communities." Paper presented at the Conference on the Reinterpretation of American Catholic History, Notre Dame University, South Bend, Indiana, October 4-5, 1974.

Caroli, Betty B. "Italian Repatriation from the United States, 1900-1914." Ph.D. dissertation, University of Chicago, 1972.

Cole, Bruce M. "The Chicago Press and the Know-Nothings, 1850-1856." Master's thesis, University of Chicago, 1948.

Covello, Leonard. "The Social Background of the Italo-American School Child." Ph.D. dissertation, New York University, 1944.

Dobbert, Guido A. "The Disintegration of an Immigrant Community: The Cincinnati Germans, 1870-1920." Ph.D. dissertation, University of Chicago, 1965.

Dolan, Jay. "American Catholics and Popular Religion." Paper presented at the Conference on the Reinterpretation of American Catholic History, Notre Dame University, South Bend, Indiana, October 4-5, 1974.

──────. "Urban Catholicism: New York City 1815-1865." Ph.D. dissertation, University of Chicago, 1970.

Funchion, Michael F. "Chicago's Irish Nationalists, 1881-1890." Ph.D. dissertation, Loyola University of Chicago, 1963.

Horak, Jakub. "Assimilation of Czechs in Chicago." Ph.D. dissertation, University of Chicago, 1920.

Iorizzo, Luciano J. "Italian Immigration and the Immigrant of the Padrone System." Ph.D. dissertation, Syracuse University, 1966.

Jammes, Jean. "The Catholic People and Their Priests." Ph.D. dissertation, University of Chicago, 1954.

Kantowicz, Edward R. "American Politics in Polonia's Capital, 1888-1940." Ph.D. dissertation, University of Chicago, 1972.

Kohlhoff, Dean Wayne. "Missouri Synod Lutherans and the Image of Germany, 1914-1945." Ph.D. dissertation, University of Chicago, 1973.

Krisciunas, Joseph. "Lithuanians in Chicago." Master's thesis, DePaul University, 1935.

McCarthy, Eugene R. "The Bohemians in Chicago and Their Benevolent Societies: 1875-1946." Master's thesis, University of Chicago, 1950.

McLaughlin, Virginia Y. "Like the Fingers of the Hand: the Family and Community Life of First-Generation Italian-Americans in Buffalo, New York, 1880-1930." Ph.D. dissertation, State University of New York at Buffalo, 1970.

Mondello, Salvatore. "The Italian Immigrant in Urban America, 1880-1920." Ph.D. dissertation, New York University, 1960.

Nelli, Humbert S. "Role of the 'Colonial' Press in the Italian-American Community of Chicago, 1886-1921." Ph.D. dissertation, University of Chicago, 1965.

Ozog, Julius J. "A Study of Polish Home Ownership in Chicago." Master's thesis, University of Chicago, 1942.

Palmer, Vivien M., gen. ed. "History of Communities." 6 vols. Chicago Historical Society, 1928. (Mimeographed.)

Parot, Joseph J. "The American Faith and the Persistence of Chicago Polonia, 1870-1920." Ph.D. dissertation, Northern Illinois University, 1971.

Piper, Ruth M. "The Irish of Chicago, 1848 to 1871." Master's thesis, University of Chicago, 1936.

Puzzo, Virgil P. "The Italians in Chicago, 1890-1930." Master's thesis, University of Chicago, 1937.

Quaintance, Esther C. "Rent and Housing Conditions in the Italian District of the Lower North Side of Chicago." Master's thesis, University of Chicago, 1937.

Rothan, Emmet H. "The German Catholic Emigrant in the United States (1830-1860)." Ph.D. dissertation, Catholic University of America, 1946.

Russo, Nicholas J. "The Religious Acculturation of the Italians in New York City." Ph.D. dissertation, St. John's University, 1968.

Sanders, James. "The Education of Chicago Catholics: An Urban History." Ph.D. dissertation, University of Chicago, 1970.

Schafer, Marvin R. "The Catholic Church in Chicago, its Growth and Administration." Ph.D. dissertation, University of Chicago, 1929.

Schanabruch, Charles H. "The Catholic Church's Role in the Americanization of Chicago's Immigrants: 1833-1928." Ph.D. dissertation, University of Chicago, 1975.

Townsend, Andrew J. "The Germans of Chicago." Ph.D. dissertation, University of Chicago, 1927.

Valletta, Clement L. "A Study of Americanization in Carneta: Italian American Identity through Three Generations." Ph.D. dissertation, University of Pennsylvania, 1968.

Vecoli, Rudolph J. "Chicago's Italians prior to World War I: A Study of Their Social and Economic Adjustment." Ph.D. dissertation, University of Wisconsin, 1963.

Walsh, John P. "The Catholic Church in Chicago and the Problems of an Urban Society, 1893-1915." Ph.D. dissertation, University of Chicago, 1948.

Interviews

Charbonneau, George, O.S.M. St. Dominic Parish, Chicago, Illinois. October 18, 1977.

Gentili, Joseph, C.PP.S. St. Mary of Mt. Carmel Parish, Chicago, Illinois. May 10, 1976.

Habig, Marion, 0.F.M. St. Augustine Parish, Chicago, Illinois. April 26, 1976.

Hahn, Henry J., Mrs. 6646 West Raven Street, Chicago, Illinois. May 30, 1978.

Gilbert, Otto. Logansport, Indiana. October 25, 1977.

Krutz, Theresa. Chicago Historical Society, Chicago, Illinois. August 20, 1978.

Serritella, Anthony. 1252 West Lexington Street, Chicago, Illinois. October 13, 1978,

Serritella, Anthony, Mrs. 1252 West Lexington Street, Chicago, Illinois. October 13, 1978.

Serritella, Anthony, Jr. 7051 North Kenton Street, Lincolnwood, Illinois. October 13, 1978.

Stobba, Hugo. 6621 South Mozart Avenue, Chicago, Illinois. April 26, 1976.

Index

Abbot, Edith, 46-47
Abendpost, 53
Addams, Jane, 123-25
Adenauer, Konrad, 160n
African-Americans, 41, 131
    Italian prejudice against, 105-6
    migration to Chicago, 6
    missions to, 19
    and George William Mundelein, 152n
Albrecht, Philip, 75
Alexian Brothers, 44
Alighieri, Dante, 61
Althoff, Henry J., 160n
Amberg, Mary Agnes, 124, 125, 126, 127
Amberg, William A., 124
Amberg, Mrs. William A., 101-3, 125
Americanization, 173n
    and attendance at public schools, 49, 51
    and Catholic Church, xv-xvi, 15-16, 109, 128-29, 157n
    Catholic opposition to melting pot, 149n
    Catholic settlement houses foster, 125, 126-27
    and Catholic Youth Organization, 24
    encouraged by German parochial schools, 92, 94
    ethnic opposition to, 27
    ethnic parishes foster, 88, 90, 107, 114-18
    fostered by dispersion of German immigrant community, 132
    of German and Italian immigrants, 31
    of German Catholic parishes, 73
    of Otto Hilbert, 132-33
    of Irish immigrants, 30-31
    of Italian immigrants, 67-68, 139-40
    of Italian neighborhoods, 106
    and Knights of Columbus, 23
    Charles E. Merriam's views on, 146n
    parochial schools foster, 21, 119-20, 122-23
    and provincialism, 62
    James Quigley's views on, 17-18, 20, 21
    resistance to in St. Michael's Parish, 102-3
    as result of World War I, 97
    in Santa Maria Incoronata Parish, 102
    in schools, 43-44
    and sports, 24, 118
    and support for World War I, 25-26
Ancient Order of Hibernians, 16
Angel Guardian Orphanage, 44
Annenberg, Max, 63
Austria
    immigrants from, 42, 157n-58n

Bandini, Pietro, 156n
Barabino, Peter, 106
Barsi, Angelico, 107
Bennet, William S., 52
Berger, Mary, 125
Bismarck, Otto von, 56-57, 161
Black Hand, The, 52
Blacks
    See African-Americans
Bogan, William A., 101-3, 173n
Bohemia
    immigrants from, 5, 11, 131
Bonzano, John, 98
Boone, Levi, 33
Brecht, Bertolt, 174n

Breckinridge, Sophonisba, 46
Brentano, Lorenz, 44
Breweries, 32, 41, 154n
Bridgeport, Northwest Territory, 1
Bronne, Traugott, 32
Brown, Edward E., 173n
Brown, Thomas, 30
Butz, Caspar, 33

Cabrini, Francis X., 104, 153n
Cahensly, Peter Paul, 12
Cahill, W. H., 173n
Calvin, John, 97
Canada
    immigrants from, 144n
Catherine Kasper Industrial School, 44
Catholic Benevolent Legion, 16
Catholic Church
    ambivalence of toward Jane Addams, 124
    and Americanization, xv-xvi, 15-16, 157n
    among German immigrants, 69-70
    anti-Italian sentiment in, 37-38
    attempts to deal with Italian immigrants, 37-38
    celebrations uniting Italian immigrants with, 39
    and charities, 16, 19-20, 22-24, 44, 54-55, 69, 78, 84, 90, 97-98, 112, 127, 151n, 156n
    Chicago parishes, 14
    conflicts among ethnic groups, 70, 78, 108-9
    cooperation with other religions, 147n
    creation of Italian seminary, 111
    diocesan system, 146n
    dominated by Irish in America, 140
    as element of Americanization, 109
    establishment of ethnic parishes, 71-75, 101-3, 106-7, 153n, 165
    establishment of parishes, 9-10, 18, 30
    and ethnicity, 96-99
    ethnic parades in, 148n
    ethnic parishes and Americanization, 88, 90, 114-18
    ethnic parishes foster ethnicity, xvi, 82, 88, 128, 133-34, 138-39
    ethnic schisms in, 12-13, 17-18, 147n
    fosters Americanization, 128-29

German parishes, 33-34
Germans more tolerant of Protestants than other Catholics, 97
goals of ethnic parishes, 172n
growth of, 16-17, 27-28
in Illinois's development, 8-9
and immigration restriction, 18
importance of ethnic parishes, 34, 38-39, 43, 55, 155n
and Italian celebrations, 110-11
and Italian festivals, 139
Italian parishes support Mussolini, 114
and language, 15
links Italians with other ethnic groups, 118-19
liturgies as unifier for German immigrants, 85-86
and missions, 19-20
and morality, 84-85, 96
and newspapers, 16, 84-85, 158n, 159n, 159n-60n
opposes idea of melting pot, 149n
parish as focus of Italian liturgical events, 109-10
parish histories, 75-82, 104-8
and *Pfarrbote*, 84-85
population of in Chicago, 131
priests foster Italian culture and tradition, 107-9
religious leaders promote ethnicity, 83-84
school system, xv, 20, 21, 27, 43-44, 55, 62-65, 69, 80-81, 91-94, 119-23, 159n, 167n
and settlement houses, 126-27, 173n
support for World War I, 25
view of women, 171n
Catholic Church Extension Society, 19
Catholic Colonization Society, 18
Catholic Home, 148n
Catholic Knights and Ladies of America, 16
Catholic Missionary Congress, 19
Catholic Mutual Benefit Association, 16
Catholic Order of Foresters, 16
Catholic Youth Organization, 90, 117-18, 151n-52n
    importance of, 23-24
    and sports, 24
    St. Rose of Lima Chapter, 24
    Working Boys' Home, 24

Cavellier, Robert, 143n
Charbonneau, George, 139
Charities, 16, 19-20, 22-24, 44, 54-55, 69, 78, 84, 90, 97-98, 112, 127, 151n, 156n
Chicago
  attracts immigrants from rural Illinois, 3
  bilingualism in public schools, xv
  Black migrants to, 4, 6
  breweries in, 32, 41, 154n
  Catholic Church in, 8, 9, 11, 11-12, 16, 16-17, 19-20, 24, 70, 76, 88, 96, 131, 167n
  Catholic Church links ethnic groups in, 118-19
  Catholic parishes in, 14
  Civil War role, 2
  clashes between Germans and native-born in, 33
  communities defined, 146n
  conflicts among ethnic groups in, 5, 144n, 145n, 157n
  crime in, 52, 159n
  early history of, 143n
  elections in, 32, 144n
  epidemics in, 2
  establishment of, 2
  establishment of parishes in, 9-10, 13
  ethnicity in, 19-20
  ethnic neighborhoods in, 30, 33, 35, 37, 40-43, 46-49, 50, 71-75, 101-3, 131, 136-37, 138, 139, 145n
  and fire of 1871, 3, 11-12
  foreign-language newspapers in, 53
  geographic area, 144n
  German Catholic parishes in, 33-34
  German parishes in, 133
  immigrants avoid political life in, 51
  immigration to, 2, 3, 4, 5, 6-7, 8, 9, 16-17, 19, 29, 31, 32-33, 35, 36-37, 39-46, 46-52, 59, 66-67, 75, 131, 136-37, 154n, 174n
  industry in, 2-3, 6
  International Eucharistic Congress in, 98-99, 119, 134
  Italian celebrations in, 39
  Italian parochial schools in, 119-23
  Jews in, 131
  living conditions in, 5, 37, 46-47, 71-72, 105, 144n-45n
  as military outpost, 1-2
  newspapers and, 16-17
  origin of name, 1
  parochial schools in, 21, 91
  physical expansion, 4
  politics of, 58
  population growth of, 3-4, 16-17, 33
  Protestants in, 35, 131
  provincialism among German immigrants in, 56-60, 62
  provincialism among Italian immigrants in, 60-62
  public works in, 144n
  relations among ethnic groups in, 105-6
  role in Indian trade, 1
  settlement houses in, 123-27
  and suburban migration, 4, 7
  tolerance of German immigrants in during World War II, 135
  use of German in public schools, 44-45
Chicago Ketteler Study House, 27
Chicago Lokal-Vaerband, 27
Chicago Times
  and teaching of German in public schools, 45
Chicago Tribune
  and teaching of German in public schools, 45
Chicago Volksfreund, 53
Cincinnati
  German Catholic population in, 33, 44
Clark, George Rogers, 1
Clergy
  foster Italian culture and tradition, 107-9
  need for American, 21
Cleveland, Grover, 20
Cogo, Anthony, 169n
Colosimo, Jim, 5
Columbus, Christopher, 61, 114
Commons, John R., 47
Condon, James A., 25
Cook County, 2
Corsi, Edward, 51, 67-68
Cottmann, Joseph, 134-35
Cottmann, Paula, 134-35
Crime in Chicago, 52, 159n
Cronau, Rudolph, 63
CYO
  See Catholic Youth Organization

Czechoslovakia
   immigrants from, 3, 29, 42
Czernoch, John, 98

Damen, Arnold, 10-11
Davis, Allen F., 123-27
della Vecchia, Angelo, 101-3, 108
Dettmer, John, 163n
Dettmer, William H., 81, 83
Dettmer, William J., 55
Deutsch-Amerikanische Geschichtsblatter, 54
Dewey, John, 124
Diversey, Michael, 73
Douglas, Stephen, 156n
Dreher, Nicholas, 164n
Dubois, Louis, 98
Duden, Gottfried, 32
Duggan, James, 11, 34, 75
Dunne, Edmund M., 18, 101-3
Durante, Oscar, 53, 159n, 159n-60n
Du Sable, Jean Baptiste Point, 1

Education
   See Schools
Einstein, Albert, 160n, 174n
England
   immigrants from, 2
   and imperialism, 143n
Ethnicity
   African-American, 4
   and Catholic Church, 16-17, 96-99
   Catholic Church links different groups, 118-19
   Catholic liturgies as unifier for German immigrants, 85-86
   Catholic parishes help Italians maintain, 128
   in Chicago, 19
   clashes between Germans and native-born, 33
   conflicts among different groups, 35, 37-38, 42, 108-9
   effect of World War I on German, 97
   and establishment of Catholic parishes, 18
   ethnic societies, 16
   fostered in ethnic parishes, xvi, 133-134, 138-39
   French Canadian, 15
   German, 7, 12-13, 15, 20, 31, 35, 41-42, 44-45, 51, 58, 62-65, 66, 68-69, 81, 82, 88, 91, 131, 160n, 163n
   German religious leaders promote, 83-84
   harmony among groups, 41-42
   and immigrant-aid societies, 87
   importance of German parish, 34, 43, 55
   importance of Italian parish, 38-39
   institutions of, 53-56
   Irish, 31
   Italian, 20, 31, 38, 51, 62-65, 67-68, 106, 107-14, 126, 128
   maintenance of in St. Michael's Parish, 103
   George William Mundelein's lack of support for, 26-27
   and neighborhoods, 30, 33, 35, 37, 40-43, 46-49, 50, 71-75, 101-3, 131, 136-37, 138, 139, 145n
   parish's role in Americanization, 88, 90
   Pfarrbote promotes German, 84-85
   Polish, 7
   and provincialism, 56-62
   and rituals of life and death, 88
   and schools, 21
   Scottish, 42
   societies fostering German, 94-96
Evers, Albert, 76-77

Fasnacht, Walter L., 83
Faulhaber, Michael von, 98
Feehan, Patrick A., 13, 15-16, 30, 44, 46, 74, 76, 78, 80, 101-3, 148n, 153n
Fischer, Matthew, 96
Fischer, Peter, 71-75
Flaget, Stephen, 8
Foley, Thomas, 11-12, 71-75
Forstmann, Symphorian, 84-85
Fort Dearborn, 1
Fortnightly Review, 12
France
   immigrants from, 2
Franco-Prussian War, 35
Fremont, John C., 35
Froebel, Friedrich, 159n
Funerals
   German rituals for, 88

Gambere, James, 102
Gannon, Richard, 150n
Garibaldi, Giuseppe, 53, 55
Geiger, Edward J., 151n
Gentile, Carlo, 53
Gentili, Joseph, 108
German Achievements in America, 63
German Conspiracies in America, 63
German Roman Catholic Verein, 16
Germany
    1848 revolutions in, 32-33, 154n
    Catholicism among immigrants from, 69-70
    Catholic parishes for immigrants from, 14
    Catholics from more tolerant of Protestants than other Catholics, 97
    dispersion of immigrants from fosters Americanization, 132
    factors encouraging immigrants from, 32
    and immigrant-aid societies, 53-55
    immigrant celebrations, 87-88
    immigrants from, 2-3, 4, 5, 6, 8, 11, 13, 16, 29, 31-36, 39-46, 43, 59, 66, 71-99, 75, 131, 131-37, 144n, 156n, 157n, 158n, 174n
    immigrants from and Catholic Church schisms, 11-12
    immigrants from avoid political life, 51
    importance of education to immigrants from, 91, 159n
    importance of parochial schools to immigrants from, 62
    involvement of immigrants from in politics of, 35
    lack of sentiment against immigrants from during World War II, 134-35
    lack of unity among immigrants from, 34, 42, 155n
    loyalties of immigrants from during World War I, 62-65
    need for priests for immigrants from, 9-10
    newspapers for immigrants from, 53
    occupations of immigrants from, 32, 35-36, 39-40, 41, 103, 137
    political power of immigrants from, 167n
    politics and immigrants from, 159n
    provincialism among immigrants from, 56-60, 62, 160n, 161

Giambastiani, Luigi, 104-9, 111, 114, 116-23, 128, 138, 140, 169n, 173n
Giangrande, Peregrine, 104
Gibbons, James, 12-13, 37, 69, 98, 148n
Gilson, Fred A., 160n
Gobel, Julis, 163n
Goldschmitt, Edward T., 80
Greece
    immigrants from, 4, 5, 29
Greeley, Horace, 156n
Guier, Peter, 41

Haas, Wilhelm, 32
Hagedorn, Herman, 57
Hahn, Mrs. Henry, 58, 83-84, 92, 133
Harrison, Benjamin, 148n
Haupt, Herman, 155n
Hecker, Frederick, 32
Hilbert, Otto, 132-33, 161, 163n
Hines, Mr. and Mrs. Edward, 21
Hines, Edward Jr., 21
Hodur, Francis, 12
Hoeffgen, Robert B., 53
Hoffman, Francis A., 32
Hollegen, Baron von, 160n
Holy Name Society, 22
Hughes, Charles Evans, 162n
Hughes, John, 9
Hull House, 46, 51, 123, 124
Hungary
    immigrants from, 3, 42, 157n-58n

Illinois
    attains statehood, 2
    Catholic Church in, 8-9,
    early population of, 3-4, 143n-44n
    immigration to, 32, 144n
    prospers, 2
    under French rule, 143n
Illinois Charitable Relief Corps, 16
Illinois Staats-Zeitung, 53
Immigrants
    occupations of German, 32, 35-36, 39-40, 41, 103, 137
    occupations of Irish, 103
    occupations of Italian, 48, 49, 67, 74
    pull factors for Germans, 32

push factors for Germans, 32
Immigrant Societies, 53-56, 58, 60, 68-69, 75-76, 87, 89, 112-13, 117, 135-36
and Americanization, 88, 90
Immigration
proposed restrictions on, 17-18
"Immigration a Foe to America?," 18
Immigration Restriction Law of 1921, 6
Immigration Restriction Law of 1924, 6
Indians
See Native Americans
Ireland
immigrants from, 2, 4, 5, 7, 11, 13, 16, 29, 30-31, 32, 131, 153n
immigrants from dominate American-style Catholic Church, 140
occupations of immigrants from, 103
Italy
Catholic Church preserves festivals for immigrants from, 139
Catholic parishes for immigrants from, 14
celebrations among immigrants from, 110-11
celebrations uniting immigrants from with Catholic Church, 39
and immigrant-aid societies, 55-56
immigrants from, 3, 4, 5, 6-7, 7-8, 8, 16, 19, 29, 31, 36-39, 46-52, 66-67, 101-29, 131, 137-40, 156n, 158n, 174n
immigrants from accused of being criminals, 52
immigrants from and ethnic parishes, 170n
immigrants from avoid political life, 51
immigrants from linked to other ethnic groups by Catholic Church, 118-19
immigrants' involvement in politics, 116-17
importance of Christopher Columbus to immigrants from, 114
lack of parochial schools among immigrants from, 62
loyalties of immigrants from during World War I, 65
newspapers for immigrants from, 53
occupations of immigrants from, 48, 49, 67, 74
politics and immigrants from, 159n
prejudice by immigrants from against African-Americans, 105-6

provincialism among immigrants from, 60-62, 161
support for Mussolini among immigrants from, 114

Jarecki, Edmund, 25
Jews, 77
cooperation with Catholics, 147n
from Germany, 40
immigration to Chicago, 5, 29
population in Chicago, 131
Jordan, Catherine, 125, 126

Kalvelage, Ferdinand, 75, 77
Kelley, Edward J., 150n
Ketteler German Manual Training School, 44
Kinzie, John, 1
Kipling, Rudyard, 144n
Kluetsch, Nicholas Q., 160n
Knights of Columbus, 23
Knopf, Oscar, 65
Kolping, Adolph, 94
Kolping Society, 83, 94-96, 168n
Kranz Family, 39-40
Krutz, Theresa, 58, 69, 83-84, 87, 88, 92, 95, 135-36, 136-137
Kuhn, Fritz, 132

La Guardia, Fiorello, 159n
Language
and bilingualism in public schools, xv
Italian parochial schools emphasize teaching of Italian, 122
and religion, 43
La Tribuna Italiana Transatlantica, 53
Laukemper, Bernard, 80, 83, 95
Lee, Charles, 1
Lespina, Mr. and Mrs. Andrea, 126
Lewis, Sinclair, 124
Liebreich, John, 80
Lill, Wilhelm, 32
Lincoln, Abraham, 35
L'Italia, 53
Lithuania
immigrants from, 4, 29
Littleton, Henry, 126

Lopreato, James, 31
Lopreato, Joseph, 39
Lucas, Scott, 153n
Ludwig I (King of Bavaria), 44
Ludwigsmissionverein, 43
L'Unione Italiana, 53
Luther, Martin, 97

McCaffrey, D. J., 13
McClellan, George, 156n
McGann, Daniel, 20
McGavick, Bishop, 173n
McGivney, Michael J., 23
McKeon, Catherine, 104
Madaj, M. J., 19
Mafia, 52
Malzacher, Louis, 32
Marquette, Jacques, 1, 143n
Marschall, James, 75
Mastrovalerio, Alessandro, 53
Mattern, Friedrich, 32
Mayer, Levy, 65
Mazzini, Giuseppe, 53
Meder, Leonora Z., 173n
Mencken, H. L., 131
Merriam, Charles E., 8, 51, 146n
Mexico
 immigrants from, 4
Meyer, Albert, 83
Meyer, Mathias, 32
Miele, Stefano, 67-68
Milwaukee
 German Catholic population in, 44
Missions, 19
Missouri and Illinois—A Handbook For Immigrants, 32
Molinari, Caesar, 102
Morality and Catholic Church, 84-85, 96
Morrison, Monsignor, 108
Muldoon, Peter J., 18, 149n
Munch, Friedrich, 36
Mundelein, George William, 20-22, 23, 24-28, 54, 70, 73, 77, 78, 80, 81, 82, 86, 95, 98, 106, 108, 117, 119-23, 125, 133, 139, 140, 150n, 150n-51n, 151n, 152n, 152n-53n, 169n-70n
Mussolini, Benito, 67-68, 114, 137-38, 170n

Nacker Family, 39-40
National Catholic Women's League, 16
National Liberal Immigration League, 18
Native Americans, 19, 143n
Nativism, 63
 and anti-German sentiment, 62-63, 162n
 and anti-Italian sentiment, 37-38, 51-52
 and liquor laws, 33
 and teaching of German in public schools, 45, 63
 and World War II, 134-35
Naturalization
 ethnic parishes support, 116
Nelli, Humbert, 56
Newspapers
 foreign-language, 53
 promote ethnicity, 84-85
New World, 16, 53, 148n
 opposes immigration restrictions, 18
 and World War I, 63
New York City
 German Catholic population in, 33
Northwest Ordinance, 1
Norton, Grace, 47
Norway
 immigrants from, 29, 32
 See also Scandinavia

O'Connor, Richard, 45
O'Connor, William, 64
O'Donnell, Patric, 98
Ogden, William E., 144n
O'Hearn, Michael, 118
O'Regan, Anthony, 10-11
Ostlangenberg, C. H., 9
Ozanam, Frederick, 22

Pacelli, Eugenio, 26, 153n
Parochial schools. *See* Schools, Parochial.
Patterson, Joseph, 63
Pershing, John J., 151n
Peutz, Anselm, 72
Pfarrbote, 84-85
Philadelphia
 German Catholic population in, 33
Piffl, Gustave, 98
Plamondon, Charles A., 173n

Plamondon, Marie, 126, 127
Poland
  immigrants from, 3, 4, 6, 11, 13, 16, 29, 73, 131, 149n, 174n
  immigrants from and Catholic Church schisms, 12
Polish National Catholic Church of America, 12
Polish Roman Catholic Union, 16
Politics
  and ethnic provincialism, 58
  Italian immigrants' involvement in, 116-17
Ponziglione, Paul, 124
Pope Leo XIII, 13, 148n
Pope Pius IV, 150n
Pope Pius X, 96
Powers, Johnny, 51
Pozzi, Aloysius, 119-23
Preising, Otto von, 83
Preuss, Arthur, 12
Priests
  See Clergy
Protestants
  in Chicago, 35, 131
  and cooperation with Catholic Church, 147n
  German Catholics more tolerant of than other Catholics, 97
  and proselytizing, 104-6, 119
Provincialism, ethnic, 56-62
  of German immigrants, 160n, 161
  of Italian immigrants, 161
Public schools. *See* Schools, public.
Purcell, Joseph, 9

Quarter, William, 73, 147n
Quigley, James, 17-20, 21, 46, 48, 75, 78, 102, 104, 106, 107, 119-20, 122-23, 140, 149n, 149n-50n
Quigley Preparatory Seminary, 21

Rehm family, 39-40
Reich, Michael, 73
Reisel, Joseph, 76
Religion
  and language, 43
  and provincialism, 58

Rempe, Charles A., 77-78, 85, 86, 98, 140
Rempe, Francis, 75
Rempe, R. A., 55
Report on a Trip to the Western States of North America, 32
Reuter, Fritz, 161
Rhode, Paul P., 19, 149n
Richard, Gabriel, 8-9
Rocca, Eva, 104
Roman Catholic Union, 20
Ronga, Giuseppe, 53
Roosevelt, Theodore, 62-63, 162n
Rosatti, Joseph, 9
Rosencrans, William, 155n
Rossini, 61
Russia
  immigrants from, 29, 174n
Ryan, Archbishop, 15

St. Boniface Parish
  as example of ethnic parish, 75-80
  statistics, 79
St. Cyr, John Mary, 9
St. Louis
  German Catholic population in, 44
St. Martin's Parish, 163n
St. Mary of the Lake Seminary, 21
St. Mary's Training School, 19-20
St. Patrick's Day, 31
St. Vincent De Paul Society, 16, 22-23, 90
Sangerbund, 40
Scalabrini, Giovanni Battista, 38
Scandinavia
  immigrants from, 29, 131
  See also Norway; Sweden
Schikowski, J., 73
Schiller, Frederick von, 60
Schlacks, Henry J., 71-75
Schlueter, Charles, 90
Schmidt, Ernst, 33
Schmidt, Martin F., 70
Schneider, George, 32-33
Schoenhofen, Peter, 63
Scholesser, Kilian, 72
Schools, Parochial, xv, 20, 21, 27, 43-44, 62-65, 69, 80-81, 91-94, 159n
  foster Americanization, 119-20, 122-23
  in Italian parishes, 119-23

Italians not concerned with, 55
  and retention of German culture, 167n
Schools, public
  bilingualism in, xv
  Italians realize importance of children attending, 49, 51
  Italians satisfied with, 55
  use of German in, 44-45
Schurz, Carl, 155n, 156n
Schweizer, Robert, 58
Scotland
  immigrants from, 2
Seipp Family, 39-40
Serritella, Anthony, 61-62, 111, 116, 139
Serritella, Anthony, Jr., 128-29
Serritella, Mrs. Anthony, 61-62, 109-10, 127, 139
Serritella, James, 139
Settlement Houses, 123-27, 173n
Sheet, Julian, 145n
Sheil, Bernard, 23
Siedenberg, Frederick, 18, 173n
Sigel, Franz, 66
Skaggs, William K., 63
Slavery
  German position on, 35
Slovakia
  immigrants from, 3, 29
Smith, Al, 118
Social workers, 46-47
Society of St. Charles Borromeo, 38
Spinale, Sam, 122-23
Sports
  and Americanization, 24, 118
Stahlke, Lorna, 134-35
Stahlke, Walter, 134-35
Steffens, Lincoln, 144n
Steinwehr, Adolph von, 155n
Steuben, General von, 66
Stobba, Hugo, 70
Stose, Clement C., 32
Strauss, Richard, 160n
Stritch, Samuel, 128, 134, 151n, 173n
Stuart, William, 162n
Stump, Peter, 40-41
Sunday Visitor, 85
Sweden
  immigrants from, 29, 144n, 174n
  See also Scandinavia

Taylor, Graham, 5-6, 38-39, 39, 159n, 171n
Thiele, Aloysius J., 78, 80, 82, 97
Thompson, "Big Bill," 58, 116
Tillich, Paul, 174n
Tippecanoe, Battle of, 1
Tomasi, Silvano, 38
Townsend, Andrew Jacke, 46
Trout, Charles, 138

Van de Velde, James Oliver, 10-11, 30, 73
Venn, Clement, 75-76, 164n
Vercelli, John, 150n
Victor Emmanuel (King of Italy), 68
Vincennes, Battle of, 1
Visitation and Aid Society, The, 16
Vitum, Harriet, 125, 173n
Vollmer, Henry, 64
von Held, Friedrich, 43

Wacker, Charles H., 65
Wales
  immigrants from, 2
Walker, Natalie, 47
Ward, Robert, 126
War of 1812, 1
Weber, Hermann, 95
Weber, Max, 3
Wellmacher, John, 32
Wentworth, "Long John," 154n
Women
  protection of, 171n
World War I
  Catholic support for, 25-26
  effect on German ethnicity, 97
  and German and Italian immigrants, 31
  and immigrant loyalties during, 62-65
World War II
  lack of virulent anti-Germanism during, 134-35
Wright, Frank Lloyd, 124

Yerkes, Charles, 51
Yugoslavia
  immigrants from, 4, 29, 42, 73

Ziegler, David, 154n
Zimmerman, Joseph, 81, 83
Zwingli, Ulrich, 97

TITLES IN THE SERIES

Chicago Studies in the History of American Religion

Editors

JERALD C. BRAUER & MARTIN E. MARTY

1. Ariel, Yaakov. *On Behalf of Israel: American Fundamentalist Attitudes toward Jews, Judaism, and Zionism, 1865-1945*
2. Bundy, James F. *Fall from Grace: Religion and the Communal Ideal in Two Suburban Villages, 1870-1917*
3. Butler, Jonathan M. *Softly and Tenderly Jesus is Calling: Heaven and Hell in American Revivalism, 1870-1920*
4. Dvorak, Katharine L. *An African-American Exodus: The Segregation of the Southern Churches*
5. Hardesty, Nancy A. *Your Daughters Shall Prophesy: Revivalism and Feminism in the Age of Finney*
6. Harding, Vincent. *A Certain Magnificence: Lyman Beecher and the Transformation of American Protestantism, 1775-1863*
7. Hewitt, Glenn A. *Regeneration and Morality: A Study of Charles Finney, Charles Hodge, John W. Nevin and Horace Bushnell*
8. Hillis, Bryan V. *Can Two Walk Together Unless They Be Agreed?: American Religious Schisms in the 1970s*
9. Jacobsen, Douglas G. *An Unprov'd Experiment: Religious Pluralism in Colonial New Jersey*
10. Kloos, John M., Jr. *A Sense of Deity: The Republican Spirituality of Dr. Benjamin Rush*

(continued, over)

TITLES IN THE SERIES

11. Kountz, Peter. *Thomas Merton as Writer and Monk: A Cultural Study, 1915-1951*
12. Lagerquist, L. DeAne. *In America the Men Milk the Cows: Factors of Gender, Ethnicity, and Religion in the Americanization of Norwegian-American Women*
13. Markwell, Bernard Kent. *The Anglican Left: Radical Social Reformers in the Church of England and the Protestant Episcopal Church, 1846-1954*
14. Morris, William Sparkes. *The Young Jonathan Edwards: A Reconstruction*
15. Pellauer, Mary D. *Toward a Tradition of Feminist Theology: The Religious Social Thought of Elizabeth Cady Stanton, Susan B. Anthony, and Anna Howard Shaw*
16. Potash, P. Jeffrey. *Vermont's Burned-Over District: Patterns of Community Development and Religious Activity, 1761-1850*
17. Queen, Edward L., II. *In the South the Baptists are the Center of Gravity: Southern Baptists and Social Change, 1930-1980*
18. Schmidt, Jean Miller. *Souls or the Social Order: The Two-Party System in American Protestantism*
19. Shaw, Stephen J. *The Catholic Parish as a Way-Station of Ethnicity and Americanization: Chicago's Germans and Italians, 1903-1939*
20. Shepard, Robert S. *God's People in the Ivory Tower: Religion in the Early American University*
21. Snyder, Stephen H. *Lyman Beecher and his Children: The Transformation of a Religious Tradition*